Rhonda Kantrowitz
622 Donlon
X3737

Modern Poetry

ENGLISH MASTERPIECES · AN ANTHOLOGY OF
IMAGINATIVE LITERATURE FROM CHAUCER TO
T. S. ELIOT · UNDER THE GENERAL EDITOR-
SHIP OF MAYNARD MACK, YALE UNIVERSITY

Modern Poetry

edited by

MAYNARD MACK

*Professor of English, and Fellow of Davenport College
Yale University*

LEONARD DEAN

Professor of English, University of Connecticut

WILLIAM FROST

*Associate Professor of English, University of California,
Santa Barbara*

Second Edition

PRENTICE-HALL, INC.
Englewood Cliffs, N. J.

TO THE READER

These volumes present a carefully proportioned collection of writings in English, from Chaucer to the present, which are primarily valuable as literary works of art. Writings in the less imaginative modes have been almost entirely excluded, and complete works have been preferred to excerpts. Where cutting or selection was necessary, an effort has been made to preserve what is crucial for an understanding of the artistic value of the whole piece. Since novels cannot be condensed or excerpted satisfactorily, they have been omitted. Separate reprints of prose fiction may be used to supplement the last two volumes of this set. The introductions try to focus the reader's attention on what is imaginatively interesting and valuable in the various selections. If they succeed, they will at the same time provide the justification for this anthology and distinguish it from the many other anthologies that are available.

Current printing (last digit):
19   18   17   16   15   14   13   12   11

LIBRARY OF CONGRESS
CATALOGUE CARD NO. 61-9352

28141-C

Contents

A Note on Chronology and the Modern Temper

The poets represented in this volume are all "modern" in the sense of having gained their greatest reputations and influence in the recent past—specifically, since about the time of the First World War (1914-18).* For two of them, however, this reputation and influence were posthumous: when that war began, Emily Dickinson and Gerard Manley Hopkins had been dead for a quarter of a century. A third poet, W. B. Yeats, had begun publishing and had already attained some stature as a late romantic during the last decade of the nineteenth century; but in the twentieth his poetry underwent a considerable alteration, both in matter and manner; and the poems by which he is represented in this volume almost all appeared during or after the period of the First World War. Of the five poets to whom this volume devotes most space, W. H. Auden is the most recent: he began publishing in the 1930's.

Before considering modern poetry itself, a word may be said about the modern temper—that is, about certain nonliterary influences shaping the poetry as well as the audience who received it and gave it its reputation.

First, this audience has been, to a probably unprecedented degree, interested in the mental phenomena revealed by introspection. The growing prestige of psychology itself as a subject of investigation has been paralleled in prose literature by the works of such writers as Joyce and Proust, each of whom created enormous verbal fabrics out of the development and history of a single sensibility. In the introduction to Volume VI of this anthology, the interest of the nineteenth-century romantics in complex states of mind as subject matter for

---

* *1914-18:* A. E. Housman is a lone exception. For more detailed information about chronology, see the biographical notes at the rear of the volume.

poetry is discussed; the twentieth century has seen such preoccupations increase rather than diminish.

Second, the modern temper—at least by contrast with the Victorian —has been characterized more by anxiety and insecurity than by confidence and assurance. In a physical sense, these qualities are no doubt attributable to the high frequency of social cataclysm during the twentieth century: the thirty-six year period 1914-49 included, after all, ten years of world war, and ten of world depression—not to mention the Russian, Italian, and German revolutions, and the Span-ish Civil War. In a spiritual sense, the period induced insecurity by its widespread revolt against traditions of all kinds, a revolt which led to an uncertainty about standards in politics, morals, and other areas. Hence, probably, the large number of conversions and apos-tasies (political or religious) among modern intellectual leaders.

Third, the period has seen the spread of radical doubts about human freedom and human dignity. Determinism, in a philosophic or religious sense, is nothing new under the sun; but by many followers of Marx (1818-83) and Freud (1856-1939), determinism in human affairs has been given in recent times a seemingly scientific basis. Marxism has suggested that human societies, in their organiza-tion and historical development, are predetermined by economic or technological considerations; Freudianism has suggested that human individuals are predetermined by the formation or malformation of the unconscious parts of their minds during infancy or early childhood. As for man's relation to his environment in a larger sense, the physical universe of science is becoming progressively larger, longer-lived, and more incomprehensible to nonmathematicians. Finally, the anthropo-logical approach to human life in general has suggested that many a cherished institution or belief takes its significance and use solely from the cultural framework in which it occurs, and has, outside that framework, neither meaning nor objective validity.

↜↝

A Philosophic Problem

Modern poetry in general has the reputation of being esoteric and obscure; but the human problem which is at the heart of much of the best of it is not at all hard to understand. Stated in its broadest general terms, this problem might be said to be the contrast or conflict or disparity felt by any intelligent, sensitive person today between experience measurable or describable in the terms of physical science, and that immeasurable meaning—of whatever sort—which permeates experience in the form of value. For modern man, this problem is necessarily acute: we can split the atom—that is a physical, scientific matter; but splitting it merely faces us with the question of what to do about the bomb—which is a political or social or moral or ethical or even metaphysical matter, and much less easy for us to handle. Yet both matters are tied up inseparably in the same atom—the scientifically graspable world on the one hand, and on the other hand the same world as it exists in terms of esthetics or ethics or religion or psychology.

This contrast, this problem, is not of course peculiar to our age; but it comes before our age in a special form. Because of the success and increasing prestige of technology since the industrial revolution, and because scientific statements about experience customarily receive widespread acceptance while evaluative statements frequently meet with hot debate, there is a tendency today to regard the physical picture of the world as the *real* one, and any other picture as a comparatively illusory or a merely relative one. It is as though a critic were to say, comparing two oil paintings, "The question of which is a better picture than the other is a matter of opinion; but the number of square inches occupied by each canvas is a matter of fact!" There are even schools of philosophy today which deny meaning itself to judgments of value, on the ground that only scientific statements are verifiable. Yet individuals and societies, no less today than in the past, are continually confronting choices which have to be made on the basis of some premise about value.

What modern poetry seeks to do with this contrast between the measurable and the immeasurable facets of experience is to dramatize it. Here the attitude of a typical modern poet is different from that of a romantic. The romantics tended to attempt individual solutions of the problem; Wordsworth and Shelley had programs; Blake issued manifestoes. A great deal of modern poetry is more tentative, and has a different object in view. It seeks to understand the split in modern ways of looking at things; to understand, to diagnose, to dramatize; not necessarily to prescribe.

Thus John Crowe Ransom, in a poem whose method symbolizes much in modern poetry, presents the tension between two irreconcilable attitudes toward a situation: the metaphysical Honor, which separates his lovers, and the physical desire, which keeps them together. Choice of either excludes the other:

In Heaven you have heard no marriage is,
No white flesh tinder to your lecheries,
Your male and female tissue sweetly shaped
Sublimed away, and furious blood escaped.

Great lovers lie in Hell, the stubborn ones
Infatuate of the flesh upon the bones;
Stuprate, they rend each other when they kiss,
The pieces kiss again, no end to this.

At first the observer had been about to intervene, to resolve the "torture of equilibrium;" the pair, too "strict," were "ruined," he felt. But having analyzed the dilemma more fully, he steps back from it, content to watch the lovers, and the two incompatible decisions, "spinning, orbited nice," like twin stars "perilous and beautiful." The achievement of a perilous equilibrium, sometimes at the expense of torture but always for the purpose of beauty, is the goal of some of the greatest modern poetry.

A different approach to the same basic philosophic problem is exploited in Auden's brief, satiric "Unknown Citizen." The poem dramatizes a disparity between the fullness of the physical, statistical information presented concerning the Citizen and the crude inadequacy of the judgments made about him. Whereas in "The Equilibrists" the balance is strictly preserved between physical and metaphysical, in "The Unknown Citizen" one pan of the balance-scale has been swept seemingly empty for the purposes of irony. The Citizen

. . . had everything necessary to the Modern Man,
A phonograph, a radio, a car and a frigidaire.

The metaphysical enters the poem solely in the words "saint" in the fourth line and "free" and "happy" in the next-to-last; and it enters only to be repudiated and brushed aside by the speaker. But by its very absence, by the urgent need for it which the poem makes us aware of, equilibrium is created. Somehow the statistics will not do; the physical "facts" are incomplete.

The sense of incompleteness itself, the feeling of irrecoverable loss, of existence without spiritual center, compass, or equilibrium, has nowhere been dramatized more poignantly than in "The Hollow Men," one of the most widely and popularly known of T. S. Eliot's poems. Here, evocations of romantic love ("Lips that would kiss"), religious affirmation (broken prayers), and esthetic responsiveness ("sunlight on a broken column") delicately illuminate some twilight province of the mind like fading or dying stars. The imagined

speakers, it is clear, feel the psychical, emotional vacuum connected
with the merely physical nature of their surroundings:

> This is the dead land
> This is cactus land
> Here the stone images
> Are raised, here they receive
> The supplication of a dead man's hand
> Under the twinkle of a fading star. . . .

and are aware of a better past ("our lost kingdoms"). But an inhibi-
tion has fixed them in their scarecrow-like condition:

> Between the conception
> And the creation
> Between the emotion
> And the response
> Falls the Shadow . . .

And has robbed even their own self-analysis of logical coherence:

> Our dried voices, when
> We whisper together
> Are quiet and meaningless . . .

Hence the poem, by contrast with "The Equilibrists" or "The
Unknown Citizen," dispenses with the more formal devices of exposi-
tory prose; there is little punctuation, and much grammatical fluidity
(is "rose" in Part IV a noun or verb?). At the same time the short
lines and fairly marked rhythms give the effect of an intermittent
chant, spoken to accompany the crepuscular ring-around-the-rosy of
Part V. All aspects of the poem—sound-effects, images, language,
ideas—fuse perfectly to dramatize the experience of inadequacy, of
incompleteness.

Incompleteness is one important charge which poetry today brings
against an exclusively physical world-picture; two others are imper-
manence and incoherence.

❧

Flux

The sense of decay and transience in physical experience is hardly
a new theme for poetry; indeed, it was extensively used by the romantics—by Shelley, for example:

> When the lamp is shattered
> The light in the dust lies dead—
> When the cloud is scattered
> The rainbow's glory is shed.

With the romantics, however, it commonly issued in a rich, self-gratifying melancholy—

> No song but sad dirges
> Like the wind through a ruined cell,
> Or the mournful surges
> That ring the dead seaman's knell—

This kind of response, though strong in personal feeling, works against the detachment necessary to drama.

The modern poet is, ostensibly at least, more noncommittal, more the stage-manager than the protagonist. Having established his triple comparison between the ancient Roman inhabitant of Britain, the decaying forest in autumn, and himself, Housman comes to a rapid and laconic conclusion:

> The gale, it plies the saplings double
> It blows so hard, 'twill soon be gone:
> Today the Roman and his trouble
> Are ashes under Uricon.

Frost's "Oven Bird" and "Nothing Gold Can Stay," both variants on the same theme, pose a question or frame a paradox ("So dawn goes down to day"); they do not define a particular emotional response by embracing it. Hopkins' "Spring and Fall," though on first reading it may seem pervaded by an almost Shelleyan mournfulness, is also built around a paradox. Margaret's approaching predictable sorrow, though she will then perfectly understand its nature, will not be explicable in words or philosophical formulae: "Nor mouth had, no nor mind, expressed." And even in "The Wild Swans at Coole," despite Yeats's brief lament for the passing of nineteen years, the focus is on the magnificent swans, symbols of something eternal, unfading, and impersonal.

Auden in his lyric "As I Walked Out One Evening" objectifies even more explicitly, and with considerable humor, the tension between an asserted ideal and the mutabilities of physical experience. In his dialogue between the lover and the clocks, the lurid extravagance of the imagery results in a light, mockingly ironic tone. When the lover sings

> I'll love you till the ocean
> Is folded and hung up to dry,

> And the seven stars go squawking
> Like geese about the sky—

the clocks are able to counter with an equally hyperbolic sketch of
the vicissitudes of domesticity:

> The glacier knocks in the cupboard,
> The desert sighs in the bed,
> And the crack in the tea-cup opens
> A lane to the land of the dead.

A kindred theme is the subject of Stevens's "Peter Quince at the
Clavier," in which the immortal beauty of the heroine bathing is set
against the flickering lust she awakens in her senile spectators:

> Susanna's music touched the bawdy strings
> Of those white elders; but, escaping,
> Left only Death's ironic scraping.

More elaborate and philosophical treatments of a similar theme
occur in two of Yeats's most famous poems, "Sailing to Byzantium"
and "Among Schoolchildren." In both these poems, the general question of the flux of the physical world is crystallized into the individual problem of old age—as the recurrent image of the scarecrow
demonstrates: "a tattered coat upon a stick," "a comfortable kind of
old scarecrow." In "Sailing to Byzantium" the decrepitude of age is
contrasted with the energy of the ordinary world, ceaselessly preoccu-
pied with the cyclical processes of birth, growth, reproduction, and
decay—

> The salmon-falls, the mackerel-crowded seas,
> Fish, flesh, or fowl, commend all summer long
> Whatever is begotten, born, and dies . . .

This energy the speaker rejects in favor of an ideal symbolized by
the centuries-old, ecclesiastical, medieval-classical Eastern empire of
Byzantium—a timeless ideal compounded of philosophy ("unageing
intellect"), religion ("sages standing in God's holy fire"), and especially art (the golden bird, set upon a golden bough, "to keep a
drowsy Emperor awake"). That this goldsmith's art is a kind of
symbol or surrogate for poetry—the art Yeats himself is practicing
in writing the poem—is suggested by the mention, in every stanza,
of singing; poetry, the poem might almost be saying, takes its materials from the flux of natural life—"what is past, or passing, or to
come"—but is itself "out of nature" in so far as it has a universal
validity and is not subject to decay.

By comparison to the formality and austere splendor of the images

used in "Sailing to Byzantium," "Among Schoolchildren" sets forth
in a natural, homely manner the question of what to make of a
diminished thing—again, the decay of life in old age. The speaker,
a public school inspector, is inspired by the sight of the children to
lose himself in a reverie on his own youth and bygone passionate
love, a reverie that widens to include the sad discrepancy between
human concepts of the ideal ("Presences/That passion, piety, or affection knows"), and the mundane fruits of human enterprise ("a sixty-
year-old smiling public man"). Once again the limitations of life
are resolved by being balanced against the satisfactions of art; but
here art is seen in an aspect different from the Byzantine ideal. Now
it is art as "play," as spontaneous, unself-regarding activity, unen-
cumbered by the harassing comparison of what we should like to
be with what we are. It is art as a harmonious union of all aspects
of being; art in which the participant so loses himself that none can
"know the dancer from the dance." In the combined figure of the
tree and the dancer, the poem suggests that sensual existence is capable of form and significance by participation in a transcendent
esthetic reality.

It is worth noting that the two poems succeed, in so far as they do
succeed, by being their own demonstrations: they do not, that is,
prove their points by logical argument; instead they create the experience that they are talking about. Thus in "Sailing to Byzantium"
the line

> Of hammered gold and gold enamelling

suggests both by its literal meaning and by its strict chiastic sound-
pattern (". . . am . . . gold . . . gold . . . am . . .") the glittering finality of a great artifact; while in the next-to-last line of "Among
Schoolchildren" the anapestic intrusion into the basic iambic beat
gives an effect of spontaneous response on the part of the poem itself
to the rhythms of the dance with which it is to conclude:

> O body swayed to music, O brightening glance,
> How can we know the dancer from the dance?

❧

The Decay of Meaning

An experience which most poets of recent times—and not only
poets—have probably undergone is doubt about the authenticity of
values; they seem to have felt rational empiricism like acid eating

away at any nonutilitarian concept of life's purposes—whether the concept stems from patriotism, morals, religion, or love. Yeats, for example, his faith undermined by Victorian popularizers of science whom he hated but believed, at first retreated into a hazy Celtic dream-world of forgotten folklore and hypnotic scenery (the Lake Isle of Innisfree), but later matured his visions of art and Ireland into a hardier armor with which to face his age. Other poets used the very experience of loss as a theme for poetry—the sense, perhaps momentarily exhilarating—of the bottom dropping out of things. Housman, translating from Horace the poem he is said to have considered the most beautiful ever written, asserted again, with stoic outward unconcern, the doctrine that ethics never ultimately count—

> When thou descendest once the shades among,
> The stern assize and equal judgment o'er,
> Not thy long lineage nor thy golden tongue
> No, nor thy righteousness, shall friend thee more.

Compare MacLeish's "End of the World," or Frost's "Acquainted with the Night" and "Desert Places." In "Acquainted with the Night," the darkness is presided over "at an unearthly height" by "One luminary clock," a gadget that divides the stream of experience into equal portions efficiently but unfortunately pointlessly: it

> Proclaimed the time was neither wrong nor right.

Similarly, in "Desert Places" the snow which blankets existence has "no expression, nothing to express"; in Tate's commemorative Ode,

> The wind whirrs without recollection,

and at the conclusion of Eliot's "Gerontion" the snow's whiteness absorbs the white feathers of the wind-driven gull.

〜

Nature

The last few poems mentioned typify the passing of the romantic concept of nature. The many meanings which landscape suggested to a poet like Wordsworth—the plastic shaping Spirit rolling through hills and sunsets, the appropriate nurturer of man's nobler qualities, and so on—these have scarcely been carried over entire into the twentieth century. Nature is still used in poetry, and sometimes as a symbolic vehicle of human feeling, but not any longer as being in

itself and by virtue of its very existence a clue to Ultimate Significance.
Instead we have the detached, indifferent fauna of Frost:

> The woodchuck could say whether it's like his
> Long sleep, as I describe its coming on
> Or just some human sleep—

or the allegorical mountains of Auden:

> Wandering lost upon the mountains of our choice
>
> .   .   .   .
>
> Upon the mountains of my fear I climb—

or Tate's ominous screech-owl, spider, and serpent; or the frigid constellation which greets, in Eliot, the members of the International Set
after their demise and dissolution:

> De Bailhache, Fresca, Mrs. Cammel, whirled
> Beyond the circuit of the shuddering Bear
> In fractured atoms . . .

or, in Hopkins, oceanic horrors:

> . . . the sea flint-flake, black-backed in the regular blow
> Sitting Eastnortheast, in cursèd quarter, the wind;
> Wiry and white-fiery and whirlwind-swivellèd snow
> Spins to the widow-making unchilding unfathering deeps.

Hopkins, it is true, occasionally invests nature with something like
the old romantic awe and wonder:

> There lives the dearest freshness deep down things—

but the freshness which Hopkins discerns does not spring from the
observer of nature (as the Romantics sometimes implied that it did)
or autonomously from nature itself. Instead it exists on account of
an explicit supernature:

> Because the Holy Ghost over the bent
> World broods with warm breast and with ah! bright wings.

The placing of the word "bent" is interesting. One would expect,
perhaps, to find "the Holy Ghost *bent over the world*"; instead it is
the *world* which is "bent": literally, "spherical"; figuratively, "ob-
sessed by its own concerns," or even "warped," "distorted," "imperfect."

History

The experience of loss of meaning in nature is paralleled, in other modern poems, by the experience of loss of meaning in history. Is history an empty chain of exciting but random catastrophes? In the nineteenth century the phrase "survival of the fittest" seemed to imply a comforting answer to this question; today, many people are less sure. (How, after all, did Darwin know which species *were* the "fittest"? Simply by checking on which ones, in fact, survived. Why not, then use a more exact phrase: "the survival of the survivors"?) Though the doctrine of inevitable progress probably persists today as an unexamined assumption in the popular mind, for poetry it is no longer a source of strength.

All this is not to imply, of course, that romantic or Victorian poetry reflected any uncritical acceptance of the doctrine of universal progress; the matter is far more complicated than that. Influenced by the French Revolution and by concomitant movements for reform (intellectual or social) in England, the romantic poets tended to become either Utopians, like Shelley in his "Prometheus," or cynics, like Byron in his "Don Juan." Between these two extremes stood Wordsworth, disillusioned by the triumph of the extremists in France, yet still hoping for rational reform in England. In the less turbulent Victorian age, though many educated people became uncomfortable about the increasing mechanization and materialism of the day, the assumption that history was at least getting *somewhere* (whether you liked its destination or not) remained substantially unquestioned.

Yeats's sonnet "Leda and the Swan" presents by symbols quite a different view of events. In Greek myth the rape of Leda by the Supreme Divinity disguised as a swan had been fraught with historic consequences: two of Leda's children were Helen, who started the war which demolished an empire ("The broken wall, the burning roof and tower"), and Clytemnestra, who treacherously murdered the leading captain among the victors ("Agamemnon dead"). The sonnet envisages this chain of events and its cause as essentially violent, physical, and brutal—though the question is left open as to whether history may not have a nonphysical meaning after all; and whether, if it does, that meaning is or is not comprehensible by the human participants:

> Did she put on his knowledge with his power
> Before the indifferent beak could let her drop?

For a more abstract treatment of the theme, compare the paragraph
in "Gerontion" beginning

> After such knowledge, what forgiveness? Think now
> History has many cunning passages . . .

Compare also Pound's bitter comment on World War I:
> There died a myriad,
> And of the best, among them,
> For an old bitch gone in the teeth,
> For a botched civilization.

Now history has two aspects, social and personal. Those who do
not read the newspapers may perhaps for a time escape the import
of the first; no one escapes the second. One of Eliot's great strengths
as a poet is his ability to handle both sides of history simultaneously;
the passage referred to in "Gerontion," for example, applies equally
to the cycle of Western culture and to Gerontion's sense of his own
past. In "The Waste Land, Part III" the mating of the clerk and
typist is most notable for its machine-like quality (machines presumably do not know or care what takes place in respect to them)—

> She smoothes her hair with automatic hand
> And puts a record on the gramophone—

and the automatism is underscored by the presence of Tiresias, who,
in Sophocles' famous play, witnessed a mating charged with the
complex significance of sin and ultimate redemption.

In "The Waste Land, Part II" history is concretely dramatized not
simply by the allusions to Cleopatra, Dido, and Ophelia (heroines
whose stories were tragic because meaningful) but also by the room
itself, full of physical reminders of the past. At first the room seems
proud and magnificent; but as the poem approaches the lady whose
day consists of hot water at ten, a closed car at four, and a game of
chess, the four walls suddenly develop sinister, menacing qualities:

> And other withered stumps of time
> Were told upon the walls; staring forms
> Leaned out, leaning, hushing the room enclosed.

The stumps of time are "withered" because no one cares what they
once meant; or because for those who do care their significance has
come to be merely frivolous:

> O O O O that Shakespeherian Rag
> It's so elegant
> So intelligent . . .

Triviality is taking over, and the result is nightmare.

The sense of nightmare, after the meaning of experience has become attenuated or doubtful, is almost a staple of modern poetry. It invests the inanimate with unwelcome animation:

> Streets that follow like a tedious argument
> Of insidious intent . . .

It confounds the living and the dead:

> There I saw one I knew, and stopped him, crying: "Stetson!
> "You who were with me in the ships at Mylae!
> "That corpse you planted last year in your garden,
> "Has it begun to sprout? Will it bloom this year?
> "Or has the sudden frost disturbed its bed? . . .

It conjures up monsters:

> A shape with lion body and the head of a man,
> A gaze blank and pitiless as the sun,
> Is moving its slow thighs . . .

It discloses internal abysses:

> O the mind, mind has mountains; cliffs of fall
> Frightful, sheer, no-man-fathomed . . .

It predicts horrors:

> Where do they come from? Those whom we so much dread
> As on our dearest location falls the chill
> Of their crooked wing . . .

It is so familiar that it can even be kidded by a comic treatment:

> Death and the Raven drift above
> And Sweeney guards the hornèd gate.

Five Poets

Enough has been said, perhaps, to suggest the recurrence of a basic philosophic problem, in several of its aspects, throughout much modern poetry. For any individual poet, of course, the problem is likely to arise in a special form, depending on that individual's particular experience, talents, and insight. This anthology emphasizes five major modern poets. The characteristic projections the dilemma is given in the poems of each of these five is worth a brief discussion.

1. *Hopkins:* G. M. Hopkins was a convert to Catholicism in a skeptical age; a Jesuit priest; and a human being with a very acute perception of the sensuous qualities of experience. He was especially sensitive, that is (if one may judge from his poetry), to sounds, shapes, colors, physical forms, and the feel of things. Thus it was natural for the equilibrium mentioned at the start of this essay to take shape in his verse as a tension or dramatic contrast between sheer brute energy, exemplified in nature, and transcendent religious significance which sometimes seemed to repudiate sense experience, sometimes to transform or hallow it.

Each of the two sonnets "Felix Randal" and "The Windhover" illustrates the contrast. In "Felix Randal" the religiously oriented picture of Randal in old age, helpless like a child, at first cursing and then piously accepting his own approaching death, is set against the sudden secular vision of the youthful horse-shoer:

When thou at the random grim forge, powerful amidst peers,
Did fettle for the great gray drayhorse his bright and battering sandal!

In "The Windhover" the vision of physical energy comes first, the sense of rapturous admiration for the falcon who "Rebuffed the big wind." The poem concludes, however, with the falling apart of physical things presented as a source of even greater beauty.

In other poems—several of the later sonnets—the tension takes a different form: it is a psychological contrast in which different parts of the speaker's own mind struggle towards and resist faith. The dramatic machinery is still, however, generally drawn from some aspect of physical nature. The storm that wrecked the Deutschland corresponds to the storm in the poet's mind; the speaker's sense of his own failure (in "Thou art indeed just, Lord") is counterbalanced by the flourishing successes of bird and bush; the blackness and bleak light of evening (in "Spelt from Sibyl's Leaves") correspond to perceptions of evil and good.

2. *Yeats:* W. B. Yeats was an Irish patriot; a romantic with a keen interest in the legendary past of the Irish and of other peoples (the Greeks, the Mohammedans, the Hebrews, the Japanese); a playwright and a public figure in his native country. He was attracted by occultism, spiritualism, and other nonscientific lore; and he constructed, like Blake, a complex private mythology.

In some of his poems, such as "Easter, 1916," heroic values of self-sacrifice in behalf of a declining national culture suddenly emerge from the "casual comedy" of modern daily life. Elsewhere, as in "Leda and the Swan," "The Second Coming," and "Two Songs from a Play," the "mere anarchy" now being let loose upon the world is accounted for in terms of an apocalyptic vision of rotating cycles of history. The age of Leda or Dionysus (Greek culture) yields to the age of Christ, which will now (2000 years having almost elapsed) yield to—what? Certainly to something; but we are not to expect a comfortable transition if the next rotation of the great wheel starts off with as much of a wrench as did the last:

> Odour of blood when Christ was slain
> Made all Platonic tolerance vain
> And vain all Doric discipline.

3. *Frost:* Robert Frost is a California-born New England farmer and academician. By contrast to the sweep of Yeats's symbols his pastoral and woodland imagery seems and is parochial; but for a purpose. What he does with the flux of time is to arrest it, investing an isolated moment of experience with self-justifying and purely human satisfactions. From these ephemeral but crystallized pleasures he then stands back, with an air of detached irony, like an adult half-amused, half-sympathetic with a child. A woodpile about to collapse in a swamp, an apple-harvest dream about to begin, a motionless grindstone slowly being snowed under—such images expand into concrete and elaborate symbols of human restlessness, or satiety, or anger. Like Lamb he would fain lay an ineffectual finger on the spoke of Time's great wheel. A characteristic lyric is "Spring Pools," in which he exhorts the seasons to delay:

> The trees that have it in their pent-up buds
> To darken nature and be summer woods—
> Let them think twice before they use their powers
> To blot out and drink up and sweep away
> These flowery waters and these watery flowers
> From snow that melted only yesterday.

4. *Eliot.* T. S. Eliot is a convert to Anglo-Catholicism, a publisher and former banker, an American-born British citizen, and a Londoner. Sensitive, highly educated, acutely aware of the European past as it impinges on the present, he probably has conveyed with greater success than any other modern poet the sense, discussed earlier in this essay, of pointless physical flux in time coupled with decay of meaning and value. Take for example these lines from "Burnt Norton":

> Only a flicker
> Over the strained time-ridden faces
> Distracted from distraction by distraction
> Filled with fancies and empty of meaning . . .

Towards the end of the poem, by means of a play on the term "word," he dramatizes these processes in respect to both literature and religion:

> Words strain,
> Crack and sometimes break, under the burden,
> Under the tension, slip, slide, perish,
> Decay with imprecision, will not stay in place,
> Will not stay still. Shrieking voices
> Scolding, mocking, or merely chattering,
> Always assail them. The Word in the desert
> Is most attacked by voices of temptation . . .

The process for him is usually staged in an urban setting: "the gloomy hills of London . . . this twittering world."

To balance this realization of a kind of chaos, "Burnt Norton" offers two counterweights: the moment of transcendent insight and the implication of an orderly pattern somehow permeating experience. In this pattern, symbolized as a wheel, the moment of insight corresponds to the geometric center of the hub—the point which theoretically does not turn but which accounts for and controls the turning of all the rest. Thus the moment of insight is both inside and outside of time: "Only through time is time conquered." It corresponds in Eliot's thought to the Christian doctrine of the Incarnation, through which history receives meaning from an event both inside and outside history—as the "Word in the desert" passage would indicate.

The way in which "Burnt Norton" confronts a dramatized perception of modern emotional or spiritual inadequacy with a set of symbols rooted in the past but presented as vigorously relevant to the present is typical of much of Eliot's poetry. In "Prufrock" we have Prufrock himself and Hamlet (or Prufrock and the mermaids, or Prufrock and Lazarus, or Prufrock and John the Baptist, or Prufrock and Guido da Montefeltro). In "Gerontion" we have the speaker and Christ. In "The Waste Land" we have Sweeney, Mr. Eugenides, and Thames maidens, etc., set over against Percivale, Ferdinand, and a host of others.

5. *Auden:* W. H. Auden is one of a group of young English poets who, especially during the decade (1929-39) of economic depression, rising fascism, and approaching war, felt and reflected the impact of a deeply disordered Europe. Much of his best poetry concerns itself, in highly symbolic terms, with a non-winnable battle imposed by freedom and fought in behalf of love. Thus his prayer, in "Petition," is for an inner strengthening:

> Prohibit sharply the rehearsed response
> And gradually correct the coward's stance;

> Cover in time with beams those in retreat
> That, spotted, they turn though the reverse were great . . .

The battle is conceived of as both external (political) and internal (psychological):

> In the nightmare of the dark
> All the dogs of Europe bark,
> And the living nations wait,
> Each sequestered in its hate;
>
> Intellectual disgrace
> Stares from every human face
> And the seas of pity lie
> Locked and frozen in each eye . . .

Although, as "Law like Love" suggests, it is difficult to formulate even tentatively an absolute value (for the way back to Eden is defended by angels "Against the poet and the legislator"), nevertheless the mere fact of being human, of having reason and freedom of choice, imposes on us a responsibility we cannot escape:

> We live in freedom by necessity,
> A mountain people dwelling among mountains.

We cannot, that is, content ourselves with being wolves in the evergreen forests, brokers roaring like beasts on the floor of the stock-exchange, or "short-haired mad executives" (who presumably stand for fashionable efficiency without direction)—we must, instead, by effort come to know ourselves fully so as to vanquish evil within and without; for guilt as well as freedom is inescapable. Thus the mysterious enemy in "Which Side Am I Supposed To Be On?" turns out to be the Seven Deadly Sins.

〜〆

The Vehicle

So far we have been examining some of the characteristic themes of modern poetry in general; a further matter to be looked into is modern poems and how they are built. It seems to be the problem of every age of poetry to find out new ways of using language; a Donne rejects the profuse elaboration of a Spenser; a Wordsworth or Keats repudiates the wit and concision of a Pope. Three areas in which innovations will ordinarily be found whenever a revolution in poetry occurs are versification, diction and imagery.

1. *Versification:* From the time of Milton down through the nineteenth century the iamb (a light syllable followed by a heavy) has been the dominant rhythmic unit in English poetry—so much so that poets have seemed almost to take it for granted. In practice, the dominance of the iamb means that, normally, if a line has five beats, it will also have ten syllables; if four beats, eight; and so on. Flexibility is ordinarily attained by varying the number of beats in a given line while holding the total number of syllables constant. Milton's line

> Rocks, caves, lakes, fens, bogs, dens, and shades of death

has ten syllables, of which eight receive at least some stress; while Pope's

> And curses wit, and poetry and Pope

has ten syllables but only four stresses. Thus the tradition has been to establish a basic iambic pattern with a fixed number of syllables per line, and then to vary the accents within the framework.

This tradition by no means began with Milton. Nor did it end with Tennyson: Yeats and Frost, for example, are moderns in whose works it is preserved and continued. Hopkins, however, developed a system of his own which has had considerable influence since his time. Like his frequent and strongly marked alliteration, it derives partly from the older (fourteenth-century or earlier) English poetry, of which "Sir Gawain and the Green Knight" is an example. Its most salient feature, exemplified very fully in "The Wreck of the Deutschland," is a reversal of the traditional roles of the stress-count and syllable-count of any line: the number of main accents is held fairly constant, but the total number of syllables is deliberately allowed to fluctuate within very wide limits. This can readily be illustrated by comparing the last line in stanza 11 with the last line in stanza 12:

> The sour scythe cringe, and the blear share come.
>
> Not vault them, the millions of rounds of thy mercy not reeve even them in?

Each line has six accents: in the first, every word except "and" and the two "the's" gets a beat; while in the second, there are no less than twelve unaccented syllables.

Influenced by the later blank verse of Shakespeare and other Elizabethan dramatists, Eliot has developed a rhythm which, in its frequent disregard of the iamb, has something in common with Hopkins. With the first of the two Hopkins lines quoted above, compare this line from "Gerontion":

> Rocks, moss, stonecrop, iron, merds

In this poem, in "The Journey of the Magi," in parts of "The Waste Land," and elsewhere, Eliot is equally free with blank verse itself: that is, he occasionally asserts the traditional pattern, as in a line like

> She gives when our attention is distracted—

but frequently allows himself anywhere from two to seven or eight feet per line. Compare the versification of Auden's "Musée des Beaux Arts."

2. *Diction:* An important tendency in modern poetic diction has been the general effort on the part of most poets to make dramatic use of natural, unself-conscious language drawn from ordinary modern speech. This is not wholly an innovation, since of course Byron and Browning practiced it in the nineteenth century and Pope in the eighteenth; but such lines as Eliot's

> And the villages dirty and charging high prices,

or Auden's

> And fake with ease a leopard or a dove,

or Frost's

> What if it wasn't all it should be? I'd
> Be satisfied if he'd be satisfied—

certainly run counter in their tone to the general romantic tradition:

> It little profits that an idle king,
> By this still hearth, among these barren crags,
> Matched with an agèd wife . . .

A further contrast with the romantics lies in the variations of mood made possible by such diction. Romantic poetry (Byron, again, is an outstanding exception) customarily treats almost any subject with intense seriousness; modern poetry, with its increased use of drama, is fully capable of anticlimax, understatement, and other witty or ironic or mock-heroic devices. Auden's sonnet "Who's Who," for example, is mock-heroic in the most literal sense of that term. The opening lines of "Prufrock," in which the glow of the setting sun's last rays on the clouds is compared to the slight flush induced by ether in a patient undergoing an operation, have become famous or notorious. A romantic or Victorian elegist (Shelley or Tennyson, for example) would scarcely have spoken of the day on which the subject of his elegy died in such terms as Auden uses concerning Yeats's death:

> A few thousand will think of this day
> As one thinks of a day when one did something slightly unusual.

Nor would a romantic or Victorian—compare Tennyson's "Ulysses"—
have let a traveler who had gone far to witness the birth of Christ
speak of the climax of his journey in language like this:

> ... and so we continued
> And arrived at evening, not a moment too soon
> Finding the place; it was (you may say) satisfactory.

At their best, such sudden drops in tone are integrally related to
the total meaning of the poems in which they occur. Prufrock com-
pares the evening to an unconscious patient because he feels that his
own powers of action are anesthetized by hesitation and self-conscious-
ness; the metaphor about the evening is an extension of his self-
awareness into his surroundings. Auden's elegy on Yeats develops a
paradox about the power and impotence of poetry. Poetry survives and
changes our ways of looking at the world; yet it "makes nothing
happen," and the death of a writer looks small in the newspapers
compared to the movements of the stock exchange. "The Journey of
the Magi" dramatizes the disheartening difficulties entailed by the
attainment of faith among "an alien people clutching their gods";
rapture like that of Milton's Nativity Ode would be out of character
in Eliot's aging Wise Man.

3. *Imagery:* The surest and best approach to many a supposedly
"difficult" modern poem is through its imagery. A reader who begins
by asking "What is the central metaphor (or metaphors) of this
poem, and what are its implications?" will probably arrive more
quickly at a fuller enjoyment and comprehension of the poem as a
whole than will a reader on the lookout only for a story or an explicit
general statement of the poem's theme. The importance of imagery
today, and the structural weight it often carries, can readily be demon-
strated by a few examples.

Hopkins's sonnet "The Caged Skylark" offers an example of an
extended comparison whose meaning is gradually developed as the
poem proceeds. The octet states the basic simile clearly: man's spirit
imprisoned in his body is like a skylark in a cage:

> As a dare-gale skylark scanted in a dull cage
>   Man's mounting spirit in his bone-house, mean house, dwells—
>   That bird beyond the remembering his free fells;
> This in drudgery, day-labouring-out life's age.
> Though aloft on turf or perch or poor low stage,
>   Both sing sometimes the sweetest, sweetest spells,
>   Yet both droop deadly sometimes in their cells
> Or wring their barriers in bursts of fear or rage.

The sestet frees the skylark from the cage altogether:

> Not that the sweet-fowl, song-fowl, needs no rest—
> Why, hear him, hear him babble and drop down to his nest,
>   But his own nest, wild nest, no prison.

Logic might expect the poem to conclude with a corresponding picture of man's soul freed (by death) from its body; but Hopkins is now concerned with unlikeness rather than likeness:

> Man's spirit will be flesh-bound when found at best,
> But uncumbered: meadow-down is not distressed
>   For a rainbow footing it nor he for his bones risen.

For man at his best, that is, the bodily "cage" is only a seeming prison; he is really "uncumbered," and spiritual vitality is no more incompatible with physical circumstance than the colors of the rainbow are with the earth out of which the bow seems to rise. The "meadow down" of the next-to-last line takes us back to the *uncaged* skylark with which man is finally compared.

T. S. Eliot's "Waste Land," a puzzling poem on the surface, can be readily approached even by a reader wholly ignorant of French, German, Italian, and Sanscrit if it is seen as a study in the analogy between two central images: a modern city and a desert. As in a documentary motion picture, the city-image is presented partly by direct description of such things as the crowd flowing over London Bridge or the cigarette boxes along the Thames; and partly by a series of dramatized glimpses into the lives and thoughts of various inhabitants, ranging from the archduke's cousin of the opening lines to the Thames maidens of Part III, and including along the way the contrasted upper- and lower-class scenes of Part II. The desert image frames the poem by its appearances in the first and last sections; it crops up in such passages as the "Burning burning burning burning" at the end of Part III; and it evokes various contrasting water-images, notably in Part IV. (Similarly, the modern city and its inhabitants also evoke contrasts; these are drawn from the past—from Elizabethan London, for example.) Linking the two images of the desert and the city is the figure of the king who, at the end of the poem, sits "Fishing, with the arid plain behind me"; the king's voice may be imagined as speaking to us through the mouths of other commentators (like Tiresias) at various points in the poem. In summary, then, "The Waste Land" might be said to be about a king whose city has become, or is becoming, a desert. The problem of reading the poem is mostly a problem of getting at the implications of the desert metaphor by means of an analysis of the kinds of lives led by the city-dwellers.

Auden's "The Climbers" is a sonnet in which the use of nature to dramatize psychology approaches pure allegory. The method is announced by the phrase "mountains of my fear" in the third line. In trying to penetrate these mountains (and obtain self-knowledge) the speaker stumbles and consoles himself with his own faults that have flowered "on a lower alp." In the sestet, accompanied by his mistress, he scales the mountain with ease. overcoming his fear with the aid of love. But the method turns out to nave its drawbacks. Pre-occupation with his companion has made him lose sight of his object, and the job of critical self-analysis remains undone. The two climbers

> Returned to shore, the rich interior still
> Unknown. Love gave the power, but took the will.

Again the implications of the extended image are the key to the poem.

Finally, it is well not to try to pin an image down too tightly, or limit it to a single possible meaning. In Eliot's dramatic monologue "Gerontion," for example, the "house" in which the old man lives is evidently both a literal and a metaphorical edifice. It is first the real house in which the homeless speaker, abandoned, hostile, and suspicious, is living out his old age; but as the poem proceeds it merges into the house of the past, a kind of museum of the old man's memories: a house in which Mr. Silvero walks in the next room; a house with booby-traps in the form of deceptive passages and corridors. Suddenly the whole bearing of the image shifts, and the house becomes the old man's body. Gerontion fears that even after death, even after he "stiffens in a rented house" he cannot evade Christ the tiger. His vain attempts to rekindle physical delight in old age are like furnishing the bodily house with "a wilderness of mirrors;" decrepitude (the spider and the weevil) cannot be forestalled. The last metamorphosis of the house is into Gerontion's mind; his musings are finally said to have been

> Tenants of the house
> Thoughts of a dry brain in a dry season.

〜✿〜

"For the Time Being"

Most of the characteristics of modern poetry discussed so far are apparent in Auden's adaptation of the traditional Christmas-pageant form, "For the Time Being." The chasm separating tangible and intangible sorts of value is dramatized in the contrast between the Fugal-Chorus in praise of technology—

> Instead of building temples, we build laboratories;
> Instead of offering sacrifices, we perform experiments;
> Instead of reciting prayers, we note pointer-readings;
> Our lives are no longer erratic but efficient—

and the meditation of Simeon on the transcendent meaning of the birth of Christ—

> By the event of this birth the true significance of all other events is defined, for of every other occasion it can be said that it could have been different, but of this birth it is the case that it could in no way be other than it is. And by the existence of this Child, the proper value of all other existences is given, for of every other creature it can be said that it has extrinsic importance but of this Child it is the case that He is in no sense a symbol.

The sense of transience and decay in physical experience is communicated most vividly in the third speech of Intuition:

> I have observed
> The sombre valley of an industry
> In dereliction. Conduits, ponds, canals,
> Distressed with weeds; engines and furnaces
> At rust in rotting shed; and their strong users
> Transformed to spongy heaps of drunken flesh . . .

The decay of meaning itself, culminating in nightmare, recurs again and again throughout the entire oratorio. In the first chorus "Darkness and snow descend/On all personality"; in the first speech of the Narrator, Horror "scratches its way in" at the back of the brain; in one of Feeling's speeches "Insects with ladders stormed a virgin's house"; the Star of the Nativity calls on the three Wise Men to "Take the cold hand of Terror for a guide"; and in the "well-run" desert through which the Holy Family flee into Egypt "anguish arrives by cable."

As for the idea of nature, Auden here as elsewhere in his poetry uses the sense of close communion between man and nature (a sense which to the Romantics had been theoretically as natural as breath itself) as a symbol of an innocence now lost and irrecoverable: "as long as there remained the least understanding between Adam and the stars, rivers, and horses with whom he had once known complete intimacy . . . there was still a hope that the effects of the poison would wear off, that the exile from Paradise was only a bad dream . . ."

Auden's treatment of history involves an implicit repudiation of the ideas of utopianism and progress. As the Narrator's final speech suggests, the Vision recurs annually even though its recipients fail to do anything more than entertain it as an agreeable possibility; and the constant interchange of imagery drawn from the first-century Roman world with up-to-date imagery like "the truck-drivers no longer carry guns" constantly implies that the problems of reason versus revelation, the absolute versus the relative, the One and the Many are no less alive or nearer solution today than they were a millennium ago. For the purposes of this poem history is what it was to many a medieval intellectual: a chronicle of varied events, sometimes bloody and discouraging, but evaluated and ordered once and for all by the ingression of the Eternal into the Temporal at Bethlehem. Thus all time is always present, and Auden is constantly enabled to suggest witty or satiric parallels between the century of Augustus and the century of Winston Churchill. And as in the popular theater of Chaucer's age, the familiar traditional machinery of Christian stories is revivified and made immediate by the infusion of sharply contemporary language, rhythms, scenery, and even gags.

POSTSCRIPT: 1961

The past ten years have seen the increasing growth of several previously established reputations in modern poetry, most notably those of Pound and Stevens; the emergence of new poets, such as Prince and Lowell, on both sides of the Atlantic; but not any basic change in preoccupations or procedures. A gulf that has perhaps widened is that between iambic and non-iambic approaches to verse form. On the one hand there is the still vigorous "rebel" tradition exemplified by Pound's "Cantos," much of Eliot's "Waste Land" and "Quartets," and the poetry of William Carlos Williams—it is pretty hard to see how the following passage, for example, though undoubtedly rhythmic, falls into any recurrent pattern of scansion:

> For heaven's sake though see to the driver!
> Take off the silk hat! In fact
> that's no place at all for him
> up there unceremoniously
> dragging our friend out to his own dignity!
> Bring him down—bring him down!

On the other hand, the Robinson-Yeats-Frost tradition of slight but significant variation on a relatively rigid iambic base—

> Upon the floor of light, and time,
> Unmurmuring, of polyp made,
> We rest; we are, as light withdraws,
> Twin atolls on a shelf of shade—

shows no signs of abandonment by younger writers like Wilbur or Amis.

A poem that takes advantage of the iambic-quatrain norm in order to try what can be done by warping it is Eberhart's "The Fury of Aerial Bombardment":

> You would think the fury of aerial bombardment
> Would rouse God to relent; the infinite spaces
> Are still silent. He looks on shock-pried faces.
> History, even, does not know what is meant.
>
> You would feel that after so many centuries
> God would give man to repent; yet he can kill
> As Cain could, but with multitudinous will,
> No farther advanced than in his ancient furies.
>
> Was man made stupid to see his own stupidity?
> Is God by definition indifferent, beyond us all?
> Is the eternal truth man's fighting soul
> Wherein the Beast ravens in its own avidity?
>
> Of Van Wettering I speak, and Averill,
> Names on a list, whose faces I do not recall
> But they are gone to early death, who late in school
> Distinguished the belt feed lever from the belt holding pawl.

How can the first line be accented so that "bombardment" will suggest an approximate rime with "meant" in line four?—or the fifth so that "furies" will seem to echo "centuries"? Do the strongly riming first and last lines of stanza three have the same number of feet? If the poem's theoretical norm is iambic pentameter, is there some way of squeezing the two concluding lines into it? Or should they be read in the easiest way, with six beats each? And if the theoretical rime scheme—or scheme of near-rimes—is ABBA, how can "recall" and "pawl" in the fourth stanza be prevented from yanking the pattern out of shape by their clear harmony? Or are we supposed to see "averill-pawl" as bracketing "recall-school"? And what has become of the internal rimes in the second line of each stanza: "relent," "repent," and (possibly) "indifferent"? Why has this ripple vanished? In short, why does the poet take the trouble to construct what looks at various points like a heavily deliberate machinery of sound effects, only to throw monkey-wrenches into the works?

An answer is suggested, perhaps, by the word "shock-pried" in stanza one. Not only are the faces of the air-raid victims pried apart by concussion—so also are the poet-philosopher's meditations on war and the verse-forms in which he couches these meditations. Not that the result is chaos: individual effects justify themselves on inspection. The last two lines, for example, need setting apart from the rest because they introduce the poem's single vivid and particular bit of diction and imagery, the sudden unmasking of the machine gun; and they need the regularity of

But THEY are GONE to EARly DEATH . . .

to suggest the rhythm of marching feet, the steadiness of well-running machinery, and the marmoreal dignity of the epitaph offered by the speaker.

In conclusion it might be added that this marmoreal dignity, and the general intense brooding seriousness of "The Fury of Aerial Bombardment," are in some ways less modern than its meters. The tendency of twentieth-century verse, by contrast to Victorian, to use casual, off-hand diction for serious purposes, or to shift a poem's mood from solemn to light in midstream, begins at least as long ago as Hardy's "Ruined Maid" or "Channel Firing" and can be observed in this volume in poems by Auden, Pound, Cummings, Amis, Robinson, and Reed.

"The Fury of Aerial Bombardment" is, then, in its metrical technique an extension of the iambic-formal method, deriving some of its effectiveness from its approximate resemblance, in size and shape, to a sonnet. It is not a sonnet—it has sixteen lines, not fourteen, and they are not all of the right length—but its quatrain shape and its taut ending show a strenuous thrust toward the sort of well-margined neatness elegantly achieved in Robinson's "New England." At the other extreme from Robinson stands the Propertius and "Cantos" poetry of Ezra Pound—

When, when, and whenever death closes our eyelids,
Moving naked over Acheron
Upon the one raft, victor and conquered together,
Marius and Jugurtha together,
        one tangle of shadows.

Pound's poetry offers a contrast to many of the poems in this volume in more than just technique: it is a kaleidoscopic attempt to communicate by means of an anthology of moods, attitudes, and techniques drawn from the European, and sometimes the Asiatic, past. A minor experimenter like E. E. Cummings may construct a special language —"Any one lived in a pretty how town"—for a single poem; Pound, writing from inside a Pisan prison camp with the ruins of Europe about him and the wreckage of his private life confronting him, uses a series of languages (translations of Chaucer, scraps of Italian or Middle English thrown together for the occasion) just as he had done a generation earlier in the major experiments that inspired Eliot's "Waste Land." Poems like Larkin's "Church-going," Thomas's "Fern Hill," and Warren's "Bearded Oaks," which derive strength from evocations of particular, localized, static scenes in the American South or the English or Welsh countryside, perpetuate an opposing tradition in twentieth-century verse:

> Back at the door
> I sign the book, donate an Irish sixpence,
> Reflect the place was not worth stopping for . . .

It has to be Irish and a sixpence because the experience can only take place on a bicycle excursion through present-day rural England. Pound's centaur-ants in their dragon world belong to every time and place.

Five Poets

Gerard Manley Hopkins

GOD'S GRANDEUR

(1918)

The world is charged with the grandeur of God.
　　It will flame out, like shining from shook foil;
　　It gathers to a greatness, like the ooze of oil
Crushed. Why do men then now not reck his rod?
Generations have trod, have trod, have trod;　　　　　　　　　　5
　　And all is seared with trade; bleared, smeared with toil;
　　And wears man's smudge and shares man's smell: the soil
Is bare now, nor can foot feel, being shod.

And for all this, nature is never spent;
　　There lives the dearest freshness deep down things;　　　10
And though the last lights off the black West went
　　Oh, morning, at the brown brink eastward, springs—
Because the Holy Ghost over the bent
　　World broods with warm breast and with ah! bright wings.

The selections from Gerard Manley Hopkins are used with the permission of the Oxford University Press.

THE WINDHOVER:
To Christ Our Lord
(1918)

I caught this morning morning's minion, king-
    dom of daylight's dauphin, dapple-dawn-drawn Falcon, in his
    riding
  Of the rolling level underneath him steady air, and striding
High there, how he rung upon the rein of a wimpling wing
In his ecstasy! then off, off forth on swing,
    As a skate's heel sweeps smooth on a bow-bend: the hurl and
    gliding   5
  Rebuffed the big wind. My heart in hiding
Stirred for a bird,—the achieve of, the mastery of the thing!

Brute beauty and valor and act, oh, air, pride, plume, here
  Buckle! AND the fire that breaks from thee then, a billion
Times told lovelier, more dangerous, O my chevalier! *Christ* 10

  No wonder of it: shéer plód makes plow down sillion
Shine, and blue-bleak embers, ah my dear,
    Fall, gall themselves, and gash gold-vermilion.

Christ's buckling:
Crucifixion & Ressurection, Fall (same thing)

THE WINDHOVER: 3. *rung upon the rein:* "to ring" in falconry means to
rise in the air spirally, and this image is combined with that of a horse
circling at the end of a long rein, and then with wimpling, which suggests
both the plaited feathers of the wings and their undulation. 11. *sillion:*
furrow.

Hopkins attempts to emulate Christ
HUBRIS.

Tmesis - device of sep elements
that would normally go together
by junk in between.

Metonymy - met - one part of the whole
stands for one thing.

32

THE CAGED SKYLARK

(1918)

As a dare-gale skylark scanted in a dull cage
  Man's mounting spirit in his bone-house, mean house, dwells—
  That bird beyond the remembering his free fells;
This in drudgery, day-laboring-out life's age.

Though aloft on turf or perch or poor low stage,   5
  Both sing sometímes the sweetest, sweetest spells,
  Yet both droop deadly sómetimes in their cells
Or wring their barriers in bursts of fear or rage.

Not that the sweet-fowl, song-fowl, needs no rest—
Why, hear him, hear him babble and drop down to his nest,   10
  But his own nest, wild nest, no prison.

Man's spirit will be flesh-bound when found at best,
But uncumbered: meadow-down is not distressed
  For a rainbow footing it nor he for his bónes rísen.

❧

THE CAGED SKYLARK: 3. *fells:* moors. 5. *turf:* a reference to the custom of placing a turf full of clover inside the skylark's cage. Cf. John Webster's *The Duchess of Malfi*, IV, ii, 135 ff: "Didst thou ever see a lark in a cage? Such is the soul in the body: this world is like her little turf of grass, and the heaven o'er our heads, like her looking-glass, only gives us a miserable knowledge of the small compass of our prison."

FELIX RANDAL

(1918)

Felix Randal the farrier, O he is dead then? my duty all ended,
Who have watched his mold of man, big-boned and hardy-handsome
Pining, pining, till time when reason rambled in it and some
Fatal four disorders, fleshed there, all contended?

Sickness broke him. Impatient he cursed at first, but mended   5
Being anointed and all; though a heavenlier heart began some
Months earlier, since I had our sweet reprieve and ransom
Tendered to him. Ah well, God rest him all road ever he offended!

This seeing the sick endears them to us, us too it endears.   9
My tongue had taught thee comfort, touch had quenched thy tears,
Thy tears that touched my heart, child, Felix, poor Felix Randal;

How far from then forethought of, all thy more boisterous years,
When thou at the random grim forge, powerful amidst peers,
Didst fettle for the great grey drayhorse his bright and battering
    sandal!

❧

FELIX RANDAL: 13. *random:* from Old French *randon*—violence, rapidity,
and used in architecture to mean built with irregular stones. 14. *fettle:*
beat and make ready.

SPRING AND FALL:
To a Young Child
(1918)

Márgarét, are you gríeving
Over Goldengrove unleaving?
Leáves, líke the things of man, you
With your fresh thoughts care for, can you?
Áh! Ás the heart grows older   5
It will come to such sights colder
By a ¹ by, nor spare a sigh
Though worlds of wanwood leafmeal lie;
And yet you wíll weep and know why.
Now no matter, child, the name: 10
Sórrow's spríngs áre the same.
Nor mouth had, no nor mind, expressed
What heart heard of, ghost guessed:
It ís the blight man was born for,
It is Margaret you mourn for.   15

❧

SPRING AND FALL: 8. *leafmeal:* a word formed on the analogy of "piece-meal."

35

SPELT FROM SIBYL'S LEAVES

(1918)

Earnest, earthless, equal, attunable, | vaulty, voluminous, . . . stupen-
    dous
Evening strains to be tíme's vást, | womb-of-all, home-of-all, hearse-of-
    all night.
Her fond yellow hornlight wound to the west, | her wild hollow
    hoarlight hung to the height
Waste; her earliest stars, earl-stars, | stárs principal, overbend us,
Fíre-féaturing heaven. For earth | her being has unbound, her dapple
    is at an end, as-   5
tray or aswarm, all throughther, in throngs; | self ín self steepèd and
    páshed—qúite
Disremembering, dísmémbering | áll now. Heart, you round me right
With: Our évening is over us; óur night | whélms, whélms, ánd will
    end us.
Only the beak-leaved boughs dragonish | damask the tool-smooth bleak
    light; black,
Ever so black on it. Óur tale, O óur oracle! | Lét life, wáned, ah lét
    life wind   10
Off hér once skéined stained véined varíety | upon, áll on twó spools;
    párt, pen, páck
Now her áll in twó flocks, twó folds—black, white; | right, wrong;
    reckon but, reck but, mind
But thése two; wáre of a wórld where bút these | twó tell, each off the
    óther; of a rack
Where, selfwrung, selfstrung, sheathe- and shelterless, | thóughts
    agaínst thoughts ín groans grínd.

❧

SPELT FROM SIBYL'S LEAVES: 5. *as-:* divided to show the rhyme. 6. *through-*
ther: dialect form of through-other; *pashed:* beaten. 7. *round:* whisper or
talk privately to.

THE LEADEN ECHO AND THE GOLDEN ECHO
Maidens' Song from "St. Winefred's Well"

(1918)

THE LEADEN ECHO

How to kéep—is there ány any, is there none such, nowhere known
    some, bow or brooch or braid or brace, láce, latch or catch or key
    to keep
Back beauty, keep it, beauty, beauty, beauty, . . . from vanishing
    away?
O is there no frowning of these wrinkles, rankèd wrinkles deep,
Dówn? no waving off of these most mournful messengers, still messen-
    gers, sad and stealing messengers of grey?
No there's none, there's none, O no there's none,   5
Nor can you long be, what you now are, called fair,
Do what you may do, what, do what you may,
And wisdom is early to despair:
Be beginning; since, no, nothing can be done
To keep at bay   10
Age and age's evils, hoar hair,
Ruck and wrinkle, drooping, dying, death's worst, winding sheets,
    tombs and worms and tumbling to decay;
So be beginning, be beginning to despair.
O there's none; no no no there's none:
Be beginning to despair, to despair,   15
Despair, despair, despair, despair.

THE GOLDEN ECHO

      Spare!
There ís one, yes I have one (Hush there!);
Only not within seeing of the sun,
Not within the singeing of the strong sun,   20
Tall sun's tingeing, or treacherous the tainting of the earth's air,
Somewhere elsewhere there is ah well where! one,
Óne. Yes I cán tell such a key, I dó know such a place,

THE LEADEN ECHO: *"St. Winefred's Well"*: an unfinished play begun by
Hopkins in 1879. According to legend a spring rose from the ground where
Winefred's head fell after it was cut off by her would-be-ravisher, the
chieftain Caradoc. She was restored to life by St. Beuno.

Where whatever's prized and passes of us, everything that's fresh and
    fast flying of us, seems to us sweet of us and swiftly away with,
    done away with, undone,
Undone, done with, soon done with, and yet dearly and dangerously
    sweet   25
Of us, the wimpled-water-dimpled, not-by-morning-matchèd face,
The flower of beauty, fleece of beauty, too too apt to, ah! to fleet,
Never fleets móre, fastened with the tenderest truth
To its own best being and its loveliness of youth: it is an everlasting-
    ness of, O it is an all youth!
Come then, your ways and airs and looks, locks, maiden gear, gallantry
    and gaiety and grace,   30
Winning ways, airs innocent, maiden manners, sweet looks, loose locks,
    long locks, lovelocks, gaygear, going gallant, girlgrace—
Resign them, sign them, seal them, send them, motion them with
    breath,
And with sighs soaring, soaring síghs deliver
Them; beauty-in-the-ghost, deliver it, early now, long before death
Give beauty back, beauty, beauty, beauty, back to God, beauty's self
    and beauty's giver.   35
See; not a hair is, not an eyelash, not the least lash lost; every hair
Is, hair of the head, numbered.
Nay, what we had lighthanded left in surly the mere mould
Will have waked and have waxed and have walked with the wind
    what while we slept,
This side, that side hurling a heavyheaded hundredfold   40
What while we, while we slumbered.
O then, weary then why should we tread?   O why are we so haggard
    at the heart, so care-coiled, care-killed, so fagged, so fashed, so
    cogged, so cumbered,
When the thing we freely fórfeit is kept with fonder a care,
Fonder a care kept than we could have kept it, kept
Far with fonder a care (and we, we should have lost it) finer,
    fonder   45
A care kept.—Where kept? Do but tell us where kept, where.—
Yonder.—What high as that! We follow, now we follow.—Yonder,
    yes yonder, yonder,
Yonder.

---

42. *fashed:* troubled.

CARRION COMFORT

(1918)

Not, I'll not, carrion comfort, Despair, not feast on thee;
Not untwist—slack they may be—these last strands of man
In me ór, most weary, cry *I can no more*. I can;
Can something, hope, wish day come, not choose not to be.
But ah, but O thou terrible, why wouldst thou rude on me   5
Thy wring-world right foot rock? lay a lionlimb against me? scan
With darksome devouring eyes my bruisèd bones? and fan,
O in turns of tempest, me heaped there; me frantic to avoid thee and
    flee?

  Why? That my chaff might fly; my grain lie, sheer and clear.
Nay in all that toil, that coil, since (seems) I kissed the rod,   10
Hand rather, my heart lo! lapped strength, stole joy, would laugh,
    chéer.
Cheer whom though? the hero whose heaven-handling flung me, fóot
    tród
Me? or me that fought him? O which one? is it each one? That night.
    that year
Of now done darkness I wretch lay wrestling with (my God!) my
    God.

NO WORST, THERE IS NONE

(1918)

No worst, there is none. Pitched past pitch of grief,
More pangs will, schooled at forepangs, wilder wring.
Comforter, where, where is your comforting?
Mary, mother of us, where is your relief?
My cries heave, herds-long; huddle in a main, a chief   5
Woe, world-sorrow; on an age-old anvil wince and sing—
Then lull, then leave off. Fury had shrieked 'No ling-
ering! Let me be fell: force I must be brief.'

   O the mind, mind has mountains; cliffs of fall
Frightful, sheer, no-man-fathomed. Hold them cheap   10
May who ne'er hung there. Nor does long our small
Durance deal with that steep or deep. Here! creep,
Wretch, under a comfort serves in a whirlwind: all
Life death does end and each day dies with sleep.

I WAKE AND FEEL THE FELL OF DARK

(1918)

I wake and feel the fell of dark, not day.
What hours, O what black hoürs we have spent
This night! what sights you, heart, saw; ways you went!
And more must, in yet longer light's delay.
    With witness I speak this. But where I say   5
Hours I mean years, mean life. And my lament
Is cries countless, cries like dead letters sent
To dearest him that lives alas! away.

   I am gall, I am heartburn. God's most deep decree
Bitter would have me taste: my taste was me;   10
Bones built in me, flesh filled, blood brimmed the curse.
   Selfyeast of spirit a dull dough sours. I see
The lost are like this, and their scourge to be
As I am mine, their sweating selves; but worse.

THOU ART INDEED JUST, LORD

Justus quidem tu es, Domine, si disputem tecum: verum tamen justa loquar ad te: Quare via impiorum prosperatur? &c.

(1918)

Thou art indeed just, Lord, if I contend
With thee; but, sir, so what I plead is just.
Why do sinners' ways prosper? and why must
Disappointment all I endeavour end?
    Wert thou my enemy, O thou my friend,   5
How wouldst thou worse, I wonder, than thou dost
Defeat, thwart me? Oh, the sots and thralls of lust
Do in spare hours more thrive than I that spend,
Sir, life upon thy cause. See, banks and brakes
Now, leavèd how thick! lacèd they are again   10
With fretty chervil, look, and fresh wind shakes
Them; birds build—but not I build; no, but strain,
Time's eunuch, and not breed one work that wakes.
Mine, O thou lord of life, send my roots rain.

❦

THOU ART INDEED JUST, LORD: *Title:* Jeremiah 12:1. The Latin is translated by the first three lines of the poem.

TO R. B.
(1918)

The fine delight that fathers thought; the strong
Spur, live and lancing like the blowpipe flame,
Breathes once and, quenchèd faster than it came,
Leaves yet the mind a mother of immortal song.
Nine months she then, nay years, nine years she long   5
Within her wears, bears, cares and combs the same:
The widow of an insight lost she lives, with aim
Now known and hand at work now never wrong.

    Sweet fire the sire of muse, my soul needs this;
I want the one rapture of an inspiration.   10
O then if in my lagging lines you miss
The roll, the rise, the carol, the creation,
My winter world, that scarcely breathes that bliss
Now, yields you, with some sighs, our explanation.

∾

<small>TO R. B. *Title:* Robert Bridges.</small>

THE WRECK OF THE *DEUTSCHLAND*

To the
happy memory of five Franciscan Nuns
exiles by the Falk Laws
drowned between midnight and morning of
Dec. 7th, 1875

(1918)

PART THE FIRST

1

Thou mastering me
  God! giver of breath and bread;
  World's strand, sway of the sea;
  Lord of living and dead;
Thou hast bound bones and veins in me, fastened me flesh,   5
And after it almost unmade, what with dread,
  Thy doing: and dost thou touch me afresh?
Over again I feel thy finger and find thee.

2

I did say yes
  O at lightning and lashed rod;   10
Thou heardst me truer than tongue confess
  Thy terror, O Christ, O God;
Thou knowest the walls, altar and hour and night:
The swoon of a heart that the sweep and the hurl of thee trod
  Hard down with a horror of height: 15
And the midriff astrain with leaning of, laced with fire of stress.

THE WRECK: *Title:* Hopkins wrote to R. W. Dixon, October 5, 1878:
". . . when in the winter of '75 the *Deutschland* was wrecked in the mouth
of the Thames and five Franciscan nuns, exiles from Germany by the Falck
Laws, aboard of her were drowned I was affected by the account and happening to say so to my rector he said that he wished some one would
write a poem on the subject. On this hint I set to work and, though my
hand was out at first, produced one. I had long had haunting my ear the
echo of a new rhythm which now I realized on paper." The Falk Laws
of May 1873 (named for the Prussian minister of public worship) were
repressive measures against the Catholics.

3

The frown of his face
Before me, the hurtle of hell
Behind, where, where was a, where was a place?
I whirled out wings that spell   20
ₐnd fled with a fling of the heart to the heart of the Host.
ₐMy heart, but you were dovewinged, I can tell,
    Carrier-witted, I am bold to boast,
To flash from the flame to the flame then, tower from the grace to the
    grace.

4

I am soft sift   25
In an hourglass—at the wall
Fast, but mined with a motion, a drift,
    And it crowds and it combs to the fall;
I steady as a water in a well, to a poise, to a pane,
But roped with, always, all the way down from the tall   30
    Fells or flanks of the voel, a vein
Of the gospel proffer, a pressure, a principle, Christ's gift.

5

I kiss my hand
To the stars, lovely-asunder
Starlight, wafting him out of it; and   35
    Glow, glory in thunder;
Kiss my hand to the dappled-with-damson west:
Since, tho' he is under the world's splendour and wonder,
    His mystery must be instressed, stressed;
For I greet him the days I meet him, and bless when I understand. 40

---

20. *spell: that* time (a noun). 24. *grace:* in his *Note-books,* p. 332, Hopkins
defined grace as "any action, activity, on God's part by which, in creating
or after creating, he carries the creature to or towards the end of its
being, which is self-sacrifice to God and its salvation." 28. *combs:* rolls and
breaks like a wave. 29. *pane:* counterpane, an equally balanced counter-
part. 31. *Fells:* pastures; *voel:* a bare hill, specifically a mountain near St.
Beuno's College in North Wales where Hopkins was studying theology
when he wrote this poem. 32. *proffer:* (a noun). 37. *damson:* a dark purple
plum. 39. *instressed:* inwardly felt; one of Hopkins' favorite words, used
both as noun and verb to suggest spiritual illumination, an insight by help
of divine grace into what Hopkins called "inscape" or ultimate reality.

6

Not out of his bliss
Springs the stress felt
Nor first from heaven (and few know this)
Swings the stroke dealt—
Stroke and a stress that stars and storms deliver,   45
That guilt is hushed by, hearts are flushed by and melt—
But it rides time like riding a river
(And here the faithful waver, the faithless fable and miss).

7

It dates from day
Of his going in Galilee;   50
Warm-laid grave of a womb-life grey;
Manger, maiden's knee;
The dense and the driven Passion, and frightful sweat;
Thence the discharge of it, there its swelling to be,
Though felt before, though in high flood yet—   55
What none would have known of it, only the heart, being hard at bay,

8

Is out with it! Oh,
We lash with the best or worst
Word last! How a lush-kept plush-capped sloe
Will, mouthed to flesh-burst,   60
Gush!—flush the man, the being with it, sour or sweet,
Brim, in a flash, full!—Hither then, last or first,
To hero of Calvary, Christ's feet—
Never ask if meaning it, wanting it, warned of it—men go.

9

Be adored among men,   65
God, three-numberèd form;
Wring thy rebel, dogged in den,
Man's malice, with wrecking and storm.
Beyond saying sweet, past telling of tongue,

Thou art lightning and love, I found it, a winter and warm;   70
    Father and fondler of heart thou hast wrung:
Hast thy dark descending and most art merciful then.

10

    With an anvil-ding
    And with fire in him forge thy will
  Or rather, rather then, stealing as Spring   75
    Through him, melt him but master him still:
Whether at once, as once at a crash Paul,
Or as Austin, a lingering-out swéet skíll,
    Make mercy in all of us, out of us all
Mastery, but be adored, but be adored King.   80

PART THE SECOND

11

    'Some find me a sword; some
    The flange and the rail; flame,
  Fang, or flood' goes Death on drum,
    And storms bugle his fame.
But wé dream we are rooted in earth—Dust!   85
Flesh falls within sight of us, we, though our flower the same,
  Wave with the meadow, forget that there must
The sour scythe cringe, and the blear share come.

12

    On Saturday sailed from Bremen,
    American-outward-bound,   90
  Take settler and seamen, tell men with women,
    Two hundred souls in the round—
O Father, not under thy feathers nor ever as guessing
The goal was a shoal, of a fourth the doom to be drowned;
  Yet did the dark side of the bay of thy blessing   95
Not vault them, the millions of rounds of thy mercy not reeve even
  them in?

---

77. *Paul:* St. Paul, who was converted with miraculous suddenness on the road to Damascus; see Acts 9. 78. *Austin:* St. Augustine (334-430), whose long and painful conversion is described in his *Confessions.* 91. *tell:* count. 93. *feathers:* cf. Psalms 91.4: "He shall cover thee with his feathers, and under his wing shalt thou trust. . . ." 95. *bay:* space in a building between columns. 96. *reeve:* fasten with ropes.

13

Into the snows she sweeps,
   Hurling the haven behind,
The Deutschland, on Sunday; and so the sky keeps,
   For the infinite air is unkind,   100
And the sea flint-flake, black-backed in the regular blow,
Sitting Eastnortheast, in cursed quarter, the wind;
   Wiry and white-fiery and whirlwind-swivellèd snow
Spins to the widow-making unchilding unfathering deeps.

14

She drove in the dark to leeward,   105
   She struck—not a reef or a rock
But the combs of a smother of sand: night drew her
   Dead to the Kentish Knock;
And she beat the bank down with her bows and the ride of her keel:
The breakers rolled on her beam with ruinous shock;   110
   And canvas and compass, the whorl and the wheel
Idle for ever to waft her or wind her with, these she endured.

15

Hope had grown grey hairs,
   Hope had mourning on,
Trenched with tears, carved with cares,   115
   Hope was twelve hours gone;
And frightful a nightfall folded rueful a day
Nor rescue, only rocket and lightship, shone,
   And lives at last were washing away:
To the shrouds they took,—they shook in the hurling and horrible
   airs.   120

16

One stirred from the rigging to save
   The wild woman-kind below,
With a rope's end round the man, handy and brave—
   He was pitched to his death at a blow,
For all his dreadnought breast and braids of thew: 125
They could tell him for hours, dandled the to and fro

---

107. *combs:* wave crests, breakers. 108. *Kentish Knock:* sandbank near the
mouth of the Thames. 111. *whorl:* propeller.

Through the cobbled foam-fleece, what could he do
With the burl of the fountains of air, buck and the flood of the wave?

17

They fought with God's cold—
  And they could not and fell to the deck   130
(Crushed them) or water (and drowned them) or rolled
  With the sea-romp over the wreck.
Night roared, with the heart-break hearing a heart-broke rabble,
The woman's wailing, the crying of child without check—
  Till a lioness arose breasting the babble,   135
A prophetess towered in the tumult, a virginal tongue told.

18

Ah, touched in your bower of bone
  Are you! turned for an exquisite smart,
Have you! make words break from me here all alone,
  Do you!—mother of being in me, heart.   140
O unteachably after evil, but uttering truth,
  Why, tears! is it? tears; such a melting, a madrigal start!
  Never-eldering revel and river of youth,
What can it be, this glee? the good you have there of your own?

19

Sister, a sister calling   145
  A master, her master and mine!—
And the inboard seas run swirling and hawling;
  The rash smart sloggering brine
Blinds her; but she that weather sees one thing, one;
Has one fetch in her: she rears herself to divine   150
  Ears, and the call of the tall nun
To the men in the tops and the tackle rode over the storm's brawling.

20

She was first of a five and came
  Of a coifèd sisterhood.
(O Deutschland, double a desperate name!   155
  O world wide of its good!

---

127. *cobbled:* as if covered with patches. 128. *burl:* a large flat knot on a tree; generally used by Hopkins to suggest fullness and roundness. 147. *hawling:* hauling. 148. *rash:* violent; *sloggering:* slugging. 150. *fetch:* idea, resource.

But Gertrude, lily, and Luther, are two of a town,
   Christ's lily and beast of the waste wood:
      From life's dawn it is drawn down,
Abel is Cain's brother and breasts they have sucked the same.)   160

21

      Loathed for a love men knew in them,
         Banned by the land of their birth,
      Rhine refused them. Thames would ruin them;
         Surf, snow, river and earth
   Gnashed: but thou art above, thou Orion of light;   165
      Thy unchancelling poising palms were weighing the worth,
         Thou martyr-master: in thy sight
Storm flakes were scroll-leaved flowers, lily showers—sweet heaven was
   astrew in them.

22

      Five! the finding and sake
         And cipher of suffering Christ.   170
      Mark, the mark is of man's make
         And the word of it Sacrificed.
   But he scores it in scarlet himself on his own bespoken,
      Before-time-taken, dearest prizèd and priced—
         Stigma, signal, cinquefoil token   175
For lettering of the lamb's fleece, ruddying of the rose-flake.

---

157. *Gertrude:* a German saint and mystic (c.1256-c.1302) who lived in a convent near Eisleben, Luther's birthplace. 158. *beast of the waste wood:* cf. Jeremiah 5.6: "Wherefor a lion out of the forest shall slay them, and a wolf of the evenings shall spoil them, a leopard shall watch over their cities: every one that goeth out thence shall be torn in pieces: because their transgressions are many, and their backslidings are increased." Cf. Dante's *Inferno,* Canto 1: "In the midway of this our mortal life, / I found me in a gloomy wood, astray / Gone upon the path direct. . . ." (tr. H. F. Cary) 165. *Orion:* God the hunter, from the representation of the constellation of Orion by a hunter with belt and sword; cf. Job 9.8-9: "Which alone spreadeth out the heavens, and treadeth upon the waves of the sea. Which maketh Arcturus, Orion, and Pleiades. . . ." 166. *unchancelling:* removing from the chancel, the part of the church reserved for the clergy. 169. *Five:* the number of Christ's wounds; *finding:* symbol through which it is found or known; *sake:* defined by Hopkins as "the being a thing has outside itself . . . a man by his name, fame, or memory, and also that in the thing by virtue of which especially it has this being abroad." (Letter to Robert Bridges, May 26, 1879.) 175. *stigma:* marks resembling Christ's wounds; *cinquefoil:* a rose or a rose-shaped design with five petals.

23

Joy fall to thee, father Francis,
  Drawn to the Life that died;
With the gnarls of the nails in thee, niche of the lance, his
  Lovescape crucified   180
And seal of his seraph-arrival! and these thy daughters
And five-livèd and leavèd favour and pride,
  Are sisterly sealed in wild waters,
To bathe in his fall-gold mercies, to breathe in his all-fire glances.

24

Away in the loveable west,   185
  On a pastoral forehead of Wales,
I was under a roof here, I was at rest,
  And they the prey of the gales;
She to the black-about air, to the breaker, the thickly
Falling flakes, to the throng that catches and quails   190
  Was calling 'O Christ, Christ, come quickly':
The cross to her she calls Christ to her, christens her wild-worst Best.

25

The majesty! what did she mean?
  Breathe, arch and original Breath.
Is it love in her of the being as her lover had been?   195
  Breathe, body of lovely Death.
They were else-minded then, altogether, the men
Woke thee with a *we are perishing* in the weather of Gennesareth.
  Or is it that she cried for the crown then,   199
The keener to come at the comfort for feeling the combating keen?

26

For how to the heart's cheering
  The down-dugged ground-hugged grey
Hovers off, the jay-blue heavens appearing
  Of pied and peeled May!

---

180. *Lovescape:* the pattern of Christ's wounds, the stigmata which were
believed to have appeared on the body of St. Francis of Assisi. 186. *forehead:* hill, site of St. Beuno College in the Vale of Clwyd. 198. *Gennesareth:*
Sea of Galilee, where Peter walked on the water, and Christ calmed the
storm; cf. Matthew 14. 204. *pied:* parti-colored; *peeled:* clean and polished;
cf. Isaiah 18.2-3: "Go, ye swift messengers, to a nation scattered and
peeled. . . ." (the marginal gloss in the Bible is *polished*).

Blue-beating and hoary-glow height; or night, still higher,   205
With belled fire and the moth-soft Milky Way,
   What by your measure is the heaven of desire,
The treasure never eyesight got, nor was ever guessed what for the
   hearing?

27

No, but it was not these.
   The jading and jar of the cart,   210
Time's tasking, it is fathers that asking for ease
   Of the sodden-with-its-sorrowing heart,
Not danger, electrical horror; then further it finds
The appealing of the Passion is tenderer in prayer apart:
   Other, I gather, in measure her mind's   215
Burden, in wind's burly and beat of endragonèd seas.

28

But how shall I . . . make me room there:
   Reach me a . . . Fancy, come faster—
Strike you the sight of it? look at it loom there,
   Thing that she . . . there then! the Master,   220
Ipse, the only one, Christ, King, Head:
He was to cure the extremity where he had cast her;
   Do, deal, lord it with living and dead;
Let him ride, her pride, in his triumph, despatch and have done with
   his doom there.

29

Ah! there was a heart right   225
   There was single eye!
Read the unshapeable shock night
   And knew the who and the why;
Wording it how but by him that present and past,
Heaven and earth are word of, worded by?—   230
   The Simon Peter of a soul! to the blast
Tarpeian-fast, but a blown beacon of light.

---

208. *eyesight:* cf. I Corinthians 2. 9: "Eye hath not seen, nor ear heard,
neither have entered into the heart of man, the things which God hath
prepared for them that love him." 211. *fathers:* turmoil fathers (produces)
the asking (desire) for quiet in which to pray apart. 217 ff. The broken
syntax is a deliberate attempt to merge the account of the wreck with that
of the nun's spiritual exaltation. 226. *eye:* cf. Matthew 6. 22: The light of
the body is the eye: if therefore thine eye be single, thy whole body shall
be full of light." 230. *word:* cf. John 1.1: "In the beginning was the Word,
and the Word was with God, and the Word was God." 231. *Simon Peter:*
who walked on the water to Christ; see Matthew 14. 24-33. 232. *Tarpeian-
fast:* as firm as the Tarpeian rock, a part of the Roman Capitoline.

30

Jesu, heart's light,
Jesu, maid's son,
What was the feast followed the night   235
Thou hadst glory of this nun?—
Feast of the one woman without stain.
For so conceivèd, so to conceive thee is done;
But here was heart-throe, birth of a brain,
Word, that heard and kept thee and uttered thee outright.   240

31

Well, she has thee for the pain, for the
Patience; but pity of the rest of them!
Heart, go and bleed at a bitterer vein for the
Comfortless unconfessed of them—
No not uncomforted: lovely-felicitous Providence   245
Finger of a tender of, O of a feathery delicacy, the breast of the
Maiden could obey so, be a bell to, ring of it, and
Startle the poor sheep back! is the shipwrack then a harvest, does tem-
pest carry the grain for thee?

32

I admire thee, master of the tides,
Of the Yore-flood, of the year's fall;   250
The recurb and the recovery of the gulf's sides,
The girth of it and the wharf of it and the wall;
Stanching, quenching ocean of a motionable mind;
Ground of being, and granite of it: past all
Grasp God, throned behind   255
Death with a sovereignty that heeds but hides, bodes but abides;

33

With a mercy that outrides
The all of water, an ark
For the listener; for the lingerer with a love glides
Lower than death and the dark;   260

---

237. *Feast:* of the Immaculate Conception of the Blessed Virgin Mary, December 8. 250. *Yore:* old, Noah's flood. 251. *recurb:* cf. Job 38. 8-11: "Or
who shut up the sea with doors, when it brake forth. . . ." 260. *Lower
than death:* souls in Purgatory.

A vein for the visiting of the past-prayer, pent in prison,
The-last-breath penitent spirits—the uttermost mark
    Our passion-plungèd giant risen,
The Christ of the Father compassionate, fetched in the storm of his
    strides.

34

Now burn, new born to the world,   265
    Doubled-naturèd name,
The heaven-flung, heart-fleshed, maiden-furled
    Miracle-in-Mary-of-flame,
Mid-numbered He in three of the thunder-throne!
Not a dooms-day dazzle in his coming nor dark as he came;   270
    Kind, but royally reclaiming his own;
A released shower, let flash to the shire, not a lightning of fire hard-
    hurled.

35

Dame, at our door
    Drowned, and among our shoals,
Remember us in the roads, the heaven-haven of the Reward: 275
    Our King back, oh, upon English souls!
Let him easter in us, be a dayspring to the dimness of us, be a
    crimson-cresseted east,
More brightening her, rare-dear Britain, as his reign rolls,
    Pride, rose, prince, hero of us, high-priest,
Our hearts' charity's hearth's fire, our thoughts' chivalry's throng's
    Lord.   280

262-64. The subject of the clause is Christ, the giant, who fetched the mark.
275. *roads:* a haven or roadstead where ships may ride at anchor. 277.
crimson-cresseted: as if lighted by cressets, iron vessels filled with burning
oil or wood.

William Butler Yeats

THE LAKE ISLE OF INNISFREE

(1893)

I WILL arise and go now, and go to Innisfree,
And a small cabin build there, of clay and wattles made:
Nine bean-rows will I have there, a hive for the honey-bee,
And live alone in the bee-loud glade.

And I shall have some peace there, for peace comes dropping slow,   5
Dropping from the veils of the morning to where the cricket sings;
There midnight's all a glimmer, and noon a purple glow,
And evening full of the linnet's wings.

I will arise and go now, for always night and day
I hear lake water lapping with low sounds by the shore;   10
While I stand on the roadway, or on the pavements grey,
I hear it in the deep heart's core.

WHEN YOU ARE OLD

(1893)

WHEN you are old and grey and full of sleep,
And nodding by the fire, take down this book,
And slowly read, and dream of the soft look
Your eyes had once, and of their shadows deep;

How many loved your moments of glad grace,   5
And loved your beauty with love false or true;
But one man loved the pilgrim soul in you,
And loved the sorrows of your changing face.

And bending down beside the glowing bars,
Murmur, a little sadly, how Love fled   10
And paced upon the mountains overhead
And hid his face amid a crowd of stars.

ADAM'S CURSE

(1904)

We sat together at one summer's end,
That beautiful mild woman, your close friend,
And you and I, and talked of poetry.
I said, 'A line will take us hours maybe;
Yet if it does not seem a moment's thought, 5
Our stitching and unstitching has been naught.

Better go down upon your marrow-bones
And scrub a kitchen pavement, or break stones
Like an old pauper, in all kinds of weather;
For to articulate sweet sounds together 10
Is to work harder than all these, and yet
Be thought an idler by the noisy set
Of bankers, schoolmasters, and clergymen
The martyrs call the world.'

          And thereupon
That beautiful mild woman for whose sake 15
There's many a one shall find out all heartache
On finding that her voice is sweet and low
Replied, 'To be born woman is to know—
Although they do not talk of it at school—
That we must labour to be beautiful.' 20

I said, 'It's certain there is no fine thing
Since Adam's fall but needs much labouring.
There have been lovers who thought love should be
So much compounded of high courtesy
That they would sigh and quote with learned looks 25
Precedents out of beautiful old books;
Yet now it seems an idle trade enough.'

We sat grown quiet at the name of love;
We saw the last embers of daylight die,
And in the trembling blue-green of the sky 30
A moon, worn as if it had been a shell
Washed by time's waters as they rose and fell
About the stars and broke in days and years.

I had a thought for no one's but your ears:
That you were beautiful, and that I strove 35
To love you in the old high way of love;
That it had all seemed happy, and yet we'd grown
As weary-hearted as that hollow moon.

THE FOLLY OF BEING COMFORTED

(1904)

One that is ever kind said yesterday:
'Your well-belovèd's hair has threads of gray,
And little shadows come about her eyes;
Time can but make it easier to be wise
Though now it seems impossible, and so   5
All that you need is patience.'
                        Heart cries, 'No,
I have not a crumb of comfort, not a grain.
Time can but make her beauty over again:
Because of that great nobleness of hers   10
The fire that stirs about her, when she stirs,
Burns but more clearly. O she had not these ways
When all the wild summer was in her gaze.'

O heart! O heart! if she'd but turn her head,
You'd know the folly of being comforted.   15

SEPTEMBER 1913

(1914)

What need you, being come to sense,
But fumble in a greasy till
And add the halfpence to the pence
And prayer to shivering prayer, until
You have dried the marrow from the bone;   5
For men were born to pray and save:
Romantic Ireland's dead and gone,
It's with O'Leary in the grave.

Yet they were of a different kind,
The names that stilled your childish play,   10
They have gone about the world like wind,
But little time had they to pray
For whom the hangman's rope was spun,
And what, God help us, could they save?
Romantic Ireland's dead and gone,   15
It's with O'Leary in the grave.

Was it for this the wild geese spread
The grey wing upon every tide;
For this that all that blood was shed,
For this Edward Fitzgerald died,   20
And Robert Emmet and Wolfe Tone,
All that delirium of the brave?
Romantic Ireland's dead and gone,
It's with O'Leary in the grave.

SEPTEMBER 1913: 8. *O'Leary:* John O'Leary, a life-long friend of Yeats',
was a militant Irish nationalist; he died in 1907. 20-1. *Edward Fitzgerald,
Robert Emmet, Wolfe Tone:* early Irish rebels whom Yeats greatly admired in his younger days. The first traveling play of the Dublin National Literary Society, which Yeats and O'Leary founded in 1892, was to
have been on Emmet, who had been hanged as a rebel in 1803; and Yeats
was active in the Wolfe Tone Centennial celebration of 1898. After that
date Yeats withdrew more and more from active politics, but the names of
the old revolutionists were still heroic to his ears.

Yet could we turn the years again,   25
And call those exiles as they were
In all their loneliness and pain,
You'd cry, 'Some woman's yellow hair
Has maddened every mother's son':
They weighed so lightly what they gave.   30
But let them be, they're dead and gone,
They're with O'Leary in the grave.

TO A FRIEND WHOSE WORK HAS COME TO NOTHING

(1914)

Now all the truth is out,
Be secret and take defeat
From any brazen throat,
For how can you compete,
Being honour bred, with one   5
Who, were it proved he lies,
Were neither shamed in his own
Nor in his neighbours' eyes?
Bred to a harder thing
Than Triumph, turn away   10
And like a laughing string
Whereon mad fingers play
Amid a place of stone,
Be secret and exult,
Because of all things known   15
That is most difficult.

THE MAGI

(1914)

Now as at all times I can see in the mind's eye,
In their stiff, painted clothes, the pale unsatisfied ones
Appear and disappear in the blue depth of the sky
With all their ancient faces like rain-beaten stones,
And all their helms of silver hovering side by side,   5
And all their eyes still fixed, hoping to find once more,
Being by Calvary's turbulence unsatisfied,
The uncontrollable mystery on the bestial floor.

THAT THE NIGHT COME

(1914)

SHE lived in storm and strife,
Her soul had such desire
For what proud death may bring
That it could not endure
The common good of life,   5
But lived as 'twere a king
That packed his marriage day
With banneret and pennon,
Trumpet and kettledrum,
And the outrageous cannon,   10
To bundle time away
That the night come.

❧

THE WILD SWANS AT COOLE
(1919)

The trees are in their autumn beauty,
The woodland paths are dry,
Under the October twilight the water
Mirrors a still sky;
Upon the brimming water among the stones   5
Are nine-and-fifty swans.

The nineteenth autumn has come upon me
Since I first made my count;
I saw, before I had well finished,
All suddenly mount   10
And scatter wheeling in great broken rings
Upon their clamorous wings.

I have looked upon those brilliant creatures,
And now my heart is sore.
All's changed since I, hearing at twilight,   15
The first time on this shore,
The bell-beat of their wings above my head,
Trod with a lighter tread.

Unwearied still, lover by lover,
They paddle in the cold   20
Companionable streams or climb the air;
Their hearts have not grown old;
Passion or conquest, wander where they will,
Attend upon them still.

But now they drift on the still water   25
Mysterious, beautiful;
Among what rushes will they build,
By what lake's edge or pool
Delight men's eyes when I awake some day
To find they have flown away?   30

THE WILD SWANS AT COOLE: *Coole:* The home of Lady Gregory in Galway,
where Yeats spent most of his summers after 1896.

ON WOMAN

(1919)

MAY God be praised for woman
That gives up all her mind,
A man may find in no man
A friendship of her kind
That covers all he has brought   5
As with her flesh and bone,
Nor quarrels with a thought
Because it is not her own.

Though pedantry denies,
It's plain the Bible means   10
That Solomon grew wise
While talking with his queens,
Yet never could, although
They say he counted grass,
Count all the praises due   15
When Sheba was his lass,
When she the iron wrought, or
When from the smithy fire
It shuddered in the water:
Harshness of their desire   20
That made them stretch and yawn,
Pleasure that comes with sleep,
Shudder that made them one.
What else He give or keep
God grant me—no, not here,   25
For I am not so bold
To hope a thing so dear
Now I am growing old,
But when, if the tale's true,
The Pestle of the moon   30
That pounds up all anew
Brings me to birth again—
To find what once I had
And know what once I have known,

ON WOMAN: 19. *water*: often used by Yeats as symbol of the female. 31.
Pestle . . . anew: cf. *The Second Coming*, 1n, and *The Tower*, 54n.

Until I am driven mad,   35
Sleep driven from my bed,
By tenderness and care,
Pity, an aching head,
Gnashing of teeth, despair;
And all because of some one   40
Perverse creature of chance,
And live like Solomon
That Sheba led a dance.

EASTER, 1916

(1921)

I have met them at close of day
Coming with vivid faces
From counter or desk among grey
Eighteenth-century houses.
I have passed with a nod of the head   5
Or polite meaningless words,
Or have lingered awhile and said
Polite meaningless words,
And thought before I had done
Of a mocking tale or a gibe   10
To please a companion
Around the fire at the club,
Being certain that they and I
But lived where motley is worn:
All changed, changed utterly: 15
A terrible beauty is born.

That woman's days were spent
In ignorant good-will,
Her nights in argument
Until her voice grew shrill.   20
What voice more sweet than hers
When, young and beautiful,
She rode to harriers?
This man had kept a school
And rode our wingèd horse;   25

EASTER, 1916: The Easter Rising of 1916 was an armed revolt of the
Irish Republicans, who seized public buildings in Dublin, but were soon
suppressed by the British. Among the leaders executed were old friends
of Yeats —MacDonagh, Connolly, Pearse, and John MacBride, who had
been living in Dublin in separation from his wife, Maud Gonne, to whom
Yeats was devoted. Word of the Rising reached Yeats in England. It surprised and stirred him as no public event had for many years. "I am
trying to write a poem on the men executed," Yeats wrote to Lady
Gregory; " 'terrible beauty has been born again.'" 17. *woman:* Countess
Markievicz. 24. *man:* Pearse.

This other his helper and friend
Was coming into his force;
He might have won fame in the end,
So sensitive his nature seemed,
So daring and sweet his thought.   30
This other man I had dreamed
A drunken, vainglorious lout.
He had done most bitter wrong
To some who are near my heart,
Yet I number him in the song;   35
He, too, has resigned his part
In the casual comedy;
He, too, has been changed in his turn,
Transformed utterly:
A terrible beauty is born.   40

Hearts with one purpose alone
Through summer and winter seem
Enchanted to a stone
To trouble the living stream.
The horse that comes from the road,   45
The rider, the birds that range
From cloud to tumbling cloud,
Minute by minute they change;
A shadow of cloud on the stream
Changes minute by minute;   50
A horse-hoof slides on the brim,
And a horse plashes within it;
The long-legged moor-hens dive,
And hens to moor-cocks call;
Minute by minute they live: 55
The stone's in the midst of all.

Too long a sacrifice
Can make a stone of the heart.
O when may it suffice?
That is Heaven's part, our part   60
To murmur name upon name,
As a mother names her child
When sleep at last has come
On limbs that had run wild.

26. *This other:* MacDonagh. 31. *man:* MacBride.

What is it but nightfall?   65
No, no, not night but death;
Was it needless death after all?
For England may keep faith
For all that is done and said.
We know their dream; enough   70
To know they dreamed and are dead;
And what if excess of love
Bewildered them till they died?
I write it out in a verse—
MacDonagh and MacBride   75
And Connolly and Pearse
Now and in time to be,
Wherever green is worn,
Are changed, changed utterly:
A terrible beauty is born.   80

A PRAYER FOR MY DAUGHTER

(1921)

Once more the storm is howling, and half hid
Under this cradle-hood and coverlid
My child sleeps on. There is no obstacle
But Gregory's wood and one bare hill
Whereby the haystack- and roof-levelling wind,   5
Bred on the Atlantic, can be stayed;
And for an hour I have walked and prayed
Because of the great gloom that is in my mind.

I have walked and prayed for this young child an hour
And heard the sea-wind scream upon the tower,   10
And under the arches of the bridge, and scream
In the elms above the flooded stream;
Imagining in excited reverie
That the future years had come,
Dancing to a frenzied drum,   15
Out of the murderous innocence of the sea.

May she be granted beauty and yet not
Beauty to make a stranger's eye distraught,
Or hers before a looking-glass, for such,
Being made beautiful overmuch,   20
Consider beauty a sufficient end,
Lose natural kindness and maybe
The heart-revealing intimacy
That chooses right, and never find a friend.

Helen being chosen found life flat and dull   25
And later had much trouble from a fool,
While that great Queen, that rose out of the spray,
Being fatherless could have her way
Yet chose a bandy-leggèd smith for man.
It's certain that fine women eat   30

DAUGHTER: Anne Butler Yeats, b. Feb. 24, 1919. 4. *Gregory's wood:* cf. *The Tower,* note on title. 25. *Helen:* Helen (later, of Troy), wife to Menelaus of Sparta. 26. *fool:* Paris, with whom she absconded to Troy. 27. *Queen:* Aphrodite, born of the sea. 29. *smith:* Hephaestos (or Vulcan), the gods' blacksmith, Aphrodite's husband.

A crazy salad with their meat
Whereby the Horn of Plenty is undone.

In courtesy I'd have her chiefly learned;
Hearts are not had as a gift but hearts are earned
By those that are not entirely beautiful;   35
Yet many, that have played the fool
For beauty's very self, has charm made wise,
And many a poor man that has roved,
Loved and thought himself beloved,
From a glad kindness cannot take his eyes.   40

May she become a flourishing hidden tree
That all her thoughts may like the linnet be,
And have no business but dispensing round
Their magnanimities of sound,
Nor but in merriment begin a chase,   45
Nor but in merriment a quarrel.
O may she live like some green laurel
Rooted in one dear perpetual place.

My mind, because the minds that I have loved,
The sort of beauty that I have approved,   50
Prosper but little, has dried up of late,
Yet knows that to be choked with hate
May well be of all evil chances chief.
If there's no hatred in a mind
Assault and battery of the wind   55
Can never tear the linnet from the leaf.

An intellectual hatred is the worst,
So let her think opinions are accursed.
Have I not seen the loveliest woman born
Out of the mouth of Plenty's horn,   60
Because of her opinionated mind
Barter that horn and every good
By quiet natures understood
For an old bellows full of angry wind?

Considering that, all hatred driven hence,   65
The soul recovers radical innocence

32. *Horn:* cf. lines 60, 62, and 79-80. 59. *woman:* e.g., Maud Gonne, whom
Yeats saw as ideal beauty and power wasted on Irish nationalism and
revolutionary harangues (line 64).

And learns at last that it is self-delighting,
Self-appeasing, self-affrighting,
And that its own sweet will is Heaven's will;
She can, though every face should scowl   70
And every windy quarter howl
Or every bellows burst, be happy still.

And may her bridegroom bring her to a house
Where all's accustomed, ceremonious;
For arrogance and hatred are the wares   75
Peddled in the thoroughfares.
How but in custom and in ceremony
Are innocence and beauty born?
Ceremony's a name for the rich horn,
And custom for the spreading laurel tree.   80

THE SECOND COMING

(1921)

Turning and turning in the widening gyre
The falcon cannot hear the falconer;
Things fall apart; the centre cannot hold;
Mere anarchy is loosed upon the world,
The blood-dimmed tide is loosed, and everywhere   5
The ceremony of innocence is drowned;
The best lack all conviction, while the worst
Are full of passionate intensity.

Surely some revelation is at hand;
Surely the Second Coming is at hand.   10
The Second Coming! Hardly are those words out
When a vast image out of *Spiritus Mundi*
Troubles my sight: somewhere in sands of the desert
A shape with lion body and the head of a man,
A gaze blank and pitiless as the sun,   15
Is moving its slow thighs, while all about it
Reel shadows of the indignant desert birds.
The darkness drops again; but now I know
That twenty centuries of stony sleep
Were vexed to nightmare by a rocking cradle,   20
And what rough beast, its hour come round at last,
Slouches towards Bethlehem to be born?

THE SECOND COMING. 1. *gyre:* (which Yeats pronounced with a hard *g*)
is literally the spiral flight of the bird, but in Yeats' mystical system (described in *A Vision*) two interpenetrating whirling gyres or cones (or
Irish "pern"—a spool) are used to represent the movements of civilizations.
Thus gyre in this symbolic sense colors the idea of a second coming from
Revelation and ancient tradition with Yeats' belief that the Great Year,
dating from the birth of Christ, was coming to an end with an ominous
transvaluation of values. 12. *Spiritus Mundi:* another term in Yeats'
mystical system, meaning the world's collective spirit or memory.

SAILING TO BYZANTIUM

(1928)

I

That is no country for old men. The young
In one another's arms, birds in the trees,
—Those dying generations—at their song,
The salmon-falls, the mackerel-crowded seas,
Fish, flesh, or fowl, commend all summer long   5
Whatever is begotten, born, and dies.
Caught in that sensual music all neglect
Monuments of unageing intellect.

II

An agèd man is but a paltry thing,
A tattered coat upon a stick, unless   10
Soul clap its hands and sing, and louder sing
For every tatter in its mortal dress,
Nor is there singing school but studying
Monuments of its own magnificence;
And therefore I have sailed the seas and come   15
To the holy city of Byzantium.

III

O sages standing in God's holy fire
As in the gold mosaic of a wall,
Come from the holy fire, perne in a gyre,
And be the singing-masters of my soul.   20
Consume my heart away; sick with desire

SAILING TO BYZANTIUM. 16. *Byzantium:* the holy city of eastern Christendom, was a symbol of art and intellect for Yeats. He had seen and admired its mosaics in 1907 and 1924. He wrote in *A Vision* (New York, 1938, p. 279) that if he could have a month in antiquity he would spend it in Byzantium before the opening of St. Sophia and the closing of Plato's Academy, talking to some philosophical worker in mosaics and experiencing history's one union of the religious, aesthetic, and practical life. 17. *fire:* Yeats asserted that there were two antithetical realities: the terrestrial (a condition of power, heterogeneity, and strain) and fire (a condition of music and rest). 19. *perne in a gyre:* see the notes to "The Second Coming."

And fastened to a dying animal
It knows not what it is; and gather me
Into the artifice of eternity.

IV

Once out of nature I shall never take   25
My bodily form from any natural thing,
But such a form as Grecian goldsmiths make
Of hammered gold and gold enamelling
To keep a drowsy Emperor awake;
Or set upon a golden bough to sing   30
To lords and ladies of Byzantium
Of what is past, or passing, or to come.

❧

29. *Emperor:* Yeats recalled (in a note in *Collected Poems,* New York, 1933, p. 450) that he had read of artificial birds that sang on a goid and silver tree in the Byzantine emperor's palace.

THE TOWER

(1928)

I

What shall I do with this absurdity—
O heart, O troubled heart—this caricature,
Decrepit age that has been tied to me
As to a dog's tail?
     Never had I more
Excited, passionate, fantastical   5
Imagination, nor an ear and eye
That more expected the impossible—
No, not in boyhood when with rod and fly,
Or the humbler worm, I climbed Ben Bulben's back
And had the livelong summer day to spend.   10
It seems that I must bid the Muse go pack,
Choose Plato and Plotinus for a friend
Until imagination, ear and eye,
Can be content with argument and deal
In abstract things; or be derided by   15
A sort of battered kettle at the heel.

II

I pace upon the battlements and stare
On the foundations of a house, or where
Tree, like a sooty finger, starts from the earth;
And send imagination forth   20
Under the day's declining beam, and call
Images and memories
From ruin or from ancient trees,
For I would ask a question of them all.

THE TOWER: *Title:* In 1917 Yeats bought a piece of the Gregory estate in Galway on which was a Norman tower, Thoor Ballylee. It became his study and frequently appears in his poems. 12. *Plotinus:* Roman Neo-Platonic philosopher (205?-270), who held true reality to be an abstract system of ideal forms; cf. 146-147.

Beyond that ridge lived Mrs. French, and once 25
When every silver candlestick or sconce
Lit up the dark mahogany and the wine,
A serving-man, that could divine
That most respected lady's every wish,
Ran and with the garden shears 30
Clipped an insolent farmer's ears
And brought them in a little covered dish.

Some few remembered still when I was young
A peasant girl commended by a song,
Who'd lived somewhere upon that rocky place, 35
And praised the colour of her face,
And had the greater joy in praising her,
Remembering that, if walked she there,
Farmers jostled at the fair
So great a glory did the song confer. 40

And certain men, being maddened by those rhymes,
Or else by toasting her a score of times,
Rose from the table and declared it right
To test their fancy by their sight;
But they mistook the brightness of the moon 45
For the prosaic light of day—
Music had driven their wits astray—
And one was drowned in the great bog of Cloone.

Strange, but the man who made the song was blind;
Yet, now I have considered it, I find 50
That nothing strange; the tragedy began
With Homer that was a blind man,
And Helen has all living hearts betrayed.
O may the moon and sunlight seem
One inextricable beam, 55
For if I triumph I must make men mad.

---

25. *Mrs. French:* like other persons in the poem, she was associated with the neighborhood of Thoor Ballylee. She lived at Peterswell in the eighteenth century, and was related to Sir Jonah Barrington (1760-1834), an Irish judge, in whose *Sketches of His Own Time* (1827, 1832) Yeats read about the incident of the ear. **34.** *girl:* Mary Hynes, a local beauty celebrated by Raftery and still remembered in Yeats' time. **49.** *man . . . blind:* Raftery, the blind Irish poet. **54.** *moon and sunlight:* in Yeats' philosophy the moon is subjective man and the sun (the dark of the moon) is objec-

And I myself created Hanrahan
And drove him drunk or sober through the dawn
From somewhere in the neighbouring cottages.
Caught by an old man's juggleries   60
He stumbled, tumbled, fumbled to and fro
And had but broken knees for hire
And horrible splendour of desire;
I thought it all out twenty years ago:

Good fellows shuffled cards in an old bawn;   65
And when that ancient ruffian's turn was on
He so bewitched the cards under his thumb
That all but the one card became
A pack of hounds and not a pack of cards,
And that he changed into a hare.   70
Hanrahan rose in frenzy there
And followed up those baying creatures towards—

O towards I have forgotten what—enough!
I must recall a man that neither love
Nor music nor an enemy's clipped ear   75
Could, he was so harried, cheer;
A figure that has grown so fabulous
There's not a neighbour left to say
When he finished his dog's day:
An ancient bankrupt master of this house.   80

Before that ruin came, for centuries,
Rough men-at-arms, cross-gartered to the knees
Or shod in iron, climbed the narrow stairs,
And certain men-at-arms there were
Whose images, in the Great Memory stored,   85
Come with loud cry and panting breast
To break upon a sleeper's rest
While their great wooden dice beat on the board.

As I would question all, come all who can;
Come old, necessitous, half-mounted man;   90

---

tive man. These are the hypothetical extremes in the phases through which
the moon passes, and at them all opposites are united, as in "one inextricable
beam." 57. *Hanrahan:* a character in Yeats' writings who represents the
Celtic temperament. The card game described in the following stanza appears in the story "Red Hanrahan." The game and the hounds lured Red
from marrying his sweetheart. 65. *bawn:* cow shed.

And bring beauty's blind rambling celebrant;
The red man the juggler sent
Through God-forsaken meadows; Mrs. French,
Gifted with so fine an ear;
The man drowned in a bog's mire,   95
When mocking muses chose the country wench.

Did all old men and women, rich and poor,
Who trod upon these rocks or passed this door,
Whether in public or in secret rage
As I do now against old age?   100
But I have found an answer in those eyes
That are impatient to be gone;
Go therefore; but leave Hanrahan,
For I need all his mighty memories.

Old lecher with a love on every wind,   105
Bring up out of that deep considering mind
All that you have discovered in the grave,
For it is certain that you have
Reckoned up every unforeknown, unseeing
Plunge, lured by a softening eye,   110
Or by a touch or a sigh,
Into the labyrinth of another's being;

Does the imagination dwell the most
Upon a woman won or woman lost?
If on the lost, admit you turned aside   115
From a great labyrinth out of pride,
Cowardice, some silly over-subtle thought
Or anything called conscience once;
And that if memory recur, the sun's
Under eclipse and the day blotted out.   120

III

It is time that I wrote my will;
I choose upstanding men
That climb the streams until
The fountain leap, and at dawn

---

92. *red man:* Hanrahan. 105. *old lecher:* Red Hanrahan, now grown old.
He began as a romantic young lover in *The Secret Rose* and *Stories of Red
Hanrahan.*

Drop their cast at the side   125
Of dripping stone; I declare
They shall inherit my pride,
The pride of people that were
Bound neither to Cause nor to State,
Neither to slaves that were spat on,   130
Nor to the tyrants that spat,
The people of Burke and Grattan
That gave, though free to refuse—
Pride, like that of the morn,
When the headlong light is loose,   135
Or that of the fabulous horn,
Or that of the sudden shower
When all streams are dry,
Or that of the hour
When the swan must fix his eye   140
Upon a fading gleam,
Float out upon a long
Last reach of glittering stream
And there sing his last song.
And I declare my faith: 145
I mock Plotinus' thought
And cry in Plato's teeth,
Death and life were not
Till man made up the whole,
Made lock, stock and barrel   150
Out of his bitter soul,
Aye, sun and moon and star, all,
And further add to that
That, being dead, we rise,
Dream and so create   155
Translunar Paradise.
I have prepared my peace
With learned Italian things
And the proud stones of Greece,
Poet's imaginings   160
And memories of love,

---

132. *Burke and Grattan:* Edmund Burke (1729-97) and Henry Grattan
(1746-1820), the Irish statesmen and orators, were much read and admired
by Yeats. 136. *horn:* Roland, the leader of Charlemagne's rear guard, refused out of pride to blow his horn for help when ambushed at Roncevaux
in 778, and he was killed with his men.

Memories of the words of women,
All those things whereof
Man makes a superhuman
Mirror-resembling dream.   165

As at the loophole there
The daws chatter and scream,
And drop twigs layer upon layer.
When they have mounted up,
The mother bird will rest   170
On their hollow top,
And so warm her wild nest.
I leave both faith and pride
To young upstanding men
Climbing the mountain side,   175
That under bursting dawn
They may drop a fly;
Being of that metal made
Till it was broken by
This sedentary trade.   180

Now shall I make my soul,
Compelling it to study
In a learned school
Till the wreck of body,
Slow decay of blood,   185
Testy delirium
Or dull decrepitude,
Or what worse evil come—
The death of friends, or death
Of every brilliant eye   190
That made a catch in the breath—
Seem but the clouds of the sky
When the horizon fades;
Or a bird's sleepy cry
Among the deepening shades.   195

TWO SONGS FROM A PLAY

(1928)

I

I saw a staring virgin stand
Where holy Dionysus died,
And tear the heart out of his side,
And lay the heart upon her hand
And bear that beating heart away;   5
And then did all the Muses sing
Of Magnus Annus at the spring,
As though God's death were but a play.

Another Troy must rise and set,
Another lineage feed the crow,   .   10
Another Argo's painted prow
Drive to a flashier bauble yet.
The Roman Empire stood appalled:
It dropped the reins of peace and war
When that fierce virgin and her Star   15
Out of the fabulous darkness called.

TWO SONGS FROM A PLAY. See notes to "The Second Coming," which deals
with the end of the *Magnus Annus* or Great Year, while these Songs deal
with its beginning when Christ replaced Dionysus, the pagan god of fertility. In *A Vision*, Yeats wrote that the passage of the sun from Pisces
(Feb. 19) to Aries (Mar. 21) was associated with the death and resurrection
of Dionysus, and that at night during the transition the full moon separated
from the constellation Virgo, with the star in the wheatsheaf or in the child.
Elsewhere in *A Vision* Yeats emphasizes a contrast between classic reason
and order and Christian irrationality, confusion and vulgarity. The transition from one civilization to another Yeats symbolizes by the change from
full to new moon. In the dark of the new moon appears the Babylonian
starlight which represented for Yeats not only the eastern origin of Chris-
tianity, but also a primary and elemental force (likewise symbolized by
blood) antithetical to classic culture. 9-12. Yeats's adaptation of the cyclical
theme of Vergil's fourth eclogue—and particularly of Shelley's version of
it in the final chorus of his *Hellas*. The *Argo* of 11 is the name of the
vessel in which Jason and his men sought the golden fleece.

II

In pity for man's darkening thought
He walked that room and issued thence
In Galilean turbulence;
The Babylonian starlight brought   20
A fabulous, formless darkness in;
Odor of blood when Christ was slain
Made all Platonic tolerance vain
And vain all Doric discipline.

Everything that man esteems   25
Endures a moment or a day.
Love's pleasure drives his love away,
The painter's brush consumes his dreams;
The herald's cry, the soldier's tread
Exhaust his glory and his might: 30
Whatever flames upon the night
Man's own resinous heart has fed.

LEDA AND THE SWAN

(1928)

A sudden blow: the great wings beating still
Above the staggering girl, her thighs caressed
By the dark webs, her nape caught in his bill,
He holds her helpless breast upon his breast.

How can those terrified vague fingers push   5
The feathered glory from her loosening thighs?
And how can body, laid in that white rush,
But feel the strange heart beating where it lies?

A shudder in the loins engenders there
The broken wall, the burning roof and tower   10
And Agamemnon dead.
                              Being so caught up,
So mastered by the brute blood of the air,
Did she put on his knowledge with his power
Before the indifferent beak could let her drop?

LEDA AND THE SWAN. Leda, wife of Tyndareus, king of Sparta, was seen
bathing in the river Eurotas by Zeus, who descended in the form of a swan
and made love to her, so that she bore Castor, Pollux, Clytemnestra, and
Helen. Leda and the swan, then, usher in the cycle of classic civilization,
with the burning of Troy and the murder of Agamemnon (to be followed
by Mary and the dove).

AMONG SCHOOL CHILDREN
(1928)

I

I walk through the long schoolroom questioning;
A kind old nun in a white hood replies;
The children learn to cipher and to sing,
To study reading-books and history,
To cut and sew, be neat in everything   5
In the best modern way—the children's eyes
In momentary wonder stare upon
Sixty year old smiling public man.

II

I dream of a Ledaean body, bent
Above a sinking fire, a tale that she   10
Told of a harsh reproof, or trivial event
That changed some childish day to tragedy—
Told, and it seemed that our two natures blent
Into a sphere from youthful sympathy,
Or else, to alter Plato's parable,   15
Into the yolk and white of the one shell.

III

And thinking of that fit of grief or rage
I look upon one child or t'other there
And wonder if she stood so at that age—
For even daughters of the swan can share   20
Something of every paddler's heritage—
And had that colour upon cheek or hair,

AMONG SCHOOL CHILDREN. When Yeats was senator he inspected some primary schools, and he particularly liked the progressive program of a convent school in Waterford. One of the students in that school, on being asked to recite, repeated the information about Yeats from *Who's Who*. 14. *sphere:* a symbol of harmony and repose in Yeats' poetry and philosophy. 15. *parable:* In Plato's parable of the origin of love, Zeus, angered at human beings, divided them in two, and ever since they have been trying to reunite as the parts of an egg might be rejoined. The speaker in the poem alters the parable to suggest that he and his childhood friend were as close together as the undivided egg.

And thereupon my heart is driven wild:
She stands before me as a living child.

IV

Her present image floats into the mind—   25
Did Quattrocento finger fashion it
Hollow of cheek as though it drank the wind
And took a mess of shadows for its meat?
And I though never of Ledaean kind
Had pretty plumage once—enough of that,   30
Better to smile on all that smile, and show
There is a comfortable kind of old scarecrow.

V

What youthful mother, a shape upon her lap
Honey of generation had betrayed,
And that must sleep, shriek, struggle to escape   35
As recollection or the drug decide,
Would think her son, did she but see that shape
With sixty or more winters on its head,
A compensation for the pang of his birth,
Or the uncertainty of his setting forth?   40

VI

Plato thought nature but a spume that plays
Upon a ghostly paradigm of things;
Solider Aristotle played the taws
Upon the bottom of a king of kings;
World-famous golden-thighed Pythagoras   45
Fingered upon a fiddle stick or strings
What a star sang and careless Muses heard:
Old clothes upon old sticks to scare a bird.

---

26. *Quattrocento:* fifteenth century. 34. *Honey of generation:* Yeats noted that he took the phrase from *The Cave of the Nymphs,* by Porphyry (233-c. 306), a Neo-Platonic philosopher, but that there was no warrant in Porphyry for considering it the *drug* (36) which destroys the recollection of pre-natal freedom. 42. *ghostly paradigm:* pattern of abstract forms, the forms being the only realities. 43-4. *taws . . . kings:* Aristotle tried to form or discipline his student Alexander the Great by spanking his bottom. 45. *golden thighed:* Diogenes Laertius (VII ii) reports of Pythagoras that "once, when he was disrobed, his thigh was seen to be of gold." 47. *star sang:* Pythagoras, a Greek philosopher of the sixth century B.C., based his metaphysics on music and mathematics, supposing that the heavenly bodies were divided according to the laws of harmony.

VII

Both nuns and mothers worship images,
But those the candles light are not as those   50
That animate a mother's reveries,
But keep a marble or a bronze repose.
And yet they too break hearts—O Presences
That passion, piety or affection knows,
And that all heavenly glory symbolize—   55
O self-born mockers of man's enterprise;

VIII

Labour is blossoming or dancing where
The body is not bruised to pleasure soul,
Nor beauty born out of its own despair,
Nor blear-eyed wisdom out of midnight oil.   60
O chestnut tree, great rooted blossomer,
Are you the leaf, the blossom or the bole?
O body swayed to music, O brightening glance,
How can we know the dancer from the dance?

CRAZY JANE TALKS WITH THE BISHOP
(1932)

I met the Bishop on the road
And much said he and I.
'Those breasts are flat and fallen now,
Those veins must soon be dry;
Live in a heavenly mansion,   5
Not in some foul sty.'

'Fair and foul are near of kin,
And fair needs foul,' I cried.
'My friends are gone, but that's a truth
Nor grave nor bed denied,   10
Learned in bodily lowliness
And in the heart's pride.

'A woman can be proud and stiff
When on love intent;
But Love has pitched his mansion in   15
The place of excrement;
For nothing can be sole or whole
That has not been rent.'

COOLE AND BALLYLEE, 1931
(1933)

Under my window-ledge the waters race,
Otters below and moor-hens on the top,
Run for a mile undimmed in Heaven's face
Then darkening through 'dark' Raftery's 'cellar' drop,
Run underground, rise in a rocky place   5
In Coole demesne, and there to finish up
Spread to a lake and drop into a hole.
What's water but the generated soul?

Upon the border of that lake's a wood
Now all dry sticks under a wintry sun,   10
And in a copse of beeches there I stood,
For Nature's pulled her tragic buskin on
And all the rant's a mirror of my mood:
At sudden thunder of the mounting swan
I turned about and looked where branches break   15
The glittering reaches of the flooded lake.

Another emblem there! That stormy white
But seems a concentration of the sky;
And, like the soul, it sails into the sight
And in the morning's gone, no man knows why;   20
And is so lovely that it sets to right
What knowledge or its lack had set awry,
So arrogantly pure, a child might think
It can be murdered with a spot of ink.

Sound of a stick upon the floor, a sound   25
From somebody that toils from chair to chair;
Beloved books that famous hands have bound,
Old marble heads, old pictures everywhere;
Great rooms where travelled men and children found
Content or joy; a last inheritor   30
Where none has reigned that lacked a name and fame
Or out of folly into folly came.

COOLE AND BALLYLEE, 1931. 4. *dark Raftery*: the blind Irish poet; Yeats
described him and the tower at Ballylee in *The Celtic Twilight*.

A spot whereon the founders lived and died
Seemed once more dear than life; ancestral trees,
Or gardens rich in memory glorified   35
Marriages, alliances, and families,
And every bride's ambition satisfied.
Where fashion or mere fantasy decrees
Man shifts about—all that great glory spent—
Like some poor Arab tribesman and his tent.   40

We were the last romantics—chose for theme
Traditional sanctity and loveliness;
Whatever's written in what poets name
The book of the people; whatever most can bless
The mind of man or elevate a rhyme;   45
But all is changed, that high horse riderless,
Though mounted in that saddle Homer rode
Where the swan drifts upon a darkening flood.

FOR ANNE GREGORY

(1933)

'Never shall a young man,   8
Thrown into despair
By those great honey-coloured
Ramparts at your ear,
Love you for yourself alone   5
And not your yellow hair.'

'But I can get a hair-dye
And set such colour there,
Brown, or black, or carrot,
That young men in despair   10
May love me for myself alone
And not my yellow hair.'

'I heard an old religious man
But yesternight declare
That he had found a text to prove   15
That only God, my dear,
Could love you for yourself alone
And not your yellow hair.'

BYZANTIUM

(1933)

The unpurged images of day recede;
The Emperor's drunken soldiery are abed;
Night resonance recedes, night-walkers' song
After great cathedral gong;
A starlit or a moonlit dome disdains   5
All that man is,
All mere complexities,
The fury and the mire of human veins.

Before me floats an image, man or shade,
Shade more than man, more image than a shade·   10
For Hades' bobbin bound in mummy-cloth
May unwind the winding path;
A mouth that has no moisture and no breath
Breathless mouths may summon;
I hail the superhuman;   15
I call it death-in-life and life-in-death.

Miracle, bird or golden handiwork,
More miracle than bird or handiwork,
Planted on the star-lit golden bough,
Can like the cocks of Hades crow,   20
Or, by the moon embittered, scorn aloud
In glory of changeless metal
Common bird or petal
And all complexities of mire or blood.

At midnight on the Emperor's pavement flit   25
Flames that no faggot feeds, nor steel has lit,

BYZANTIUM. See notes to "Two Songs" and "Sailing to Byzantium." In 1930, before writing the poem, Yeats jotted in his manuscript-book a reminder to describe Byzantium as it is in the system (*A Vision*) toward the end of the first Christian millennium. "A walking mummy, flames in the street corners where the soul is purified, birds of hammered gold singing in the golden trees." 11. *bobbin:* compare the perne or spool on which experience is wound by one epoch and unwound or re-experienced by a succeeding one. 20. *cocks of Hades:* cocks which crowed one age out and another in.

Nor storm disturbs, flames begotten of flame,
Where blood-begotten spirits come
And all complexities of fury leave,
Dying into a dance,   30
An agony of trance,
An agony of flame that cannot singe a sleeve.

Astraddle on the dolphin's mire and blood,
Spirit after spirit! The smithies break the flood,
The golden smithies of the Emperor!   35
Marbles of the dancing floor
Break bitter furies of complexity,
Those images that yet
Fresh images beget,
That dolphin-torn, that gong-tormented sea.   40

❦

35. The Emperor in this poem represents (among other things) the artist, whose 'smithies' receive the weltering images of temporal experience and master them, form them, into a timeless work—'glory of changeless metal.'

AFTER LONG SILENCE

(1933)

Speech after long silence; it is right,
All other lovers being estranged or dead,
Unfriendly lamplight hid under its shade,
The curtains drawn upon unfriendly night,
That we descant and yet again descant   5
Upon the supreme theme of Art and Song:
Bodily decrepitude is wisdom; young
We loved each other and were ignorant.

LONG-LEGGED FLY

(1939)

That civilisation may not sink,
Its great battle lost,
Quiet the dog, tether the pony
To a distant post;
Our master Caesar is in the tent   5
Where the maps are spread,
His eyes fixed upon nothing,
A hand under his head.
Like a long-legged fly upon the stream
His mind moves upon silence.   10

That the topless towers be burnt
And men recall that face,
Move most gently if move you must
In this lonely place.
She thinks, part woman, three parts a child,   15
That nobody looks; her feet
Practise a tinker shuffle
Picked up on a street.
Like a long-legged fly upon the stream
Her mind moves upon silence.   20

That girls at puberty may find
The first Adam in their thought,
Shut the door of the Pope's chapel,
Keep those children out.
There on that scaffolding reclines   25
Michael Angelo.
With no more sound than the mice make
His hand moves to and fro.
Like a long-legged fly upon the stream
His mind moves upon silence.   30

LONG-LEGGED FLY: 10. *silence:* Yeats's emblem for the quasi-divine source from which genius (whether in leaders of men or beautiful women or great artists) draws its power. 12. *that face:* Helen's (of Troy). 23. *chapel:* the Vatican's Sistine Chapel, famous for its frescoes by Michael Angelo, especially that of God creating Adam.

THE CIRCUS ANIMALS' DESERTION
(1939)

I

I sought a theme and sought for it in vain,
I sought it daily for six weeks or so.
Maybe at last, being but a broken man,
I must be satisfied with my heart, although
Winter and summer till old age began   5
My circus animals were all on show,
Those stilted boys, that burnished chariot,
Lion and woman and the Lord knows what.

II

What can I but enumerate old themes?
First that sea-rider Oisin led by the nose   10
Through three enchanted islands, allegorical dreams,
Vain gaiety, vain battle, vain repose,
Themes of the embittered heart, or so it seems,
That might adorn old songs or courtly shows;
But what cared I that set him on to ride,   15
I, starved for the bosom of his færy bride?

And then a counter-truth filled out its play,
The Countess Cathleen was the name I gave it;
She, pity-crazed, had given her soul away,
But masterful Heaven had intervened to save it.   20

THE CIRCUS ANIMALS' DESERTION: 6. *circus animals:* the poet's symbols. 7.
stilted boys: the heroes of his early poetry, stilted in their Victorianism,
but stilted, too, in the sense that all art is on stilts—bigger and more
emphatic than life. *burnished chariot:* the chariot of Cuchulain, hero of
Irish legend, who became for Yeats the image of humanity at its
best and whose battle with the sea typified man's brave but doomed encounter with temporal life (cf. *Byzantium,* 7-8, 24, 29, 37, 40). 8. *Lion
and woman:* although the lion figure appears specifically in *The Second
Coming* (and elsewhere), it perhaps includes here the various beast-sym-
bols of Yeats's world, as the woman includes the various woman-symbols.
Lion-and-woman, taken together, give the sphinx figure, which also
haunted Yeats. 10. *Oisin:* In *The Wanderings of Oisin* (1889), the hero
moves among islands that have, among other possible meanings, those
assigned in line 12. 16. *bride:* Niamh, inspired by Maud Gonne. 18.
The . . . Cathleen: an early Yeats play (1892).

I thought my dear must her own soul destroy,
So did fanaticism and hate enslave it,
And this brought forth a dream and soon enough
This dream itself had all my thought and love.

And when the Fool and Blind Man stole the bread   25
Cuchulain fought the ungovernable sea;
Heart-mysteries there, and yet when all is said
It was the dream itself enchanted me:
Character isolated by a deed
To engross the present and dominate memory.   30
Players and painted stage took all my love,
And not those things that they were emblems of.

III

Those masterful images because complete
Grew in pure mind, but out of what began?
A mound of refuse or the sweepings of a street,   35
Old kettles, old bottles, and a broken can,
Old iron, old bones, old rags, that raving slut
Who keeps the till. Now that my ladder's gone,
I must lie down where all the ladders start,
In the foul rag-and-bone shop of the heart.   40

---

21. *my dear:* Maud Gonne, whose misuse of her great beauty Yeats also
comments on in *Prayer For My Daughter,* 59 ff. 25. *Fool and Blind Man:*
two recurring figures in Yeats's poetry (drawn perhaps from *King Lear*)
who in his play *On Baile's Strand* steal bread from the ovens while Cuchulain fights the sea. 40. *the . . . heart:* i.e., the welter of existence out of
which art climbs.

LAPIS LAZULI
(*For Harry Clifton*)
(1939)

I HAVE heard that hysterical women say
They are sick of the palette and fiddle-bow,
Of poets that are always gay,
For everybody knows or else should know
That if nothing drastic is done   5
Aeroplane and Zeppelin will come out,
Pitch like King Billy bomb-balls in
Until the town lie beaten flat.

All perform their tragic play,
There struts Hamlet, there is Lear,   10
That's Ophelia, that Cordelia;
Yet they, should the last scene be there,
The great stage curtain about to drop,
If worthy their prominent part in the play,
Do not break up their lines to weep.   15
They know that Hamlet and Lear are gay;
Gaiety transfiguring all that dread.
All men have aimed at, found and lost;
Black out; Heaven blazing into the head:
Tragedy wrought to its uttermost.   20
Though Hamlet rambles and Lear rages,
And all the drop-scenes drop at once
Upon a hundred thousand stages,
It cannot grow by an inch or an ounce.

LAPIS LAZULI: Dedication—*Harry Clifton:* Henry Talbot DeVere Clifton, who reprints Yeats's poem at the beginning of his own *Gleams Britain's Day* (1942), and who is said to have been the donor of the carved lapis lazuli celebrated in the peom: "a great piece carved by some Chinese sculptor into the semblance of a mountain, with temple, trees, paths, and an ascetic and pupil about to climb the mountain" (Yeats to Dorothy Wellesley, 6 July 1935). 7. *King Billy:* William III of England, whose army's bombardment of Limerick in 1691 reduced whole streets to ashes. 19. *Black . . . head:* alluding (in theatrical terms) to tragic suffering, madness, death, on the one hand, and, on the other, to tragic illumination.

On their own feet they came, or on shipboard,   25
Camel-back, horse-back, ass-back, mule-back,
Old civilizations put to the sword.
Then they and their wisdom went to rack:
No handiwork of Callimachus,
Who handled marble as if it were bronze,   30
Made draperies that seemed to rise
When sea-wind swept the corner, stands;
His long lamp-chimney shaped like the stem
Of a slender palm, stood but a day;
All things fall and are built again,   35
And those that build them again are gay.

Two Chinamen, behind them a third,
Are carved in lapis lazuli,
Over them flies a long-legged bird,
A symbol of longevity;   40
The third, doubtless a serving-man,
Carries a musical instrument.

Every discoloration of the stone,
Every accidental crack or dent,
Seems a water-course or an avalanche,   45
Or lofty slope where it still snows
Though doubtless plum or cherry-branch
Sweetens the little half-way house
Those Chinamen climb towards, and I
Delight to imagine them seated there;   50
There, on the mountain and the sky,
On all the tragic scene they stare.
One asks for mournful melodies;
Accomplished fingers begin to play.
Their eyes mid many wrinkles, their eyes,   55
Their ancient, glittering eyes, are gay.

---

29. *Callimachus:* 5th-century (B.C.) Athenian sculptor, whose fame has
survived but not his works, among which was a famous lamp (line 33)
for the Erechtheum.

JOHN KINSELLA'S LAMENT FOR
MRS. MARY MOORE
(1940)

A bloody and a sudden end,
  Gunshot or a noose,
For death who takes what man would keep,
  Leaves what man would lose.
He might have had my sister,   5
  My cousins by the score,
But nothing satisfied the fool
  But my dear Mary Moore,
None other knows what pleasures man
  At table or in bed.   10
What shall I do for pretty girls
  Now my old bawd is dead?

Though stiff to strike a bargain,
  Like an old Jew man,
Her bargain struck we laughed and talked   15
  And emptied many a can;
And O! but she had stories,
  Though not for the priest's ear,
To keep the soul of man alive,
  Banish age and care,   20
And being old she put a skin
  On everything she said.
What shall I do for pretty girls
  Now my old bawd is dead?

The priests have got a book that says   25
  But for Adam's sin
Eden's Garden would be there,
  And I there within.
No expectation fails there,
  No pleasing habit ends,   30
No man grows old, no girl grows cold,
  But friends walk by friends.
Who quarrels over halfpennies

That plucks the trees for bread?
What shall I do for pretty girls   35
  Now that my old bawd is dead?

Robert Frost

REVELATION

(1913)

We make ourselves a place apart
   Behind light words that tease and flout,
But oh, the agitated heart
   Till someone find us really out.

'Tis pity if the case require   5
   (Or so we say) that in the end
We speak the literal to inspire
   The understanding of a friend.

But so with all, from babes that play
   At hide-and-seek to God afar,   10
So all who hide too well away
   Must speak and tell us where they are.

These selections from Robert Frost are used with the permission of Henry Holt and Company, Inc., from COMPLETE POEMS OF ROBERT FROST, 1949, *copyright 1930, 1939, 1949, by Henry Holt and Company, Inc.; copyright 1936 by Robert Frost:* "Revelation," "The Tuft of Flowers," "After Apple-Picking," "The Wood-Pile," "The Oven Bird," "The Grindstone," "Fire and Ice," "Dust of Snow," "Nothing Gold Can Stay," "Stopping by Woods on a Snowy Evening," "The Onset," "Spring Pools," "Acquainted with the Night," "Desert Places" *are from* THE COMPLETE POEMS OF ROBERT FROST, 1949, *copyright 1930, 1939, 1949, by Henry Holt and Company, Inc.; copyright 1936 by Robert Frost.* "Mending Wall," "The Road Not Taken," "Once By the Pacific," "Two Tramps in Mud Time," "The Most of It," "Provide, Provide" *are from* THE COMPLETE POEMS OF ROBERT FROST, *copyright 1930, 1949 by Henry Holt and Co., Inc.* By permission of Holt, Rinehart, & Winston, Inc.

THE TUFT OF FLOWERS

(1913)

I went to turn the grass once after one
Who mowed it in the dew before the sun.

The dew was gone that made his blade so keen
Before I came to view the levelled scene.

I looked for him behind an isle of trees;   5
I listened for his whetstone on the breeze.

But he had gone his way, the grass all mown,
And I must be, as he had been,—alone,

'As all must be,' I said within my heart,
'Whether they work together or apart.'   10

But as I said it, swift there passed me by
On noiseless wing a bewildered butterfly,

Seeking with memories grown dim o'er night
Some resting flower of yesterday's delight.

And once I marked his flight go round and round,   15
As where some flower lay withering on the ground.

And then he flew as far as eye could see,
And then on tremulous wing came back to me.

I thought of questions that have no reply,
And would have turned to toss the grass to dry;   20

But he turned first, and led my eye to look
At a tall tuft of flowers beside a brook,

A leaping tongue of bloom the scythe had spared
Beside a reedy brook the scythe had bared.

I left my place to know them by their name,   25
Finding them butterfly-weed when I came.

The mower in the dew had loved them thus,
By leaving them to flourish, not for us,

Nor yet to draw one thought of ours to him,
But from sheer morning gladness at the brim.   30

The butterfly and I had lit upon,
Nevertheless, a message from the dawn,

That made me hear the wakening birds around,
And hear his long scythe whispering to the ground,

And feel a spirit kindred to my own;   35
So that henceforth I worked no more alone;

But glad with him, I worked as with his aid,
And weary, sought at noon with him the shade;

And dreaming, as it were, held brotherly speech
With one whose thought I had not hoped to reach.   40

'Men work together,' I told him from the heart,
'Whether they work together or apart.'

AFTER APPLE-PICKING

(1914)

My long two-pointed ladder's sticking through a tree
Toward heaven still,
And there's a barrel that I didn't fill
Beside it, and there may be two or three
Apples I didn't pick upon some bough.
But I am done with apple-picking now.
Essence of winter sleep is on the night,
The scent of apples: I am drowsing off.
I cannot rub the strangeness from my sight
I got from looking through a pane of glass   10
I skimmed this morning from the drinking trough
And held against the world of hoary grass.
It melted, and I let it fall and break.
But I was well
Upon my way to sleep before it fell,   15
And I could tell
What form my dreaming was about to take.
Magnified apples appear and disappear,
Stem end and blossom end,
And every fleck of russet showing clear.   20
My instep arch not only keeps the ache,
It keeps the pressure of a ladder-round.
I feel the ladder sway as the boughs bend.
And I keep hearing from the cellar bin
The rumbling sound   25
Of load on load of apples coming in.
For I have had too much
Of apple-picking: I am overtired
Of the great harvest I myself desired.
There were ten thousand thousand fruit to touch,   30
Cherish in hand, lift down, and not let fall.
For all
That struck the earth,
No matter if not bruised or spiked with stubble,
Went surely to the cider-apple heap   35
As of no worth.
One can see what will trouble

This sleep of mine, whatever sleep it is.
Were he not gone,
The woodchuck could say whether it's like his   40
Long sleep, as I describe its coming on,
Or just some human sleep.

THE WOOD-PILE

(1914)

Out walking in the frozen swamp one grey day,
I paused and said, 'I will turn back from here.
No, I will go on farther—and we shall see.'
The hard snow held me, save where now and then
One foot went through. The view was all in lines   5
Straight up and down of tall slim trees
Too much alike to mark or name a place by
So as to say for certain I was here
Or somewhere else: I was just far from home.
A small bird flew before me. He was careful   10
To put a tree between us when he lighted,
And say no word to tell me who he was
Who was so foolish as to think what *he* thought.
He thought that I was after him for a feather—
The white one in his tail; like one who takes   15
Everything said as personal to himself.
One flight out sideways would have undeceived him.
And then there was a pile of wood for which
I forgot him and let his little fear
Carry him off the way I might have gone,   20
Without so much as wishing him good-night.
He went behind it to make his last stand.
It was a cord of maple, cut and split
And piled—and measured, four by four by eight.
And not another like it could I see.   25
No runner tracks in this year's snow looped near it.
And it was older sure than this year's cutting,
Or even last year's or the year's before.
The wood was grey and the bark warping off it
And the pile somewhat sunken. Clematis   30
Had wound strings round and round it like a bundle.
What held it though on one side was a tree
Still growing, and on one a stake and prop,
These latter about to fall. I thought that only
Someone who lived in turning to fresh tasks   35
Could so forget his handiwork on which

He spent himself, the labour of his axe,
·And leave it there far from a useful fireplace
To warm the frozen swamp as best it could
With the slow smokeless burning of decay.   40

MENDING WALL

(1914)

Something there is that doesn't love a wall,
That sends the frozen-ground-swell under it,
And spills the upper boulders in the sun;
And makes gaps even two can pass abreast.
The work of hunters is another thing: **5**
I have come after them and made repair
Where they have left not one stone on a stone,
But they would have the rabbit out of hiding,
To please the yelping dogs. The gaps I mean,
No one has seen them made or heard them made,   **10**
But at spring mending-time we find them there.
I let my neighbour know beyond the hill;
And on a day we meet to walk the line
And set the wall between us once again.
We keep the wall between us as we go.   **15**
To each the boulders that have fallen to each.
And some are loaves and some so nearly balls
We have to use a spell to make them balance:
"Stay where you are until our backs are turned!"
We wear our fingers rough with handling them.   **20**
Oh, just another kind of outdoor game,
One on a side. It comes to little more:
There where it is we do not need the wall:
He is all pine and I am apple orchard.
My apple trees will never get across   **25**
And eat the cones under his pines, I tell him.
He only says, 'Good fences make good neighbours.'
Spring is the mischief in me, and I wonder
If I could put a notion in his head:
'*Why* do they make good neighbors? Isn't it   **30**
Where there are cows? But here there are no cows.
Before I built a wall I'd ask to know
What I was walling in or walling out,
And to whom I was like to give offence.
Something there is that doesn't love a wall,   **35**
That wants it down.' I could say 'Elves' to him,
But it's not elves exactly, and I'd rather

He said it for himself. I see him there
Bringing a stone grasped firmly by the top
In each hand, like an old-stone savage armed.   40
He moves in darkness as it seems to me,
Not of woods only and the shade of trees.
He will not go behind his father's saying,
And he likes having thought of it so well
He says again, 'Good fences make good neighbours.'   45

THE OVEN BIRD
(1916)

There is a singer everyone has heard,
Loud, a mid-summer and a mid-wood bird,
Who makes the solid tree trunks sound again.
He says that leaves are old and that for flowers
Mid-summer is to spring as one to ten.   5
He says the early petal-fall is past
When pear and cherry bloom went down in showers
On sunny days a moment overcast;
And comes that other fall we name the fall.
He says the highway dust is over all.   10
The bird would cease and be as other birds
But that he knows in singing not to sing.
The question that he frames in all but words
Is what to make of a diminished thing.

THE ROAD NOT TAKEN

(1916)

Two roads diverged in a yellow wood,
And sorry I could not travel both
And be one traveller, long I stood
And looked down one as far as I could
To where it bent in the undergrowth;   5

Then took the other, as just as fair,
And having perhaps the better claim,
Because it was grassy and wanted wear;
Though as for that the passing there
Had worn them really about the same,   10

And both that morning equally lay
In leaves no step had trodden black.
Oh, I kept the first for another day!
Yet knowing how way leads on to way,
I doubted if I should ever come back.   15

I shall be telling this with a sigh
Somewhere ages and ages hence:
Two roads diverged in a wood, and I—
I took the one less travelled by,
And that has made all the difference.   20

THE GRINDSTONE

(1923)

Having a wheel and four legs of its own
Has never availed the cumbersome grindstone
To get it anywhere that I can see.
These hands have helped it go, and even race;
Not all the motion, though, they ever lent,   5
Not all the miles it may have thought it went,
Have got it one step from the starting place.
It stands beside the same old apple tree.
The shadow of the apple tree is thin
Upon it now, its feet are fast in snow.   10
All other farm machinery's gone in,
And some of it on no more legs and wheel
Than the grindstone can boast to stand or go.
(I'm thinking chiefly of the wheelbarrow.)
For months it hasn't known the taste of steel,   15
Washed down with rusty water in a tin.
But standing outdoors hungry, in the cold,
Except in towns at night, is not a sin.
And, anyway, its standing in the yard
Under a ruinous live apple tree   20
Has nothing any more to do with me,
Except that I remember how of old
One summer day, all day I drove it hard,
And someone mounted on it rode it hard,
And he and I between us ground a blade.   25

I gave it the preliminary spin,
And poured on water (tears it might have been);
And when it almost gayly jumped and flowed,
A Father-Time-like man got on and rode,
Armed with a scythe and spectacles that glowed.   30
He turned on will-power to increase the load
And slow me down—and I abruptly slowed,
Like coming to a sudden railroad station.
I changed from hand to hand in desperation.
I wondered what machine of ages gone   35
This represented an improvement on.
For all I knew it may have sharpened spears

And arrowheads itself. Much use for years
Had gradually worn it an oblate
Spheroid that kicked and struggled in its gait,   40
Appearing to return me hate for hate;
(But I forgive it now as easily
As any other boyhood enemy
Whose pride has failed to get him anywhere).
I wondered who it was the man thought ground—·   45
The one who held the wheel back or the one
Who gave his life to keep it going round?
I wondered if he really thought it fair
For him to have the say when we were done.
Such were the bitter thoughts to which I turned.   50

Not for myself was I so much concerned.
Oh no!—although, of course, I could have found
A better way to pass the afternoon
Than grinding discord out of a grindstone,
And beating insects at their gritty tune.   55
Nor was I for the man so much concerned.
Once when the grindstone almost jumped its bearing
It looked as if he might be badly thrown
And wounded on his blade. So far from caring,
I laughed inside, and only cranked the faster,   60
(It ran as if it wasn't greased but glued);
I'd welcome any moderate disaster
That might be calculated to postpone
What evidently nothing could conclude.
The thing that made me more and more afraid   65
Was that we'd ground it sharp and hadn't known,
And now were only wasting precious blade.
And when he raised it dripping once and tried
The creepy edge of it with wary touch,
And viewed it over his glasses funny-eyed,   70
Only disinterestedly to decide
It needed a turn more, I could have cried
Wasn't there danger of a turn too much?
Mightn't we make it worse instead of better?
I was for leaving something to the whetter.   75
What if it wasn't all it should be? I'd
Be satisfied if he'd be satisfied.

FIRE AND ICE

(1923)

Some say the world will end in fire,
Some say in ice.
From what I've tasted of desire
I hold with those who favor fire.
But if it had to perish twice,   5
I think I know enough of hate
To say that for destruction ice
Is also great
And would suffice.

DUST OF SNOW

(1923)

The way a crow
Shook down on me
The dust of snow
From a hemlock tree

Has given my heart   5
A change of mood
And saved some part
Of a day I had rued.

NOTHING GOLD CAN STAY

(1923)

Nature's first green is gold,
Her hardest hue to hold.
Her early leaf's a flower;
But only so an hour.
Then leaf subsides to leaf.   5
So Eden sank to grief,
So dawn goes down to day.
Nothing gold can stay.

STOPPING BY WOODS ON A SNOWY EVENING

(1923)

Whose woods these are I think I know.
His house is in the village though;
He will not see me stopping here
To watch his woods fill up with snow.

My little horse must think it queer   5
To stop without a farmhouse near
Between the woods and frozen lake
The darkest evening of the year.

He gives his harness bells a shake
To ask if there is some mistake.   10
The only other sound's the sweep
Of easy wind and downy flake.

The woods are lovely, dark and deep.
But I have promises to keep,
And miles to go before I sleep,   15
And miles to go before I sleep.

THE ONSET

(1923)

Always the same, when on a fated night
At last the gathered snow lets down as white
As may be in dark woods, and with a song
It shall not make again all winter long
Of hissing on the yet uncovered ground,   5
I almost stumble looking up and round,
As one who overtaken by the end
Gives up his errand, and lets death descend
Upon him where he is, with nothing done
To evil, no important triumph won,   10
More than if life had never been begun.

Yet all the precedent is on my side:
I know that winter death has never tried
The earth but it has failed: the snow may heap
In long storms an undrifted four feet deep   15
As measured against maple, birch, and oak,
It cannot check the peeper's silver croak;
And I shall see the snow all go down hill
In water of a slender April rill
That flashes tail through last year's withered brake   20
And dead weeds, like a disappearing snake.
Nothing will be left white but here a birch,
And there a clump of houses with a church.

SPRING POOLS

(1928)

These pools that, though in forests, still reflect
The total sky almost without defect,
And like the flowers beside them, chill and shiver,
Will like the flowers beside them soon be gone,
And yet not out by any brook or river,   5
But up by roots to bring dark foliage on.

The trees that have it in their pent-up buds
To darken nature and be summer woods—
Let them think twice before they use their powers
To blot out and drink up and sweep away   10
These flowery waters and these watery flowers
From snow that melted only yesterday.

ACQUAINTED WITH THE NIGHT
(1928)

I have been one acquainted with the night.
I have walked out in rain—and back in rain.
I have outwalked the furthest city light.

I have looked down the saddest city lane.
I have passed by the watchman on his beat   5
And dropped my eyes, unwilling to explain.

I have stood still and stopped the sound of feet
When far away an interrupted cry
Came over houses from another street,

But not to call me back or say good-bye;   10
And further still at an unearthly height,
One luminary clock against the sky

Proclaimed the time was neither wrong nor right.
I have been one acquainted with the night.

ONCE BY THE PACIFIC

(1928)

The shattered water made a misty din.
Great waves looked over others coming in,
And thought of doing something to the shore
That water never did to land before.
The clouds were low and hairy in the skies,
Like locks blown forward in the gleam of eyes
You could not tell, and yet it looked as if
The shore was lucky in being backed by cliff,
The cliff in being backed by continent;
It looked as if a night of dark intent
Was coming, and not only a night, an age.
Someone had better be prepared for rage.
There would be more than ocean-water broken
Before God's last *Put out the Light* was spoken.

TWO TRAMPS IN MUD TIME

or, A Full-Time Interest

(1936)

Out of the mud two strangers came
And caught me splitting wood in the yard.
And one of them put me off my aim
By hailing cheerily "Hit them hard!"
I knew pretty well why he dropped behind   5
And let the other go on a way.
I knew pretty well what he had in mind:
He wanted to take my job for pay.

Good blocks of oak it was I split,
As large around as the chopping block;   10
And every piece I squarely hit
Fell splinterless as a cloven rock.
The blows that a life of self-control
Spares to strike for the common good
That day, giving a loose to my soul,   15
I spent on the unimportant wood.

The sun was warm but the wind was chill.
You know how it is with an April day
When the sun is out and the wind is still,
You're one month on in the middle of May.   20
But if you so much as dare to speak,
A cloud comes over the sunlit arch,
A wind comes off a frozen peak,
And you're two months back in the middle of March.

A bluebird comes tenderly up to alight   25
And turns to the wind to unruffle a plume
His song so pitched as not to excite
A single flower as yet to bloom.
It is snowing a flake: and he half knew
Winter was only playing possum.   30
Except in colour he isn't blue,
But he wouldn't advise a thing to blossom.

The water for which we may have to look
In summertime with a witching-wand,
In every wheelrut's now a brook,   35
In every print of a hoof a pond.
Be glad of water, but don't forget
The lurking frost in the earth beneath
That will steal forth after the sun is set
And show on the water its crystal teeth.   40

The time when most I loved my task
These two must make me love it more
By coming with what they came to ask.
You'd think I never had felt before
The weight of an axe-head poised aloft,   45
The grip on earth of outspread feet.
The life of muscles rocking soft
And smooth and moist in vernal heat.

Out of the woods two hulking tramps
(From sleeping God knows where last night,   50
But not long since in the lumber camps).
They thought all chopping was theirs of right.
Men of the woods and lumberjacks,
They judged me by their appropriate tool.
Except as a fellow handled an axe,   55
They had no way of knowing a fool.

Nothing on either side was said.
They knew they had but to stay their stay
And all their logic would fill my head:
As that I had no right to play   60
With what was another man's work for gain.
My right might be love but theirs was need.
And where the two exist in twain
Theirs was the better right—agreed.

But yield who will to their separation,   65
My object in living is to unite
My avocation and my vocation
As my two eyes make one in sight.
Only where love and need are one,
And the work is play for mortal stakes,   70
Is the deed ever really done
For Heaven and the future's sakes.

DESERT PLACES
(1936)

Snow falling and night falling fast oh fast
In a field I looked into going past,
And the ground almost covered smooth in snow,
But a few weeds and stubble showing last.

The woods around it have it—it is theirs.   5
All animals are smothered in their lairs.
I am too absent-spirited to count;
The loneliness includes me unawares.

And lonely as it is that loneliness
Will be more lonely ere it will be less—   10
A blanker whiteness of benighted snow
With no expression, nothing to express.

They cannot scare me with their empty spaces
Between stars—on stars where no human race is.
I have it in me so much nearer home   15
To scare myself with my own desert places.

PROVIDE, PROVIDE

(1936)

The witch that came (the withered hag)
To wash the steps with pail and rag,
Was once the beauty Abishag,

The picture pride of Hollywood.
Too many fall from great and good   5
For you to doubt the likelihood.

Die early and avoid the fate.
Or if predestined to die late,
Make up your mind to die in state.

Make the whole stock exchange your own!   10
If need be occupy a throne,
Where nobody can call *you* crone.

Some have relied on what they knew;
Others on being simply true.
What worked for them might work for you.   15

No memory of having starred
Atones for later disregard,
Or keeps the end from being hard.

Better to go down dignified
With boughten friendship at your side   20
Than none at all. Provide, provide!

THE MOST OF IT

(1942)

He thought he kept the universe alone;
For all the voice in answer he could wake
Was but the mocking echo of his own
From some tree-hidden cliff across the lake.
Some morning from the boulder-broken beach   5
He would cry out on life, that what it wants
Is not its own love back in copy speech,
But counter-love, original response.
And nothing ever came of what he cried
Unless it was the embodiment that crashed   10
In the cliff's talus on the other side,
And then in the far distant water splashed,
But after a time allowed for it to swim,
Instead of proving human when it neared
And someone else additional to him,   15
As a great buck it powerfully appeared,
Pushing the crumpled water up ahead,
And landed pouring like a waterfall,
And stumbled through the rocks with horny tread,
And forced the underbrush—and that was all.   20

Thomas Stearns Eliot

THE LOVE SONG OF J. ALFRED PRUFROCK

(1917)

S'io credesse che mia riposta fosse
A persona che mai tornasse al mondo,
Questa fiamma staria senza piu scosse.
Ma perciocche giammai di questo fondo
Non torno vivo alcun, s'i'odo il vero,
Senza tema d'infamia ti rispondo.

Let us go then, you and I,
When the evening is spread out against the sky
Like a patient etherised upon a table;
Let us go, through certain half-deserted streets,
The muttering retreats   5
Of restless nights in one-night cheap hotels
And sawdust restaurants with oyster-shells:
Streets that follow like a tedious argument
Of insidious intent
To lead you to an overwhelming question . . .   10
Oh, do not ask, "What is it?"
Let us go and make our visit.
In the room the women come and go
Talking of Michelangelo.

The selections from T. S. Eliot are used with the permission of Harcourt, Brace and Company, Inc., from COLLECTED POEMS 1909-1935, *by T. S. Eliot, copyright 1936, by Harcourt, Brace and Company, Inc.*

PRUFROCK: *Epigraph:* "If I thought my answer were to one who ever could return to the world, this flame should shake no more; but since no one did ever return alive from this depth, if what I hear be true, without fear of infamy I answer thee." These are the words of Guido da Montefeltro to Dante (*Inferno,* XXVII, 61-6), when asked why he is being punished: he is still fearful of what people on earth will say, and only answers Dante's query because he thinks him one of the dead. This motif of fear of the world's judgment pervades Prufrock's confession, too.

14. *Michelangelo:* The many-sided Renaissance artist, whose vigor in painting, sculpture, and architecture points the irony of his becoming the subject of hyper-cultivated chit-chat in a social group whose members have none of this quality.

The yellow fog that rubs its back upon the window-panes,   15
The yellow smoke that rubs its muzzle on the window-panes
Licked its tongue into the corners of the evening,
Lingered upon the pools that stand in drains,
Let fall upon its back the soot that falls from chimneys,
Slipped by the terrace, made a sudden leap,   20
And seeing that it was a soft October night,
Curled once about the house, and fell asleep.

And indeed there will be time
For the yellow smoke that slides along the street,
Rubbing its back upon the window-panes;   25
There will be time, there will be time
To prepare a face to meet the faces that you meet;
There will be time to murder and create,
And time for all the works and days of hands
That lift and drop a question on your plate;   30
Time for you and time for me,
And time yet for a hundred indecisions,
And for a hundred visions and revisions,
Before the taking of a toast and tea.

In the room the women come and go   35
Talking of Michelangelo.

And indeed there will be time
To wonder, "Do I dare?" and, "Do I dare?"
Time to turn back and descend the stair,
With a bald spot in the middle of my hair—   40
(They will say: "How his hair is growing thin!")
My morning coat, my collar mounting firmly to the chin,
My necktie rich and modest, but asserted by a simple pin—
(They will say: "But how his arms and legs are thin!")
Do I dare   45
Disturb the universe?
In a minute there is time
For decisions and revisions which a minute will reverse.

---

29. *works and days:* This phrase recalls the title of Hesiod's *Works and Days,* a poem in praise of harsh agricultural toil and so in ironic contrast with Prufrock's world.

For I have known them all already, known them all:
Have known the evenings, mornings, afternoons,   50
I have measured out my life with coffee spoons;
I know the voices dying with a dying fall
Beneath the music from a farther room.
  So how should I presume?
And I have known the eyes already, known them all—·   55
The eyes that fix you in a formulated phrase,
And when I am formulated, sprawling on a pin,
When I am pinned and wriggling on the wall,
Then how should I begin
To spit out all the butt-ends of my days and ways?   60
  And how should I presume?

And I have known the arms already, known them all—
Arms that are braceleted and white and bare
(But in the lamplight, downed with light brown hair!)
Is it perfume from a dress   65
That makes me so digress?
Arms that lie along a table, or wrap about a shawl.
  And should I then presume?
  And how should I begin?

          .   .   .   .   .   .

Shall I say, I have gone at dusk through narrow streets   70
And watched the smoke that rises from the pipes
Of lonely men in shirt-sleeves, leaning out of windows? . . .

I should have been a pair of ragged claws
Scuttling across the floors of silent seas.

          .   .   .   .   .   .

And the afternoon, the evening, sleeps so peacefully!   75
Smoothed by long fingers,
Asleep . . . tired . . . or it malingers,
Stretched on the floor, here beside you and me.
Should I, after tea and cakes and ices,
Have the strength to force the moment to its crisis?   80
But though I have wept and fasted, wept and prayed,
Though I have seen my head (grown slightly bald) brought in
    upon a platter,
I am no prophet—and here's no great matter;

83. *no prophet:* i.e., no John the Baptist, with whose head—"brought in a

I have seen the moment of my greatness flicker,
And I have seen the eternal Footman hold my coat, and snicker,   85
And in short, I was afraid.

And would it have been worth it, after all,
After the cups, the marmalade, the tea,
Among the porcelain, among some talk of you and me,
Would it have been worth while,   90
To have bitten off the matter with a smile,
To have squeezed the universe into a ball
To roll it toward some overwhelming question,
To say: "I am Lazarus, come from the dead,
Come back to tell you all, I shall tell you all"—   95
If one, settling a pillow by her head,
    Should say: "That is not what I meant at all;
    That is not it, at all."

And would it have been worth it, after all,
Would it have been worth while,   100
After the sunsets and the dooryards and the sprinkled streets,
After the novels, after the teacups, after the skirts that trail along the
    floor—
And this, and so much more?—
It is impossible to say just what I mean!
But as if a magic lantern threw the nerves in patterns on a
    screen: 105
Would it have been worth while
If one, settling a pillow or throwing off a shawl,
And turning toward the window, should say:
    "That is not it at all,
    That is not what I meant, at all."   110

.   .   .   .   .   .

No! I am not Prince Hamlet, nor was meant to be;
Am an attendant lord, one that will do
To swell a progress, start a scene or two,
Advise the prince; no doubt, an easy tool,

charger"—Herod rewarded the dancing of Herodias's daughter Salome
(Matthew, 14: 1-11). 94. *Lazarus:* The brother of Mary and Martha whom
Christ resurrects from the grave (John 11: 1-44).

Deferential, glad to be of use,   115
Politic, cautious, and meticulous;
Full of high sentence, but a bit obtuse;
At times, indeed, almost ridiculous—
Almost, at times, the Fool.

I grow old . . . I grow old . . .   120
I shall wear the bottoms of my trousers rolled.

Shall I part my hair behind? Do I dare to eat a peach?
I shall wear white flannel trousers, and walk upon the beach.
I have heard the mermaids singing, each to each.

I do not think that they will sing to me.   125

I have seen them riding seaward on the waves
Combing the white hair of the waves blown back
When the wind blows the water white and black.

We have lingered in the chambers of the sea
By sea-girls wreathed with seaweed red and brown   130
Till human voices wake us, and we drown.

---

117. *Full . . . sentence:* full of maxims and saws (like Polonius in *Hamlet*).
121. *I . . . rolled:* i.e., try to look young by wearing the latest fashion (at
the date of this poem, the fashion of cuffed—i.e., *rolled*—trousers was just
coming in).

SWEENEY AMONG THE NIGHTINGALES

(1920)

ὤμοι, πέπληγμαι καιρίαν πληγὴν ἔσω.

Apeneck Sweeney spreads his knees
Letting his arms hang down to laugh,
The zebra stripes along his jaw
Swelling to maculate giraffe.

The circles of the stormy moon   5
Slide westward toward the River Plate,
Death and the Raven drift above
And Sweeney guards the hornèd gate.

Gloomy Orion and the Dog
Are veiled; and hushed the shrunken seas;   10
The person in the Spanish cape
Tries to sit on Sweeney's knees

Slips and pulls the table cloth
Overturns a coffee-cup,
Reorganised upon the floor   15
She yawns and draws a stocking up;

SWEENEY: *Title:* Sweeney is Eliot's symbol of the permanent vulgarity, brutality, and emptiness of life when lived on the naturalistic level alone.

Epigraph: Aeschylus, *Agamemnon,* 1343: "Ah, I am struck deep with a deadly blow." This is Agamemnon's cry as he suffers at the hands of Clytemnestra the fate Sweeney is to suffer.

1. *Apeneck:* All the people in the poem are carefully dehumanized or else depersonalized ("lady in the cape," "vertebrate in brown," etc.) 4. *maculate:* spotted. 6. *River Plate:* Apparently the South American Rio de la Platta. 8. *the . . . gate:* Usually now identified as the gate of horn (*Odyssey,* xix 559 ff.; *Aeneid,* vi 892 ff.) through which come the true intimations from the world of dream. A likelier guess is that the reference is to the horns of the crescent moon, attribute of the goddess Diana, in whose sacred grove at Nemi (see below, 37n) was transacted the ritual death with which Eliot seems to be comparing and contrasting the murder of Sweeney.

The silent man in mocha brown
Sprawls at the window-sill and gapes;
The waiter brings in oranges
Bananas figs and hothouse grapes;   20

The silent vertebrate in brown
Contracts and concentrates, withdraws;
Rachel *née* Rabinovitch
Tears at the grapes with murderous paws;

She and the lady in the cape   25
Are suspect, thought to be in league;
Therefore the man with heavy eyes
Declines the gambit, shows fatigue,

Leaves the room and reappears
Outside the window, leaning in,   30
Branches of wistaria
Circumscribe a golden grin;

The host with someone indistinct
Converses at the door apart,
The nightingales are singing near   35
The Convent of the Sacred Heart,

And sang within the bloody wood
When Agamemnon cried aloud,

---

35. *nightingales:* As in the *Waste Land,* the nightingales are possibly a symbol of the potential transformation of violence and suffering to beauty (the
myth of Philomela)—hence of the ways in which a material 'death' may
lead to spiritual rebirth, which is possibly also the significance of the Convent of the Sacred Heart. According to this view, the nightingales suggest
a world antithetical to Sweeney's, in which death has meaning. Some
critics, however, have preferred to see in the nightingale's song the mark of
a universe impervious alike to the death of a Sweeney *or* an Agamemnon.
37. *bloody wood:* perhaps a two-fold reference to: (1) the wood of Nemi,
sacred to Diana, where, according to Frazer's *Golden Bough,* ch. i ("The
King of the Wood"), each priestly king was killed by a younger and
stronger successor in a vegetation ritual symbolizing death and rebirth,
winter and spring; (2) the grove of the Furies (hence, *bloody*), described
by Sophocles in *Oedipus at Colonus,* 17-8, as filled with singing nightingales.
As ministers of punishment for bloodshed, pursuing Orestes when he murdered his mother Clytemnestra in order to avenge her murder of his father
Agamemnon, the Furies are relevant to this context; and since, according to
Frazer, the cult at Nemi is said in some ancient sources to have been
brought there by Orestes, the two 'bloody woods' have a connection. In

And let their liquid siftings fall
To stain the stiff dishonoured shroud.   40

any case, both seem to suggest a world in which death has meaning—as
in our world Sweeney's clearly has not.

GERONTION

(1920)

Thou hast nor youth nor age
But as it were an after dinner sleep
Dreaming of both.

Here I am, an old man in a dry month,
Being read to by a boy, waiting for rain.
I was neither at the hot gates
Nor fought in the warm rain
Nor knee deep in the salt marsh, heaving a cutlass,   5
Bitten by flies, fought.
My house is a decayed house,
And the jew squats on the window sill, the owner,
Spawned in some estaminet of Antwerp,
Blistered in Brussels, patched and peeled in London.   10
The goat coughs at night in the field overhead;
Rocks, moss, stonecrop, iron, merds.
The woman keeps the kitchen, makes tea,
Sneezes at evening, poking the peevish gutter.
                      I an old man,
A dull head among windy spaces.

GERONTION: *Title:* "Gerontion," formed from the Greek word for old man (*geron*), means "little old man." Gerontion himself is (among other things) a representative of twentieth-century Western civilization, secularized and despiritualized, living an empty life with only memories of its heroic past and its one-time affirmations. His meditation in the poem is Eliot's history-in-brief of that civilization and its decay.
Epigraph: From Shakespeare's *Measure for Measure*, III, i, where it forms part of a speech emphasizing the vanity and futility of earthly life. These particular lines suggest both the dream-like movement of thought that Eliot's poem illustrates, and also the situation of Gerontion and the civilization he stands for.
1-2. Adapted by Eliot from a passage in A. C. Benson's life of Edward Fitzgerald, the author of the *Rubaiyat:* "Here he sits, in a dry month, old and blind, being read to by a country boy, longing for rain." 3. *hot gates:* These two words translate the Greek word Thermopylae, site of the battle where Leonidas and his Lacedaemonians died holding off the Persian invaders. 9. *estaminet:* "dive." 12. *stonecrop:* moss-like plant that grows among rocks. *merds:* feces.

Signs are taken for wonders. "We would see a sign!"
The word within a word, unable to speak a word,
Swaddled with darkness. In the juvescence of the year
Came Christ the tiger

In depraved May, dogwood and chestnut, flowering judas, 20
To be eaten, to be divided, to be drunk
Among whispers; by Mr. Silvero
With caressing hands, at Limoges
Who walked all night in the next room;

16-20. *Signs . . . May:* Adapted from Lancelot Andrewes' Nativity Sermon
of 1618 (see also that of 1611), where, after elaborating on the humility
implied by the *crèche* as Christ's "sign," Andrewes continues: "Signs are
taken for wonders. 'Master, we would fain see a sign,' that is, a miracle.
And, in this sense, it [Christ's birth in a *crèche*] is a sign, to wonder at.
Indeed, every word (here) is a wonder: . . . *an Infant, Verbum Infans, the
Word* without a *word;* the *eternal word* not able to speak a *word;* a wonder
sure. And . . . swaddled; . . . that a *wonder* too. He that (as in the 38th
of Job he saith) taketh the vast body of the main sea, turns it to and fro, as a
little child, and rolls it about with the swaddling bands of darkness . . ."
[I owe this passage to my friend D. P. Harding.] One reason (apart from
the Easter reference) for the association of Christ with "the juvescence of
the year" and "depraved May," is perhaps illuminated by Andrewes' comparison in his Nativity Sermon of 1622 between the alacrity of the Magi in
obeying the summons of the Star and the lethargy of the rest of us. We,
Andrewes says, would "fairly have put it off till the spring of the year, till
the days be longer, and the ways fairer, and the weather warmer: till better
travelling to Christ"; and we would excuse our failure to make haste by saying, " 'Why should we, Christ is no wild-Cat. . . . What needs such
haste?' " 16. *We . . . sign:* Cf. Matthew 12: 38-9: "Then certain of the
scribes and of the Pharisees answered, saying, Master, we would see a sign
from thee. But he answered and said unto them, An evil and adulterous
generation seeketh after a sign; and there shall no sign be given to it . . ."
19. *tiger:* The mystery symbolized in Blake's "Tiger, Tiger" seems relevant
here, as does also an anthropological reference to primitive habits of eating
and drinking the flesh and blood of fierce animals in order to gain their
attributes. Possibly there is also an allusion to the complacent belief cited by
Lancelot Andrewes (above, 16-20 n) that "Christ is no wild-Cat." 20. *depraved, judas:* Oblique references to the decay or betrayal of the Christian
tradition. Possibly adapted from Henry Adams's description of a Washington spring (*Education,* ch. XVIII), with its "dogwood and the judas-tree,"
and the "passionate depravity that marked the Maryland May"—"sensual,
animal, elemental." Readers of *The Education* (1918) will find much in
Adams himself to remind them of Gerontion. 22 ff. The names (like the
house, earlier) suggest the rootless internationalism of modern European
culture: "Silvero" is an Italianate name (though not Italian); "Hakagawa"
suggests a Japanese, etc.

By Hakagawa, bowing among the Titians;   25
By Madame de Tornquist, in the dark room
Shifting the candies; Fräulein von Kulp
Who turned in the hall, one hand on the door.
  Vacant shuttles
Weave the wind. I have no ghosts,   30
An old man in a draughty house
Under a windy knob.

After such knowledge, what forgiveness? Think now
History has many cunning passages, contrived corridors
And issues, deceives with whispering ambitions,   35
Guides us by vanities. Think now
She gives when our attention is distracted
And what she gives, gives with such supple confusions
That the giving famishes the craving. Gives too late
What's not believed in, or if still believed,   40
In memory only, reconsidered passion. Gives too soon
Into weak hands, what's thought can be dispensed with
Till the refusal propagates a fear. Think
Neither fear nor courage saves us. Unnatural vices
Are fathered by our heroism. Virtues   45
Are forced upon us by our impudent crimes.
These tears are shaken from the wrath-bearing tree.

The tiger springs in the new year. Us he devours. Think at last
We have not reached conclusion, when I
Stiffen in a rented house. Think at last   50
I have not made this show purposelessly
And it is not by any concitation
Of the backward devils.
I would meet you upon this honestly.
I that was near your heart was removed therefrom   55
To lose beauty in terror, terror in inquisition.
I have lost my passion: why should I need to keep it
Since what is kept must be adulterated?
I have lost my sight, smell, hearing, taste and touch:
How should I use them for your closer contact?   60

These with a thousand small deliberations
Protract the profit of their chilled delirium,

---

28. *door:* cf. *The Waste Land,* 412-5. 30. *shuttles . . . wind:* Cf. Job 7 : 6-7:
"My days are swifter than a weaver's shuttle . . . O remember that my life
is wind . . ." 32. *knob:* hill. 48. *tree:* Perhaps a reference to the tree of the
knowledge of good and evil (perhaps, also, to the cross). 52. *concitation:*
stirring up, arousing.

Excite the membrane, when the sense has cooled,
With pungent sauces, multiply variety
In a wilderness of mirrors. What will the spider do,   65
Suspend its operations, will the weevil
Delay? De Bailhache, Fresca, Mrs. Cammel, whirled
Beyond the circuit of the shuddering Bear
In fractured atoms. Gull against the wind, in the windy straits
Of Belle Isle, or running on the Horn,   7c
White feathers in the snow, the Gulf claims,
And an old man driven by the Trades
To a sleepy corner.

                    Tenants of the house,
Thoughts of a dry brain in a dry season.

⤚⤙

64-5. *multiply . . . mirrors:* The thought here is illuminated by Seneca's
account of one Hostius Quadra, who accommodated his lust by surrounding
himself "with mirrors to multiply and group his scenes of vice" (*Nat.
Quaest.,* I xvi). 66. *spider:* symbol of the destructiveness of time, from its
habit of building its webs in ruins. 68. *De Bailhache . . . Cammel:* Once
again, the names suggest an international café society. 71. *Belle Isle:* island
between Newfoundland and Canada.

THE WASTE LAND

(1922)

*"NAM Sibyllam quidem Cumis ego ipse oculis meis vidi
in ampulla pendere, et cum illi pueri dicerent: Σίβυλλα τί
θέλεις; respondebat illa: ἀποθανεῖν θέλω."*

I. THE BURIAL OF THE DEAD

April is the cruellest month, breeding
Lilacs out of the dead land, mixing

THE WASTE LAND: *Title:* Not only the title, but the plan and a good
deal of the incidental symbolism of the poem were suggested by Miss
Jessie L. Weston's book on the Grail legend: *From Ritual to Romance*
(Cambridge). Indeed, so deeply am I indebted, Miss Weston's book will
elucidate the difficulties of the poem much better than my notes can do;
and I recommend it (apart from the great interest of the book itself) to
any who think such elucidation of the poem worth the trouble. To another
work of anthropology I am indebted in general, one which has influenced
our generation profoundly; I mean *The Golden Bough;* I have used especially the two volumes *Adonis, Attis, Osiris.* Anyone who is acquainted
with these works will immediately recognise in the poem certain references
to vegetation ceremonies. [E] (*Notes or portions of notes signed E are
Eliot's.*)

In the original Grail legend a wounded king called the Fisher King rules
over a land called the Waste Land, doomed to remain waste until a knight
of surpassing purity comes to heal the king's wound, which is in the sexual
organs. This story became associated in the Middle Ages with Arthurian
stories and particularly with the story of the Holy Grail, the vessel supposed to have been used by Christ at the Last Supper. Through the efficacy
of this vessel, the Fisher King is healed by one of Arthur's knights, usually
Sir Perceval, and the land's fertility is restored. But before he can execute
this mission, the knight has had to suffer terrifying trials and temptations
in the Waste Land (as in Eliot's poem, section v), which culminate in the
ordeal of the Chapel Perilous. Miss Weston argues that the roots of this
story are to be found in the rites by which primitive men invoked spring
and new fertility after the apparent death of winter.

Epigraph: "Yes, and I myself saw with my own eyes the Sibyl of Cumae
hanging in a cage; and when the children cried at her: "Sibyl, what do you
want?' she used to reply: 'I want to die' "—Petronius, *Satyricon,* ch. xlviii.
The Sibyl's words introduce one of the poem's ambivalent concepts: (1)
that life in the Waste Land is a living death; (2) that death may be made
the means of rebirth.

Memory and desire, stirring
Dull roots with spring rain.
Winter kept us warm, covering   5
Earth in forgetful snow, feeding
A little life with dried tubers.
Summer surprised us, coming over the Starnbergersee
With a shower of rain; we stopped in the colonnade,
And went on in sunlight, into the Hofgarten,   10
And drank coffee, and talked for an hour.
Bin gar keine Russin, stamm' aus Litauen, echt deutsch.
And when we were children, staying at the archduke's,
My cousin's, he took me out on a sled,
And I was frightened. He said, Marie,   15
Marie, hold on tight. And down we went.
In the mountains, there you feel free.
I read, much of the night, and go south in the winter.

What are the roots that clutch, what branches grow
Out of this stony rubbish? Son of man,   20
You cannot say, or guess, for you know only
A heap of broken images, where the sun beats,
And the dead tree gives no shelter, the cricket no relief,
And the dry stone no sound of water. Only
There is shadow under this red rock,   25
(Come in under the shadow of this red rock),
And I will show you something different from either
Your shadow at morning striding behind you
Or your shadow at evening rising to meet you;
I will show you fear in a handful of dust.   30

---

1. Compare the opening of the *Canterbury Tales*. 12. "I am no Russian,
I come from Lithuania—real German." 20. Cf. Ezekiel 2 : 1 [E]: "And he
said unto me, Son of man, stand upon thy feet, and I will speak unto thee."
23. Cf. Ecclesiastes 12 : 5 [E]: "Also when they shall be afraid of that which
is high, and fears shall be in the way, and the almond tree shall flourish,
and the grasshopper shall be a burden, and desire shall fail; because man
goeth to his long home, and the mourners go about the streets." 24-6. Cf.
Isaiah 32 : 2, where it is said that at Christ's coming "a man shall be . . . as
rivers of water in a dry place, as the shadow of a great rock in a weary
land." In the Grail story as told by Wolfram von Eschenbach (*Parzifal,* ix
627 ff.), the Grail is said to be a stone, and those who are called to its quest
are said to be called as children and to grow up under its shadow. ("As
children the Grail doth call them, 'neath its shadow they wax and grow.")
30. *dust:* Genesis 2 : 7: "And the Lord God formed man of the dust of the
ground."

> *Frisch weht der Wind*
> *Der Heimat zu,*
> *Mein Irisch Kind,*
> *Wo weilest du?*

"You gave me hyacinths first a year ago;   35
"They called me the hyacinth girl."
—Yet when we came back, late, from the Hyacinth garden,
Your arms full, and your hair wet, I could not
Speak, and my eyes failed, I was neither
Living nor dead, and I knew nothing,   40
Looking into the heart of light, the silence.
Oed' und leer das Meer.

Madame Sosostris, famous clairvoyante,
Had a bad cold, nevertheless
Is known to be the wisest woman in Europe,   45
With a wicked pack of cards. Here, said she,
Is your card, the drowned Phoenician Sailor,
(Those are pearls that were his eyes. Look!)
Here is Belladonna, the Lady of the Rocks,
The lady of situations.   50

---

31. Wagner's *Tristan und Isolde,* I, verses 5-8 [E]: "Fresh blows the wind
homeward; my Irish child, where are you tarrying?" The verses are sung
by a sailor on the ship bringing the Irish Isolde to Cornwall. 41. *the . . .
light:* cf. Dante's phrase, *Paradiso,* xii 28: *del cor dell' una delle luci nuove"*
(from the heart of one of the new lights). 42. Tristan und Isolde, III, verse
24 [E]: "Waste and empty the sea." These are the words informing the
dying Tristan that there is no sign of Isolde's ship. 46. I am not familiar
with the exact constitution of the Tarot pack of cards, from which I have
obviously departed to suit my own convenience. The Hanged Man, a member of the traditional pack, fits my purpose in two ways: because he is
associated in my mind with the Hanged God of Frazer, and because
I associate him with the hooded figure in the passage of the disciples
to Emmaus in Part V. The Phoenician Sailor and the Merchant appear later; also the "crowds of people," and Death by Water is executed
in Part IV. The Man with Three Staves (an authentic member of the Tarot
pack) I associate, quite arbitrarily, with the Fisher King himself. [E]
   The Tarot pack of cards seems to have played a significant part in the
ancient fertility rituals. Here it has degenerated into a fortune-teller's
property. 48. *Those . . . eyes:* From Ariel's song to Prince Ferdinand in
The Tempest (I ii 398), touching on "the sea-change" of King Alonzo,
Ferdinand's father, whom Ferdinand supposes to be drowned. 49. *Belladonna . . . Rocks:* With ironic reminder of the Madonna, of whom there
is a painting by Leonardo da Vinci entitled "Madonna of the Rocks."

Here is the man with three staves, and here the Wheel,
And here is the one-eyed merchant, and this card,
Which is blank, is something he carries on his back,
Which I am forbidden to see. I do not find
The Hanged Man. Fear death by water.   55
I see crowds of people, walking round in a ring.
Thank you. If you see dear Mrs. Equitone,
Tell her I bring the horoscope myself:
One must be so careful these days.

Unreal City,   60
Under the brown fog of a winter dawn,
A crowd flowed over London Bridge, so many,
I had not thought death had undone so many.
Sighs, short and infrequent, were exhaled,
And each man fixed his eyes before his feet.   65
Flowed up the hill and down King William Street,
To where Saint Mary Woolnoth kept the hours
With a dead sound on the final stroke of nine.
There I saw one I knew, and stopped him, crying: "Stetson!
"You who were with me in the ships at Mylae!   70
"That corpse you planted last year in your garden,

60-62. Cf. [Charles] Baudelaire [*The Seven Old Men*]: "Swarming city,
city full of dreams, where the spectre in broad daylight buttonholes the
passer-by." [E] 63. Cf. [Dante's] *Inferno*, III 55-7 [E], especially 57—
Dante's comment about those souls too negative to be accepted either in hell
or heaven—of which this line is a translation. 64. Cf. *Inferno*, IV 25-7 [E].
66. *King William Street*: One of the London streets most thronged with
commuting office-workers at the morning rush hour. 67. *Saint Mary Woolnoth*: Church at the corner of King William and Lombard Streets. 68. A
phenomenon [the dead sound] which I have often noticed [E]. Nine is the
hour when the business crowd must be at work. But cf. also, Matthew 27 :
45-6: "Now from the sixth hour there was darkness over all the land unto
the ninth hour. And about the ninth hour Jesus cried with a loud voice,
saying . . . 'My God, my God, why hast thou forsaken me?' " 69. So Dante
in the *Inferno* sees and stops friends. *Stetson* is simply a typical business-
man's name. 70. *Mylae*: scene of Rome's great naval victory over the Car-
thaginians in the first Punic War—a 'business' war. 71. Romans 6 : 3-5:
"Know ye not that so many of us as were baptised into Jesus Christ were
baptised into his death? Therefore we are buried with him by baptism into
death: that like as Christ was raised up from the dead by the glory of the
Father, even so we should walk in newness of life. For if we have been
planted together in the likeness of his death, we shall be also in the likeness
of his resurrection." See the whole chapter.

"Has it begun to sprout? Will it bloom this year?
"Or has the sudden frost disturbed its bed?
"Oh keep the Dog far hence, that's friend to men,
"Or with his nails he'll dig it up again!   75
"You! hypocrite lecteur!—mon semblable,—mon frère!"

II. A GAME OF CHESS

The chair she sat in, like a burnished throne,
Glowed on the marble, where the glass
Held up by standards wrought with fruited vines
From which a golden Cupidon peeped out   80
(Another hid his eyes behind his wing)
Doubled the flames of sevenbranched candelabra
Reflecting light upon the table as
The glitter of her jewels rose to meet it,
From satin cases poured in rich profusion;   85
In vials of ivory and coloured glass

74-5. Cf. the Dirge in [John] Webster's *The White Devil* [V. iv] [E]—sung
by a mad woman to her son over the corpse of his brother whom he has
killed.

> Call for the robin redbreast and the wren,
> Since o'er shady groves they hover,
> And with leaves and flowers do cover
> The friendless bodies of unburied men.
> Call unto his funeral dole
> The ant, the field-mouse, and the mole,
> To rear him hillocks that shall keep him warm,
> And, when gay tombs are robbed, sustain no harm;
> But keep the wolf far thence, that's foe to men,
> For with his nails he'll dig them up again.

74. *the Dog:* Cf. Psalm 22:20: "Deliver my soul from the sword; my
darling from the power of the dog." Also, Eliot's lines in *Marina:*

> Those who sharpen the tooth of the dog, meaning
> Death.

76. Cf. Baudelaire, Preface [i.e., prefatory poem] to *Fleurs du Mal* [E],
where the "menagerie" of men's vices concludes with "Boredom":

> You know him, reader, this dainty monster—
> Hypocrite reader—my double—my brother.

77 ff. Cf. *Antony and Cleopatra,* II, ii, 190 [E], where Enobarbus begins his
great description of Cleopatra floating down the Nile to Antony, with the
words: "The chair she sat in, like a burnished throne, Burned on the water."
The many reminiscences in Eliot's lines of Shakespeare's description of
Imogen's room in *Cymbeline* suggests that to the atmosphere of passionate
love and lust invoked here the pretended 'rape' of Imogen is also relevant.

Unstoppered, lurked her strange synthetic perfumes,
Unguent, powdered, or liquid—troubled, confused
And drowned the sense in odours; stirred by the air
That freshened from the window, these ascended   90
In fattening the prolonged candle-flames,
Flung their smoke into the laquearia,
Stirring the pattern on the coffered ceiling.
Huge sea-wood fed with copper
Burned green and orange, framed by the coloured stone,   95
In which sad light a carvèd dolphin swam.
Above the antique mantel was displayed
As though a window gave upon the sylvan scene
The change of Philomel, by the barbarous king
So rudely forced; yet there the nightingale   100
Filled all the desert with inviolable voice
And still she cried, and still the world pursues,
"Jug Jug" to dirty ears.
And other withered stumps of time
Were told upon the walls; staring forms   105
Leaned out, leaning, hushing the room enclosed.
Footsteps shuffled on the stair.
Under the firelight, under the brush, her hair
Spread out in fiery points
Glowed into words, then would be savagely still.   110

92. *laquearia:* V. *Aeneid,* i. 726 [E]: "Lighted lamps hang out from the fretted ceiling [laquearia] of gold, and flaming torches drive out the night." The line describes the feast given by Queen Dido of Carthage for Aeneas and his men on their arrival from Troy, and invokes another of the world's great 'love' affairs. 98. *sylvan scene:* V. Milton, *Paradise Lost,* iv 140 [E], where the phrase describes the approach to Paradise as Satan first views, still from the outside, the garden he is about to violate. 99. V. Ovid, *Metamorphoses,* vi: Philomela [E]. Philomela, going to visit her sister Procne, was raped on the way by her sister's husband Tereus, who then silenced her by cutting out her tongue and imprisoning her in a lonely place. She, however, wove into a piece of tapestry the story of her sufferings and thus communicated them to her sister, who found her prison and released her. Together they took revenge on Tereus by serving up his son to him as a feast and then revealing what they had done. As he was about to stab them both, he was changed to a hoopoe bird, Procne to a swallow, and Philomela to a nightingale. In poetic tradition, this story accounts for the supposedly plaintive notes of the nightingale and swallow. 100. Cf. [*The Waste Land*] Part III, 204 [E]. 103. "Jug Jug": The words commonly used in Elizabethan poetry to represent the song of the nightingale.

"My nerves are bad to-night. Yes, bad. Stay with me.
"Speak to me. Why do you never speak. Speak.
"What are you thinking of? What thinking?
"What?
"I never know what you are thinking. Think."   115

I think we are in rats' alley
Where the dead men lost their bones.

"What is that noise?"
                          The wind under the door.
"What is that noise now? What is the wind doing?"
                              Nothing again nothing.   12c

                                              "Do
"You know nothing? Do you see nothing? Do you remember
"Nothing?"

          I remember
Those are pearls that were his eyes.   12⁴
"Are you alive, or not? Is there nothing in your head?"

                                              But
O O O O that Shakespeherian Rag—
It's so elegant
So intelligent   130
"What shall I do now? What shall I do?"
"I shall rush out as I am, and walk the street
"With my hair down, so. What shall we do to-morrow?
"What shall we ever do?"
                          The hot water at ten.   135
And if it rains, a closed car at four.
And we shall play a game of chess,
Pressing lidless eyes and waiting for a knock upon the door.

When Lil's husband got demobbed, I said—
I didn't mince my words, I said to her myself,   140
HURRY UP PLEASE ITS TIME

---

115. Cf. Part III, 195 [E]. 118. Cf. Webster [*The Devil's Law Case*, III ii
162]: "Is the wind in that door still?" [E]. 122. *Do . . . nothing?*: Cf.
Hamlet's surprised remark when he realizes his mother cannot see the ghost
(III iv 132): "Do you see nothing there?" 125. Cf. Part I, 37, 48 [E]. 126.
Is . . . head: Cf. *The Hollow Men*, 4. 138. Cf. the game of chess in
[Thomas] Middleton's *Women Beware Women* [II ii] [E]. Livia plays
chess with Bianca's mother-in-law to distract her attention while Bianca is
being seduced. 139. *demobbed*: demobilized. 141. The call of the barman
in an English "pub" at closing time

Now Albert's coming back, make yourself a bit smart.
He'll want to know what you done with that money he gave you
To get yourself some teeth. He did, I was there.
You have them all out, Lil, and get a nice set,   145
He said, I swear, I can't bear to look at you.
And no more can't I, I said, and think of poor Albert,
He's been in the army four years, he wants a good time,
And if you don't give it him, there's others will, I said.
Oh is there, she said. Something o' that, I said.   150
Then I'll know who to thank, she said, and give me a straight look.
HURRY UP PLEASE ITS TIME
If you don't like it you can get on with it, I said.
Others can pick and choose if you can't.
But if Albert makes off, it won't be for lack of telling.   155
You ought to be ashamed, I said, to look so antique.
(And her only thirty-one.)
I can't help it, she said, pulling a long face,
It's them pills I took, to bring it off, she said.
(She's had five already, and nearly died of young George.)   160
The chemist said it would be all right, but I've never been the same.
You *are* a proper fool, I said.
Well, if Albert won't leave you alone, there it is, I said,
What you get married for if you don't want children?
HURRY UP PLEASE ITS TIME   165
Well, that Sunday Albert was home, they had a hot gammon,
And they asked me in to dinner, to get the beauty of it hot—
HURRY UP PLEASE ITS TIME
HURRY UP PLEASE ITS TIME
Goonight Bill. Goonight Lou. Goonight May. Goonight.   170
Ta ta. Goonight. Goonight.
Good night, ladies, good night, sweet ladies, good night, good night.

III. THE FIRE SERMON

The river's tent is broken: the last fingers of leaf
Clutch and sink into the wet bank. The wind
Crosses the brown land, unheard. The nymphs are departed.   175
Sweet Thames, run softly, till I end my song.
The river bears no empty bottles, sandwich papers,

---

172. Cf. *Hamlet* (V iv), where Ophelia wanders onto the stage, mad, and after singing of the burial of loved ones and the betrayal of trusting maids, wanders off again with these words. 176. V. Spenser, *Prothalamion* [E]— which describes the progress of two young ladies about to be married down a somewhat lovelier Thames, and which contains this line as refrain.

Silk handkerchiefs, cardboard boxes, cigarette ends
Or other testimony of summer nights. The nymphs are departed.
And their friends, the loitering heirs of city directors;   180
Departed, have left no addresses.
By the waters of Leman I sat down and wept . . .
Sweet Thames, run softly till I end my song,
Sweet Thames, run softly, for I speak not loud or long.
But at my back in a cold blast I hear   185
The rattle of the bones, and chuckle spread from ear to ear.
A rat crept softly through the vegetation
Dragging its slimy belly on the bank
While I was fishing in the dull canal
On a winter evening round behind the gashouse   190
Musing upon the king my brother's wreck
And on the king my father's death before him.
White bodies naked on the low damp ground
And bones cast in a little low dry garret,
Rattled by the rat's foot only, year to year.   195
But at my back from time to time I hear
The sound of horns and motors, which shall bring
Sweeney to Mrs. Porter in the spring.
O the moon shone bright on Mrs. Porter
And on her daughter   200
They wash their feet in soda water

---

182. A paraphrase of Psalm 137 : 1, lamenting the captivity of the Hebrews
in Babylon: "By the rivers of Babylon, there we sat down, yea, we wept,
when we remembered Zion." Leman is a name often applied by the romantic poets to Lake Geneva. 185. Cf. Andrew Marvell's *To His Coy Mistress:*
          But ever at my back I hear
          Time's wingèd chariot, hurrying near;
          And yonder all before us lie
          Deserts of vast eternity.
192. Cf. *The Tempest,* I, ii [389-91] [E]. There Prince Ferdinand says:
          "Sitting on a bank,
     Weeping again the King my father's wrack,
     This music crept by me upon the waters . . ."
196. Cf. Marvell, *To His Coy Mistress:* [E]. 197. Cf. [John] Day, *Parliament of Bees* [c. 1607]:
          "When of the sudden, listening, you shall hear,
          "A noise of horns and hunting, which shall bring
          "Actaeon to Diana in the spring,
          "Where all shall see her naked skin . . ." [E]
Actaeon, having looked on Diana (the goddess of chastity) naked, is turned
to a stag and killed by his own hounds. The story was often mythologized
to mean pursuit and slaughter by one's lusts. 199. I do not know the
origin of the ballad from which these lines are taken: it was reported to
me from Sydney, Australia. [E]

Et O ces voix d'enfants, chantant dans la coupole!

Twit twit twit
Jug jug jug jug jug jug
So rudely forc'd.   205
Tereu

Unreal City
Under the brown fog of a winter noon
Mr. Eugenides, the Smyrna merchant
Unshaven, with a pocket full of currants   210
C.i.f. London: documents at sight,
Asked me in demotic French
To luncheon at the Cannon Street Hotel
Followed by a weekend at the Metropole.
At the violet hour, when the eyes and back   215
Turn upward from the desk, when the human engine waits
Like a taxi throbbing waiting,
I Tiresias, though blind, throbbing between two lives,
Old man with wrinkled female breasts, can see

---

202. V. [Paul] Verlaine, *Parsifal* [E], where Parsifal, at the end of his quest,
hears in the chapel of the Holy Grail—"And—O those children's voices,
singing in the choir." In the Parsifal story, this singing of the children
celebrates the healing of the Fisher King and of his land, brought about by a
washing of the feet (cf. 201); but in Verlaine's poem, the line has pederastic
implications, and so serves in Eliot's context as a further instance of the
secularization and perversion of religious values, like the Porters' foot-
washing.
203-4, 206. Again, words used in Elizabethan poetry to suggest the song
(and story) of the nightingale. 210. The currants were quoted at a price
"carriage and insurance free to London"; and the Bill of Lading etc.
were to be handed to the buyer upon payment of the sight draft. [E]
212. *demotic:* slangy. 213. *Cannon Street Hotel:* London hotel fre-
quented in the 1920's by Continental businessmen. 214. *the Metropole:*
Brighton hotel, popular for assignations. 218. *Tiresias:* Tiresias, although a mere spectator and not indeed a "character," is yet the most
important personage in the poem, uniting all the rest. Just as the
one-eyed merchant, seller of currants, melts into the Phoenician Sailor,
and the latter is not wholly distinct from Ferdinand Prince of Naples,
so all the women are one woman, and the two sexes meet in Tiresias.
What Tiresias *sees,* in fact, is the substance of the poem. The whole passage
from Ovid [*Metamorphoses* iii 322 ff.] is of great anthropological interest:
"It chanced that Jove, while warmed with wine, put care aside and bandied
good-humored jests with Juno, in an idle hour. 'I maintain,' he said, 'that
your pleasure in love is greater than we [male gods] enjoy.' She held the
opposite view. And so they decided to ask the judgment of wise Tiresias.

At the violet hour, the evening hour that strives   220
Homeward, and brings the sailor home from sea,
The typist home at teatime, clears her breakfast, lights
Her stove, and lays out food in tins.
Out of the window perilously spread
Her drying combinations touched by the sun's last rays,   225
On the divan are piled (at night her bed)
Stockings, slippers, camisoles, and stays.
I Tiresias, old man with wrinkled dugs
Perceived the scene, and foretold the rest—
I too awaited the expected guest.   230
He, the young man carbuncular, arrives,
A small house agent's clerk, with one bold stare,
One of the low on whom assurance sits
As a silk hat on a Bradford millionaire.
The time is now propitious, as he guesses,   235
The meal is ended, she is bored and tired,
Endeavors to engage her in caresses
Which still are unreproved, if undesired.
Flushed and decided, he assaults at once;
Exploring hands encounter no defence;   240
His vanity requires no response,
And makes a welcome of indifference.
(And I Tiresias have foresuffered all

He knew both sides of love. For once with a blow of his staff he
had outraged two huge serpents mating in the green forest; and, wonderful to relate, from man he was changed into a woman, and in that
form spent seven years. In the eighth year he saw the same serpent
again and said, 'Since in striking you there is such magic power as
to change the nature of the giver of the blow, now will I strike you
once more.' So saying, he struck the serpents and his former state was
restored and he became as he had been born. He therefore, being asked
to arbitrate the playful dispute of the gods, took sides with Jove. Saturnia
[Juno], they say, grieved more deeply than she should and than the issue
warranted, and condemned the arbitrator to perpetual blindness. But the
Almighty Father (for no god may undo what another god has done) in return for his loss of sight gave Tiresias the power to know the future, light-
ening the penalty by the honor." [E] 221. This may not appear as exact
as Sappho's lines, but I had in mind the "longshore" or "dory" fisherman,
who returns at nightfall. [E] Eliot refers to Sappho's iines on the evening star: "Hesperus, you bring all that bright morning scattered, the
sheep, the kid, and the child to its mother", but his poem also reflects
R. L. Stevenson's *Requiem*: "Home is the sailor, home from sea." 234.
Bradford: a manufacturing town, filled after the first World War with
"newly rich," whose breeding was somewhat uncertain.

Enacted on this same divan or bed;
I who have sat by Thebes below the wall   245
And walked among the lowest of the dead.)
Bestows one final patronising kiss,
And gropes his way, finding the stairs unlit . . .

She turns and looks a moment in the glass,
Hardly aware of her departed lover;   250
Her brain allows one half-formed thought to pass:
"Well now that's done: and I'm glad it's over."
When lovely woman stoops to folly and
Paces about her room again, alone,
She smoothes her hair with automatic hand,   255
And puts a record on the gramophone.

"This music crept by me upon the waters"
And along the Strand, up Queen Victoria Street.
O City city, I can sometimes hear
Beside a public bar in Lower Thames Street,   260
The pleasant whining of a mandoline
And a clatter and a chatter from within
Where fishmen lounge at noon: where the walls
Of Magnus Martyr hold
Inexplicable splendor of Ionian white and gold.   265

      The river sweats
      Oil and tar

---

253. V. Goldsmith, the song in *The Vicar of Wakefield*, [ch. 24] [E]:
      When lovely woman stoops to folly,
      And finds too late that men betray,
      What charm can soothe her melancholy?
      What art can wash her guilt away?

      The only art her guilt to cover,
      To hide her shame from every eye,
      To give repentance to her lover
      And wring his bosom—is to die.

257. V. *The Tempest*, as above [192] [E]. 260. *Lower Thames Street:* i. e.,
at Billingsgate fishmarket, near London Bridge. 264. The interior of St.
Magnus Martyr is to my mind one of the finest among Wren's interiors. [E]
266. The Song of the (three) Thames-daughters begins here. From line
292 to 306 inclusive they speak in turn. V. *Götterdämmerung*, III, i: the
Rhine-daughters. [E] In Wagner's *Das Rheingold* the three Rhine-daughters sing of the gold they guard, using the refrain of 277 and 290; but in
his *Götterdämmerung*, they mourn its loss. Eliot's Thames-daughters also
mourn a loss.

The barges drift
With the turning tide
Red sails   270
Wide
To leeward, swing on the heavy spar.
The barges wash
Drifting logs
Down Greenwich reach   275
Past the Isle of Dogs.
              Weialala leia
              Wallala leialala

Elizabeth and Leicester
Beating oars   280
The stern was formed
A gilded shell
Red and gold
The brisk swell
Rippled both shores   285
Southwest wind
Carried down stream
The peal of bells
White towers
              Weialala leia   290
              Wallala leialala

"Trams and dusty trees.
Highbury bore me. Richmond and Kew

275-6. *Greenwich* . . . *Dogs:* a curving stretch of the Thames, with a
dismal dock area on one side and a range of fine Wren buildings on the
other. 279. V. Froude, *Elizabeth,* Vol. I, ch. iv, letter of De Quadra to
Philip of Spain: "In the afternoon we were in a barge, watching the games
on the river. (The queen) was alone with Lord Robert and myself on the
poop, when they began to talk nonsense, and went so far that Lord Robert
at last said, as I was on the spot there was no reason why they should not
be married [De Quadra was a bishop] if the queen pleased." [E] 289.
white towers: the donjon of the Tower of London. 293-4. *Highbury* . . .
me: Cf. *Purgatorio,* V, 133:
              "Remember me, who am Pia. Siena made me,
              Maremma unmade me." [E]
Cf. also the epitaph attributed to Virgil: *"Mantua me genuit, Calabri ra-*
puere, tenet Parthenope." (Mantua bore me, Calabria was the death of me,
now Naples holds me.) 293. *Highbury:* lower-middle-class suburb. *Rich-*
mond and Kew: popular riverside vacation spots.

Undid me. By Richmond I raised my knees
Supine on the floor of a narrow canoe."   295

"My feet are at Moorgate, and my heart
Under my feet. After the event
He wept. He promised 'a new start.'
I made no comment. What should I resent?"

"On Margate Sands.   300
I can connect
Nothing with nothing.
The broken fingernails of dirty hands.
My people humble people who expect
Nothing."   305
　　　　　　　la la

To Carthage then I came

Burning, burning, burning burning
O Lord Thou pluckest me out
O Lord Thou pluckest   310

burning

IV. DEATH BY WATER

Phlebas the Phoenician, a fortnight dead,
Forgot the cry of gulls, and the deep sea swell

---

296. *Moorgate:* area in the heart of the London financial district (where this Thames-daughter may have been a secretary). 300. *Margate:* seaside resort near London. 307. V. St. Augustine's *Confessions:* "to Carthage then I came, where a cauldron of unholy loves sang all about mine ears." [E] Throughout the *Confessions* Augustine dwells on sensuality as an impediment to spirituality, and, speaking of his own case (X 34), says: "I also entangle my steps in these outward beauties: but thou wilt pluck me out, O Lord, thou wilt pluck me out" (cf. 309-10). 308. Eliot's note refers to "the complete text of the Buddha's Fire Sermon (which corresponds in importance to the Sermon on the Mount) from which these words are taken." In this sermon, Buddha says that all things bodily and sensory are on fire with the fire of desire and passion, with the endless mortal burning from which it is the wish of the Buddhist to be set free. 309. From St. Augustine's *Confessions* again. The collocation of these two representatives of eastern and western asceticism, as the culmination of this part of the poem, is not an accident. [E]

　　Section IV. Title: Water: Water and Fire (308) frequently have ambivalent meanings in Eliot's poetry. Water as (1) a destructive element in which one may drown, but (2) a fertile and saving (cf. holy water) element that a sterile land needs. Fire as (1) the ceaseless agitation of desire to which life in time is subject, (2) the purging fire of suf-

And the profit and loss.
                              A current under sea   315
Picked his bones in whispers. As he rose and fell
He passed the stages of his age and youth
Entering the whirlpool.
                              Gentile or Jew
O you who turn the wheel and look to windward,   320
Consider Phlebas, who was once handsome and tall as you.

V. WHAT THE THUNDER SAID

After the torchlight red on sweaty faces
After the frosty silence in the gardens
After the agony in stony places
The shouting and the crying   325
Prison and palace and reverberation
Of thunder of spring over distant mountains
He who was living is now dead
We who were living are now dying
With a little patience   330

Here is no water but only rock
Rock and no water and the sandy road
The road winding above among the mountains
Which are mountains of rock without water
If there were water we should stop and drink   335
Amongst the rock one cannot stop or think
Sweat is dry and feet are in the sand
If there were only water amongst the rock

---

fering that purifies us. 314. *profit and loss:* A phrase (like the pun
on "currant," 315) that associates Phlebas with Mr. Eugenides (209).
319-20. Romans 3 : 9: ". . . we have before proved both Jews and Gen-
tiles, that they are all under sin". *Ibid.,* 10: 12-13: "For there is no
difference between the Jew and the Greek: for the same Lord over all is
rich unto all that call upon him. For whosoever shall call upon the name
of the Lord shall be saved."
    Section V, *Title:* In the first part of Part V three themes are employed:
the journey to Emmaus, the approach to the Chapel Perilous (see Miss
Weston's book) and the present decay of eastern Europe. [E] 322. *torchlight:* John 18 : 3: "Judas, then, having received a band of men and officers
from the chief priests and Pharisees, cometh thither with lanterns and
torches and weapons." But the poem also commemorates all the hanged
or slain gods of anthropology, through whose deaths new life was invoked.
323. *gardens:* the Garden of Gethsemane, among others. 326. *Prison and
palace:* Christ's prison and Pilate's palace, among others.

Dead mountain mouth of carious teeth that cannot spit
Here one can neither stand nor lie nor sit   340
There is not even silence in the mountains
But dry sterile thunder without rain
There is not even solitude in the mountains
But red sullen faces sneer and snarl
From doors of mudcracked houses   345
              If there were water
    And no rock
    If there were rock
    And also water
    And water   350
    A spring
    A pool among the rock
    If there were the sound of water only
    Not the cicada
    And dry grass singing   355
    But sound of water over a rock
    Where the hermit-thrush sings in the pine trees
    Drip drop drip drop drop drop drop
    But there is no water

Who is the third who walks always beside you?   360
When I count, there are only you and I together
But when I look ahead up the white road
There is always another one walking beside you
Gliding wrapt in a brown mantle, hooded
I do not know whether a man or a woman   365
—But who is that on the other side of you?

What is that sound high in the air
Murmur of maternal lamentation

---

357. Eliot's note calls attention to the cool liquid "water-dripping song" of
the hermit thrush. 360 ff. The return of the slain god. 361. The following
lines were stimulated by the account of one of the Antarctic expeditions
(I forget which, but I think one of Shackleton's): it was related that the
party of explorers, at the extremity of their strength, had the constant de-
lusion that there was *one more member* than could actually be counted.
[E] Cf. also the journey to Emmaus, in the course of which two of the
disciples meet the newly risen Christ: "But their eyes were holden that they
should not know him" (Luke 24: 13-31). 367-77. Cf. Hermann Hesse,
Blick ins Chaos: "Already half of Europe, already at least half of Eastern
Europe, is on the way to Chaos, traveling drunken in holy illusion along
the edge of the abyss, and as she goes, sings drunken hymns, as Dmitri
Karamazov sang. Over these songs the outraged burgher laughs scorn-
fully, the saint and seer hears them with tears." [E]

Who are those hooded hordes swarming
Over endless plains, stumbling in cracked earth 370
Ringed by the flat horizon only
What is the city over the mountains
Cracks and reforms and bursts in the violet air
Falling towers
Jerusalem Athens Alexandria 375
Vienna London
Unreal

A woman drew her long black hair out tight
And fiddled whisper music on those strings
And bats with baby faces in the violet light 380
Whistled, and beat their wings
And crawled head downward down a blackened wall
And upside down in air were towers
Tolling reminiscent bells, that kept the hours
And voices singing out of empty cisterns and exhausted wells. 385

In this decayed hole among the mountains
In the faint moonlight, the grass is singing
Over the tumbled graves, about the chapel
There is the empty chapel, only the wind's home.
It has no windows, and the door swings, 390
Dry bones can harm no one.
Only a cock stood on the rooftree
Co co rico co co rico
In a flash of lightning. Then a damp gust
Bringing rain 395

Ganga was sunken, and the limp leaves
Waited for rain, while the black clouds
Gathered far distant, over Himavant.
The jungle crouched, humped in silence.

---

373. *violet:* A twilight of civilization. 385. *cisterns . . . wells:* Jeremiah
2:13: "For my people have committed two evils; they have forsaken me
the fountain of living waters and hewed them out cisterns, broken
cisterns that can hold no water." Also, Ecclesiastes 12:6. 386-95. The Chapel
Perilous, where in the Grail stories the questing knight undergoes a night
of supernatural terrors before the achievement of his quest the next day.
Here, the terror is that there may be no supernatural. 393. *Co . . . rico:*
The crowing of the cock which signalizes the departure of evil spirits.
But cf. also, Matthew 26:74-5: "Then began he to curse and swear, saying,
I know not the man. And immediately the cock crew. And Peter remem-
bered the word of Jesus which said unto him, Before the cock crow, thou
shall deny me thrice."

THE WASTE LAND 159

Then spoke the thunder   400
DA
Datta: what have we given?
My friend, blood shaking my heart
The awful daring of a moment's surrender
Which an age of prudence can never retract   405
By this, and this only, we have existed
Which is not to be found in our obituaries
Or in memories draped by the beneficent spider
Or under seals broken by the lean solicitor
In our empty rooms   410
DA
Dayadhvam: I have heard the key
Turn in the door once and turn once only
We think of the key, each in his prison
Thinking of the key, each confirms a prison   415
Only at nightfall, aethereal rumours

---

402. *"Datta, dayadhvam damyata"* (Give, sympathise, control). The fable of the meaning of the Thunder is found in the *Brihadaranyaka—Upanishad*, 5, I. . . . [E] In the fable of the thunder, Prajapati (the Lord of Creation) thunders three times—the thunder being represented by the sound "Da!" His pupils interpret the meaning in three different ways, according to three different Sanskrit words beginning with "Da"—the three that Eliot uses in the poem. The fable then closes with the instruction: "This same thing does the divine voice here, thunder, repeat: *Da! Da! Da!* that is, restrain yourselves, give, be compassionate." (Cf. R. E. Hume, *The Thirteen Principal Upanishads*, 1921). 408. Cf. Webster, *The White Devil,* V, vi:

> ". . . they'll remarry
> Ere the worm pierce your winding-sheet, ere the spider
> Make a thin curtain for your epitaphs." [E]

Also, *Gerontion, 66.* 412. Cf. *Inferno*, XXXIII, 46: ". . . and below, I heard the door of the horrible tower being nailed up." Also F. H. Bradley, *Appearance and Reality*, p. 346: "My external sensations are no less private to myself than are my thoughts or my feelings. In either case, my experience falls within my own circle, a circle closed on the outside; and, with all its elements alike, every sphere is opaque to the others which surround it. . . . In brief, regarded as an existence which appears in a soul, the whole world for each is peculiar and private to that soul." [E] The Dante quotation is from the passage in which Ugolino tells Dante how he and his sons were immured in a tower to starve. The association of the incident with a "key" (not mentioned in Dante) is perhaps owing to C. E. Norton's note on this place in his translation, where it is observed that, after the imprisonment of the actual historical Ugolino, "the keys of the tower were thrown into the Arno."

Revive for a moment a broken Coriolanus
DA
Damyata: The boat responded
Gaily, to the hand expert with sail and oar   420
The sea was calm, your heart would have responded
Gaily, when invited, beating obedient
To controlling hands

                              I sat upon the shore
Fishing, with the arid plain behind me   425
Shall I at least set my lands in order?   •
London Bridge is falling down falling down falling down
Poi s'ascose nel foco che gli affina
Quando fiam uti chelidon—O swallow swallow
Le Prince d'Aquitaine à la tour abolie   430

---

417. *Coriolanus:* A great Roman general and aristocratic despiser of the
fickle mob—hero of Shakespeare's tragedy *Coriolanus.* Through his own
pride and the mob's ingratitude he is forced into exile, joins the Volscian
enemy in his rage, returns at the head of their army to conquer Rome, is
persuaded to spare it by his Roman mother, wife, and son, and then is
killed by the Volscians in reprisal. 419-20. Cf. 31 ff. 425. V. Weston: *From
Ritual to Romance;* chapter on the Fisher King. [E] 426. *set . . . order:*
Cf. the prayer of Jacopone da Todi which Dante places as epigraph to his
Purgatorio: "Set my love in order, O thou who lovest me." 428. V. *Purgatorio,* XXVI, 148: " 'Now I pray you, by that Power which guides you to
the summit of this stairway, at due time be mindful of my pain.' Then he
hid himself in the fire that refines them." [E] The last sentence of this is
the line quoted in the poem. The person speaking is Arnaut Daniel, a Pro-
vencal troubadour, who has just said to Dante: "I am Arnaut, who weep
and go singing; contrite I see my past folly, and glad I see before me the
joy I hope for." 429. *Quando . . . chelidon:* V. *Pervigilium Veneris.* Cf.
Philomela in Parts II and III [of *The Waste Land*]. [E] As its title implies, the *Pervigilium* celebrates "The Eve of Venus," when all nature rejoices, and even Philomela the nightingale sings. The poet alone is dis-
pirited:

    She is singing: I am silent. When will spring awake in me?
    When shall I be like the swallow and from dumb distress be free?
O swallow swallow: Cf. Swinburne's *Itylus,* through which runs the cry
'O Swallow' and a reproach like that of *Pervigilium:* "How can thine
heart be full of the Spring?" 430. V. Gerard de Nerval, Sonnet *El Des-
dichado* [E] In this sonnet, the title of which is Spanish for "The Dis-
inherited One," de Nerval represents himself as the neglected and outcast
heir of the imaginative tradition of the troubadours (associated with the
fabulous castles of Aquitaine in Southern France). Hence he refers to himself in the line quoted by Eliot as "The Prince of Aquitaine, of the ruined
tower."

These fragments I have shored against my ruins
Why then Ile fit you. Hieronymo's mad againe.
Datta. Dayadhvam. Damyata.
     Shantih shantih shantih

❧

432. V. Kyd's *Spanish Tragedy* [E], IV i 67. In Kyd's tragedy, Hieronymo suffers fits of madness through grief for his murdered son. He
writes a play by means of which he hopes to kill the murderers who are
to be persuaded to act in it along with himself. When an invitation comes
from the court that will allow him to carry out his plan, he accepts eagerly,
saying to the murderers who have brought the invitation, "Why then, I'll
fit [i.e., supply] you." The second half of Eliot's line is the subtitle of the
Spanish Tragedy. 434. *Shantih:* Repeated as here, a formal ending to an
Upanishad. "The Peace which passeth understanding" is our equivalent to
this word. [E]

THE HOLLOW MEN

(1925)

Mistah Kurtz—he dead.

A penny for the Old Guy

I

We are the hollow men
We are the stuffed men
Leaning together
Headpiece filled with straw. Alas!
Our dried voices, when   5
We whisper together
Are quiet and meaningless
As wind in dry grass
Or rats' feet over broken glass
In our dry cellar   10

THE HOLLOW MEN: *Title:* On the situation and the atmosphere, cf. Dante's account (*Inferno*, III) of Hell's entrance, where dwell in "the starless air," in "air forever dark," and "without hope of death," those "who never were alive"—"the wretched souls of those who lived without infamy and without praise"—because they were not positive enough spiritually to be either good or evil. R ε G

Epigraphs: Mistah . . . dead: In Conrad's *Heart of Darkness,* this is the phrase used by the black cabin boy announcing Mr. Kurtz's death. Mr. Kurtz, a European trader, had gone into "the heart of darkness"—the mysterious primitive life of the African jungle—with high intentions, but was soon barbarized by it: "The wilderness . . . found him out early. . . . I think it whispered to him things about himself which he did not know— and the whisper . . . proved irresistibly fascinating. It echoed loudly within him because he was hollow at the core." Despite his hollowness, however, as Marlowe the narrator of the story insists, Mr. Kurtz had been "a re- markable man." His dying whisper, "The horror! The horror!" showed at least "some sort of belief; it had candour, it had conviction, it had a vibrating note of revolt . . . , it had the appalling face of a glimpsed truth."

A . . . Guy: The cry of English children on Guy Fawkes day, as they go about with straw effigies of the seventeenth-century traitor Guy Fawkes —later to be hung and burned—and ask for pennies with which to buy fireworks. But it is we who are the real hollow men, the poem hints—not the lost violent souls like Fawkes (or even Kurtz).

Shape without form, shade without colour,
Paralysed force, gesture without motion;

Those who have crossed
With direct eyes, to death's other Kingdom
Remember us—if at all—not as lost   15
Violent souls, but only
As the hollow men
The stuffed men.

II

Eyes I dare not meet in dreams
In death's dream kingdom   20
These do not appear:
There, the eyes are
Sunlight on a broken column
There, is a tree swinging
And voices are   25
In the wind's singing
More distant and more solemn
Than a fading star.
Let me be no nearer
In death's dream kingdom   30
Let me also wear
Such deliberate disguises
Rat's coat, crowskin, crossed staves
In a field
Behaving as the wind behaves   35
No nearer—

Not that final meeting
In the twilight kingdom.

13-14. *Those . . . Kingdom:* i.e., those who stood for something positive,
either evil or good, and so can really die, as the hollow men cannot.
19. *Eyes:* In the *Purgatorio,* xxx and xxxi, Beatrice's eyes are a symbol
of spiritual reality—on which account Dante both longs and dreads to behold them. Among the hollow men, in Limbo, there is no such challenge.
All phenomena are naturalistic. 28. *Star:* a symbol embracing both the
world of naturalistic flux (cf. l. 54) and the world of eternal spirit (cf.
l. 63). 33-35. *crossed . . . behaves:* i.e., effigies, scarecrows, tossing in the
wind. 37. *that . . . meeting:* i.e., with the searching eyes of spiritual
reality.

III

This is the dead land
This is cactus land   40
Here the stone images
Are raised, here they receive
The supplication of a dead man's hand
Under the twinkle of a fading star.

Is it like this   45
In death's other kingdom
Waking alone
At the hour when we are
Trembling with tenderness
Lips that would kiss   50
Form prayers to broken stone

IV

The eyes are not here
There are no eyes here
In this valley of dying stars
In this hollow valley   55
This broken jaw of our lost kingdoms.

In this last of meeting places
We grope together
And avoid speech
Gathered on this beach of the tumid river.   60

Sightless, unless
The eyes reappear
As the perpetual star
Multifoliate rose
Of death's twilight kingdom   65
The hope only
Of empty men.

---

60. *the . . . river:* The river Acheron, in Dante's *Inferno,* on the far side
of which is Hell. 64. *multifoliate rose:* Cf. Dante's Celestial Rose made of
light, *Paradiso,* XXX 116—"how vast is the spread of this rose in its outer-
most leaves." The rose is traditionally Christ's emblem (and the Virgin's).

V

Here we go round the prickly pear
Prickly pear prickly pear
Here we go round the prickly pear   70
At five o'clock in the morning.

Between the idea
And the reality
Between the motion
And the act   75
Falls the Shadow
          For Thine is the Kingdom

Between the conception
And the creation
Between the emotion   80
And the response
Falls the Shadow
          Life is very long

Between the desire
And the spasm   85
Between the potency
And the existence
Between the essence
And the descent
Falls the Shadow   90
          For Thine is the Kingdom

For Thine is
Life is
For thine is the

---

68. Eliot's variant (cf. the cactus land, 39 ff.) of the nursery rhyme, "Here we go round the mulberry bush." 74-5. Cf. *Julius Caesar*, II i 63 ff.:
          "Between the acting of a dreadful thing
          And the first motion, all the interim is
          Like a phantasma or a hideous dream."
76. *Falls . . . shadow:* Cf. Ernest Dowson's *Cynara:*
          "Last night, ah, yesternight, betwixt her lips and mine
          There fell thy shadow, Cynara!"

This is the way the world ends   95
This is the way the world ends
This is the way the world ends
Not with a bang but a whimper.

❧

98. *bang:* relevant to the fireworks of Guy Fawkes day; the violence that
Fawkes planned (blowing up the Houses of Parliament); and the positive-
ness of soul, even if evil, that the hollow men long for.

JOURNEY OF THE MAGI

(1927)

'A cold coming we had of it,
Just the worst time of the year
For a journey, and such a long journey:
The ways deep and the weather sharp,
The very dead of winter.'   5
And the camels galled, sore-footed, refractory,
Lying down in the melting snow.
There were times we regretted
The summer palaces on slopes, the terraces,
And the silken girls bringing sherbet.   10
Then the camel men cursing and grumbling
And running away, and wanting their liquor and women,
And the night-fires going out, and the lack of shelters,
And the cities hostile and the towns unfriendly
And the villages dirty and charging high prices: 15
A hard time we had of it.
At the end we preferred to travel all night,
Sleeping in snatches,
With the voices singing in our ears, saying
That this was all folly.   20

Then at dawn we came down to a temperate valley,
Wet, below the snow line, smelling of vegetation;
With a running stream and a water-mill beating the darkness,
And three trees on the low sky,
And an old white horse galloped away in the meadow.   25
Then we came to a tavern with vine-leaves over the lintel,
Six hands at an open door dicing for pieces of silver,

THE JOURNEY OF THE MAGI. 1-5. Adapted by Eliot from Lancelot Andrewes' Nativity Sermon (1622): "It was no summer progress. A cold
coming they had of it at this time of year, just the worst time of the year
to take a journey, and specially a long journey, in. The ways deep, the
weather sharp, the days short, the sun farthest off, . . . the very dead of
winter." 24. *three trees:* cf. the three crosses or "trees" on Calvary. 25.
white horse: Cf. the white horse of Revelation 6:2; and the white horse
of Revelation 19:11-14, whose rider is the Messiah. 27. Cf. the dicing after
the Crucifixion.

And feet kicking the empty wine-skins.
But there was no information, and so we continued
And arrived at evening, not a moment too soon   30
Finding the place; it was (you may say) satisfactory.

All this was a long time ago, I remember,
And I would do it again, but set down
This set down
This: were we led all that way for   35
Birth or Death? There was a Birth, certainly,
We had evidence and no doubt. I had seen birth and death,
But had thought they were different; this Birth was
Hard and bitter agony for us, like Death, our death.
We returned to our places, these Kingdoms,   40
But no longer at ease here, in the old dispensation,
With an alien people clutching their gods.
I should be glad of another death.

BURNT NORTON
(1935)

Τοῦ λόγου δ'ἐόντος ξυνοῦ ζώουσιν οἱ πολλοὶ
ὡς ἰδίαν ἔχοντες φρόνησιν.

I. p. 77. Fragment 2.

ὁδὸς ἄνω κάτω μία καὶ ὡυτή.

I. p. 89. Fragment 60.

—H. Diels, *Die fragmente der Vorsokratiker* (Herakleitos).

BURNT NORTON: *Title:* This is the first of four poems by Eliot entitled *Four Quartets.* Each of the poems has five parts—corresponding roughly to "movements" in music—which introduce a theme (usually an opposition of attitudes, a statement and counter-statement), manipulate and develop it in several different idioms and at several different levels of intensity, and finally suggest a resolution. In each poem this theme grows out of, and plays between, three concepts: (1) the concept of life as the prisoner of time: man and his universe caught in mere flux; (2) the concept of an opposing eternity or stability *somewhere,* which the concept of flux implies: "turning" presupposes reference to a "still point"; and (3) the fusion of the flux and the still point in the concept of "incarnation"— not simply the Christian Incarnation, but the concept of an eternal divine principle or Logos *always* penetrating the temporal and offering to all who will receive it the moment of illumination, the "shaft of sunlight." The title of this first *Quartet* is taken from the name of a seventeenth-century manor house in the Cotswolds (England). The identity of the house seems, however, to have nothing to do with the meaning of the poem: the house is any strange house into which the speaker might have wandered and then commenced to speculate about its history, turning it into a symbol of the individual consciousness simultaneously penetrated by past, present, and future.

Epigraph: Heracleitus: The pre-Socratic philosopher whose teachings emphasize the doctrine that all is flux. Reality for Heracleitus consisted in the four elements, Fire, Air, Water, Earth, which were constantly changing into one another in an endless cycle, moving from fire toward earth and from earth again toward fire. It is to this cyclical flux that the second quotation from Heracleitus refers: "The road up and the road down is one and the same." The first quotation, on the other hand, whatever it may have meant to Heracleitus himself, points for any reader who has the fourth Gospel in mind to an eternity and stability beyond the flux; to the Logos, the Word, the Truth, which is here rejected by the Many: "But though the Word is common, the many live as though they had a wisdom of their own."

I

Time present and time past
Are both perhaps present in time future,
And time future contained in time past.
If all time is eternally present
All time is unredeemable.   5
What might have been is an abstraction
Remaining a perpetual possibility
Only in a world of speculation.
What might have been and what has been
Point to one end, which is always present.   10
Footfalls echo in the memory
Down the passage which we did not take
Towards the door we never opened
Into the rose-garden. My words echo
Thus, in your mind.
               But to what purpose   15
Disturbing the dust on a bowl of rose-leaves
I do not know.
          Other echoes
Inhabit the garden. Shall we follow?
Quick, said the bird, find them, find them,
Round the corner. Through the first gate,   20
Into our first world, shall we follow
The deception of the thrush? Into our first world.
There they were, dignified, invisible,
Moving without pressure, over the dead leaves,
In the autumn heat, through the vibrant air,   25

1. *Time:* On the treatment of time in this poem, cf. St. Augustine's treatment of it in the *Confessions,* XI, xi and xviii, especially xviii: "For if there
be time past and time to come, fain would I know where they be: . . . yet
thus much I know, that wheresoever they now be, they are not there future
or past, but present." 11. *Footfalls:* Cf. *ibid.,* xviii: "Although as for things
past, whenever true stories are related, out of the memory are drawn not
the things themselves which are past, but such words as . . . they, in their
passing through our senses, have, as their footsteps, left imprinted in our
minds." 14. *the rose-garden:* One of Eliot's favorite symbols—possibly here
a symbol of the longing to be born again—a Paradise to be regained, an
innocence to be recovered. 16. *rose-leaves:* rose-petals. 23. *they:* i.e., the inhabitants of "our first world," the past.

And the bird called, in response to
The unheard music hidden in the shrubbery,
And the unseen eyebeam crossed, for the roses
Had the look of flowers that are looked at.
There they were as our guests, accepted and accepting.   30
So we moved, and they, in a formal pattern,
Along the empty alley, into the box circle,
To look down into the drained pool.
Dry the pool, dry concrete, brown edged,
And the pool was filled with water out of sunlight,   35
And the lotos rose, quietly, quietly,
The surface glittered out of heart of light,
And they were behind us, reflected in the pool.
Then a cloud passed, and the pool was empty.
Go, said the bird, for the leaves were full of children,   40
Hidden excitedly, containing laughter.
Go, go, go, said the bird: human kind
Cannot bear very much reality.
Time past and time future
What might have been and what has been   45
Point to one end, which is always present.

II

Garlic and sapphires in the mud
Clot the bedded axle-tree.
The trilling wire in the blood
Sings below inveterate scars   50
And reconciles forgotten wars.
The dance along the artery
The circulation of the lymph
Are figured in the drift of stars
Ascend to summer in the tree   55

---

28. *the . . . crossed:* i.e., we were conscious of their unseen glance crossing ours. (Eliot interprets sight in "our first world" on the old theory that it was caused by a "beam" of light emanating from the eye). 32. *box:* i.e., the shrub of that name. 38. One of the moments of illumination when the past (reflected in the pool) and the future (full of children) are simultaneous in the present. 47 ff. The Heracleitean pattern of opposites in ceaseless agitation: the flux in which we all participate. 47-8. Cf. Mallarmé's phrase in the sonnet *M'introduire dans ton histoire:* "Thunder and rubies in the wheel-hubs" (Tonnerre et rubis aux moyeux).

We move above the moving tree
In light upon the figured leaf
And hear upon the sodden floor
Below, the boarhound and the boar
Pursue their pattern as before   60
But reconciled among the stars.

At the still point of the turning world. Neither flesh nor fleshless;
Neither from nor towards; at the still point, there the dance is,
But neither arrest nor movement. And do not call it fixity,
Where past and future are gathered. Neither movement from nor
    towards,   65
Neither ascent nor decline. Except for the point, the still point,
There would be no dance, and there is only the dance.
I can only say, *there* we have been: but I cannot say where.
And I cannot say, how long, for that is to place it in time.

The inner freedom from the practical desire,   70
The release from action and suffering, release from the inner
And the outer compulsion, yet surrounded
By a grace of sense, a white light still and moving,
Erhebung without motion, concentration
Without elimination, both a new world   75
And the old made explicit, understood
In the completion of its partial ecstasy,
The resolution of its partial horror.
Yet the enchainment of past and future
Woven in the weakness of the changing body,   80
Protects mankind from heaven and damnation
Which flesh cannot endure.
                       Time past and time future
Allow but a little consciousness.
To be conscious is not to be in time
But only in time can the moment in the rose-garden,   85
The moment in the arbour where the rain beat,
The moment in the draughty church at smokefall
Be remembered; involved with past and future.
Only through time time is conquered.

---

62 ff. The still point that the flux implies, where awaits the moment of
illumination. 74. *Erhebung:* exaltation, elevation. 82. *Which . . . endure:*
Cf. 42-3.

III

Here is a place of disaffection   90
Time before and time after
In a dim light: neither daylight
Investing form with lucid stillness
Turning shadow into transient beauty
With slow rotation suggesting permanence   5
Nor darkness to purify the soul
Emptying the sensual with deprivation
Cleansing affection from the temporal.
Neither plenitude nor vacancy. Only a flicker
Over the strained time-ridden faces   100
Distracted from distraction by distraction
Filled with fancies and empty of meaning
Tumid apathy with no concentration
Men and bits of paper, whirled by the cold wind
That blows before and after time,   105
Wind in and out of unwholesome lungs
Time before and time after.
Eructation of unhealthy souls
Into the faded air, the torpid
Driven on the wind that sweeps the gloomy hills of London,   110
Hampstead and Clerkenwell, Campden and Putney,
Highgate, Primrose and Ludgate. Not here
Not here the darkness, in this twittering world.

Descend lower, descend only
Into the world of perpetual solitude,   115
World not world, but that which is not world,
Internal darkness, deprivation
And destitution of all property,
Desiccation of the world of sense,
Evacuation of the world of fancy,   120
Inoperancy of the world of spirit;

---

90 ff. One kind of "darkness" and "road down" (cf. the Epigraph): the imagery is drawn from the London subways. 114 ff. Another kind of "darkness" and "road down"—this time a deliberately willed abstention from the flux-world of appetency and desire.

This is the one way, and the other
Is the same, not in movement
But absention from movement; while the world moves
In appetency, on its metalled ways   125
Of time past and time future.

IV

Time and the bell have buried the day,
The black cloud carries the sun away.
Will the sunflower turn to us, will the clematis
Stray down, bend to us; tendril and spray   130
Clutch and cling?
Chill
Fingers of yew be curled
Down on us? After the kingfisher's wing
Has answered light to light, and is silent, the light is still   135
At the still point of the turning world.

V

Words move, music moves
Only in time; but that which is only living
Can only die. Words, after speech, reach
Into the silence. Only by the form, the pattern,   140
Can words or music reach
The stillness, as a Chinese jar still
Moves perpetually in its stillness.
Not the stillness of the violin, while the note lasts,
Not that only, but the co-existence,   145
Or say that the end precedes the beginning,
And the end and the beginning were always there

122-3. *This . . . same:* Cf. the second sentence in the Epigraph and note.
127 ff. The chill of twilight (and of mortality); but the flash off the kingfisher's wing high in the sky suggests that the light of the world (and the
Light of the World) is there, though invisible. 137 ff. The principle of
incarnation—movement yet stillness—intersection of the timeless with
time: in a Chinese jar, in music, in words in a poem, in the Word.

Before the beginning and after the end.
And all is always now. Words strain,
Crack and sometimes break, under the burden,　　　　150
Under the tension, slip, slide, perish,
Decay with imprecision, will not stay in place,
Will not stay still. Shrieking voices
Scolding, mocking, or merely chattering,
Always assail them. The Word in the desert　　　　155
Is most attacked by voices of temptation,
The crying shadow in the funeral dance,
The loud lament of the disconsolate chimera.

The detail of the pattern is movement,
As in the figure of the ten stairs.　　　　160
Desire itself is movement
Not in itself desirable;
Love is itself unmoving,
Only the cause and end of movement,
Timeless, and undesiring　　　　165
Except in the aspect of time
Caught in the form of limitation
Between un-being and being.
Sudden in a shaft of sunlight
Even while the dust moves　　　　170
There rises the hidden laughter
Of children in the foliage
Quick now, here, now, always—
Ridiculous the waste sad time
Stretching before and after.　　　　175

❧

153-8. *Shrieking . . . chimera:* Cf. Donne's paragraph on imperfect prayers
in Sermon LXXX, which Eliot quotes in his essay on Lancelot Andrewes:
"A memory of yesterday's pleasures, a fear of tomorrow's dangers, a straw
under my knee, a noise in mine ear, a light in mine eye, a nothing, a fancy,
a chimera in my brain, troubles me in my prayer." 158-9. *The . . .
temptation:* Alluding to Christ's (and Everyman's) temptation and distraction in the wilderness. 160. *the . . . stairs:* St. John of the Cross, a
sixteenth-century writer on spiritual exercises, describes the discipline of
religious meditation as a ladder of ten steps which the soul continually
ascends and descends in order to become perfect in love. Here is a "road
up and a road down," a cyclical movement, a pattern, a dance, which the
poem opposes to the Heracleitean flux. 169 ff. The coexistence of past,
present, and future in the moment of illumination—of incarnation.

Wystan Hugh Auden

WHICH SIDE AM I SUPPOSED TO BE ON?

(1932)

Though aware of our rank and alert to obey orders,
Watching with binoculars the movement of the grass for an ambush,
The pistol cocked, the code-word committed to memory;
    The youngest drummer
Knows all the peace-time stories like the oldest soldier,   5
    Though frontier-conscious.

About the tall white gods who landed from their open boat,
Skilled in the working of copper, appointing our feast-days,
Before the islands were submerged, when the weather was calm,
    The maned lion common,   10
An open wishing-well in every garden;
    When love came easy.

Perfectly certain, all of us, but not from the records,
Not from the unshaven agent who returned to the camp;
The pillar dug from the desert recorded only   15
    The sack of a city,

The selections from W. H. Auden are used by permission of Random House, Inc.: "Which Side Am I Supposed to Be On?," "O Where Are You Going?," "Something is Bound to Happen" and "Petition," *from* POEMS *reprinted from* THE COLLECTED POETRY OF W. H. AUDEN, *copyright 1934 and renewed 1961 by W. H. Auden;* "Look Stranger, on This Island Now," *and* "Now the Leaves are Falling Fast" *from* ON THIS ISLAND, *reprinted from* THE COLLECTED POETRY OF W. H. AUDEN, *copyright 1937 by W. H. Auden;* "Law Like Love," "Lay Your Sleeping Head, My Love," "Mussee des Beaux Arts," "As I Walked Out One Evening," "Let Me Tell a Little Story," "The Unknown Citizen," "In Memory of W. B. Yeats" *from* ANOTHER TIME, *reprinted from* THE COLLECTED POETRY OF W. H. AUDEN, *copyright 1940 by W. H. Auden;* "For the Time Being," *from* THE COLLECTED POETRY OF W. H. AUDEN, *copyright 1944 by W. H. Auden;* "In Father's Footsteps," "Paysage Moralise," "Who's Who," "The Climbers," "O Who Can Ever Gaze His Fill," "In Time of War, Parts I, II, XXI and XXIII," *and* "Crisis," *from* THE COLLECTED POETRY OF W. H. AUDEN, *copyright 1945 by W. H. Auden.*
WHICH SIDE AM I SUPPOSED TO BE ON. 68. *Acedia:* Accidia (or acedy), an old name for Sloth, one of the deadly sins.

The agent clutching his side collapsed at our feet,
    "Sorry! They got me!"

Yes, they were living here once but do not now,
Yes, they are living still but do not here;   20
Lying awake after Lights Out a recruit may speak up:
    "Who told you all this?"
The tent-talk pauses a little till a veteran answers
    "Go to sleep, Sonny!"

Turning over he closes his eyes, and then in a moment   25
Sees the sun at midnight bright over cornfield and pasture,
Our hope. . . . Someone jostles him, fumbling for boots,
    Time to change guard:
Boy, the quarrel was before your time, the aggressor
    No one you know.   30

Your childish movements of awareness were all of our world,
At five you sprang, already a tiger in the garden,
At night your mother taught you to pray for our Daddy
    Far away fighting,
One morning you fell off a horse and your brother mocked you: 35
    "Just like a girl!"

You've got their names to live up to and questions won't help,
You've a very full programme, first aid, gunnery, tactics,
The technique to master of raids and hand-to-hand fighting;
    Are you in training?   40
Are you taking care of yourself? Are you sure of passing
    The endurance test?

Now we're due to parade on the square in front of the Cathedral,
When the bishop has blessed us, to file in after the choirboys,
To stand with the wine-dark conquerors in the roped-off pews,   45
    Shout ourselves hoarse:
"They ran like hares; we have broken them up like firewood;
    They fought against God."

While in a great rift in the limestone miles away
At the same hour they gather, tethering their horses beside them; 50
A scarecrow prophet from a boulder foresees our judgment,
    Their oppressors howling;
And the bitter psalm is caught by the gale from the rocks:
    "How long shall they flourish?"

What have we all been doing to have made from Fear   55
That laconic war-bitten captain addressing them now?

"Heart and head shall be keener, mood the more
        As our might lessens":
To have caused their shout "We will fight till we lie down beside
        The Lord we have loved."   60

There's Wrath who has learnt every trick of guerrilla warfare
The shamming dead, the night-raid, the feinted retreat;
Envy their brilliant pamphleteer, to lying
        As husband true,
Expert impersonator and linguist, proud of his power   65
        To hoodwink sentries.

Gluttony living alone, austerer than us,
Big simple Greed, Acedia famed with them all
For her stamina, keeping the outposts, and somewhere Lust
        With his sapper's skill,   70
Muttering to his fuses in a tunnel "Could I meet here with Love,
        I would hug her to death."

There are faces there for which for a very long time
We've been on the look-out, though often at home we imagined,
Catching sight of a back or hearing a voice through a doorway,   75
        We had found them at last;
Put our arms round their necks and looked in their eyes and discovered
        We were unlucky.

And some of them, surely, we seem to have seen before:
Why, that girl who rode off on her bicycle one fine summer
        evening   80
And never returned, she's there; and the banker we'd noticed
        Worried for weeks;
Till he failed to arrive one morning and his room was empty,
        Gone with a suitcase.

They speak of things done on the frontier we were never told,   85
The hidden path to their squat Pictish tower
They will never reveal though kept without sleep, for their code is
        "Death to the squealer":
They are brave, yes, though our newspapers mention their bravery
        In inverted commas.   90

But careful; back to our lines; it is unsafe there,
Passports are issued no longer; that area is closed;
There's no fire in the waiting-room now at the climbers' Junction,
        And all this year

Work has been stopped on the power-house; the wind whistles
    under   95
        The half-built culverts.

Do you think that because you have heard that on Christmas Eve
In a quiet sector they walked about on the skyline,
Exchanged cigarettes, both learning the words for "I love you"
        In either language: 100
You can stroll across for a smoke and a chat any evening?
        Try it and see.

That rifle-sight you're designing; is it ready yet?
You're holding us up; the office is getting impatient;
The square munition works out on the old allotments   105
        Needs stricter watching;
If you see any loiterers there you may shoot without warning,
        We must stop that leakage.

All leave is cancelled tonight; we must say good-bye.
We entrain at once for the North; we shall see in the morning   110
The headlands we're doomed to attack; snow down to the tide-line:
        Though the bunting signals
"Indoors before it's too late; cut peat for your fires,"
        We shall lie out there.

                      ❧

---

110. *North:* In *Paradise Lost* the legions of Satan gather in the north; it is
the direction traditionally associated with Evil.

"O WHERE ARE YOU GOING?"
(1932)

"O where are you going?" said reader to rider,
"That valley is fatal when furnaces burn,
Yonder's the midden whose odours will madden,
That gap is the grave where the tall return."

"O do you imagine," said fearer to farer,　　　　　5
"That dusk will delay on your path to the pass,
Your diligent looking discover the lacking
Your footsteps feel from granite to grass?

"O what was that bird," said horror to hearer,
"Did you see that shape in the twisted trees?　　　10
Behind you swiftly the figure comes softly,
The spot on your skin is a shocking disease?"

"Out of this house"—said rider to reader,
"Yours never will"—said farer to fearer,
"They're looking for you"—said hearer to horror,　　15
As he left them there, as he left them there.

❦

_____

O WHERE ARE YOU GOING. 3. *midden:* dunghill.

180

SOMETHING IS BOUND TO HAPPEN
(1934)

Doom is dark and deeper than any sea-dingle.
Upon what man it fall
In spring, day-wishing flowers appearing,
Avalanche sliding, white snow from rock-face,
That he should leave his house,   5
No cloud-soft hand can hold him, restraint by women;
But ever that man goes
Through place-keepers, through forest trees,
A stranger to strangers over undried sea,
Houses for fishes, suffocating water,   10
Or lonely on fell as chat,
By pot-holed becks
A bird stone-haunting, an unquiet bird.

There head falls forward, fatigued at evening,
And dreams of home,   15
Waving from window, spread of welcome,
Kissing of wife under single sheet;
But waking sees
Bird-flocks nameless to him, through doorway voices
Of new men making another love.   20

Save him from hostile capture,
From sudden tiger's spring at corner;
Protect his house,
His anxious house where days are counted
From thunderbolt protect,   25
From gradual ruin spreading like a stain;
Converting number from vague to certain,
Bring joy, bring day of his returning,
Lucky with day approaching, with leaning dawn.

❧

SOMETHING IS BOUND TO HAPPEN. 11. *chat:* a variety of warbler (esp. the stone-chat) found on moors. *fell:* moorland. 12. *beck:* brook.

PETITION

(1934)

Sir, no man's enemy, forgiving all
But will its negative inversion, be prodigal:
Send to us power and light, a sovereign touch
Curing the intolerable neural itch,
The exhaustion of weaning, the liar's quinsy,   5
And the distortions of ingrown virginity.
Prohibit sharply the rehearsed response
And gradually correct the coward's stance;
Cover in time with beams those in retreat
That, spotted, they turn though the reverse were great;   10
Publish each healer that in city lives
Or country houses at the end of drives;
Harrow the house of the dead; look shining at
New styles of architecture, a change of heart.

∾

PETITION. 3. *sovereign touch:* with reference to the king's touch, which was supposed to cure sufferers of the "king's evil" (scrofula). 13. *harrow:* with reference to the "harrowing of hell," *i.e.,* Christ's visit to hell after his crucifixion to set free the souls of the righteous, who were held there until his coming.

IN FATHER'S FOOTSTEPS
(1936)

Our hunting fathers told the story
  Of the sadness of the creatures,
Pitied the limits and the lack
  Set in their finished features;
Saw in the lion's intolerant look,   5
Behind the quarry's dying glare,
Love raging for the personal glory
  That reason's gift would add,
The liberal appetite and power,
  The rightness of a god.   10

Who, nurtured in that fine tradition,
  Predicted the result,
Guessed Love by nature suited to
  The intricate ways of guilt,
That human ligaments could so   15
His southern gestures modify
And make it his mature ambition
  To think no thought but ours,
To hunger, work illegally,
  And be anonymous?   20

LOOK, STRANGER, ON THIS ISLAND
(1936)

Look, stranger, on this island now
The leaping light for your delight discovers,
Stand stable here
And silent be,
That through the channels of the ear   5
May wander like a river
The swaying sound of the sea.

Here at the small field's ending pause
When the chalk wall falls to the foam and its tall ledges
Oppose the pluck   10
And knock of the tide,
And the shingle scrambles after the sucking surf,
And the gull lodges
A moment on its sheer side.

Far off like floating seeds the ships   15
Diverge on urgent voluntary errands,
And the full view
Indeed may enter
And move in memory as now these clouds do,
That pass the harbour mirror   20
And all the summer through the water saunter.

❧

LOOK, STRANGER. 12. *shingle:* beach-pebbles.

PAYSAGE MORALISÉ

(1936)

Hearing of harvests rotting in the valleys,
Seeing at end of street the barren mountains,
Round corners coming suddenly on water,
Knowing them shipwrecked who were launched for islands,
We honour founders of these starving cities   5
Whose honour is the image of our sorrow,

Which cannot see its likeness in their sorrow
That brought them desperate to the brink of valleys;
Dreaming of evening walks through learned cities
They reined their violent horses on the mountains,   10
Those fields like ships to castaways on islands,
Visions of green to them who craved for water.

They built by rivers and at night the water
Running past windows comforted their sorrow;
Each in his little bed conceived of islands   15
Where every day was dancing in the valleys
And all the green trees blossomed on the mountains
Where love was innocent, being far from cities.

But dawn came back and they were still in cities;
No marvellous creature rose up from the water;   20
There was still gold and silver in the mountains
But hunger was a more immediate sorrow,
Although to moping villagers in valleys
Some waving pilgrims were describing islands . . .

"The gods," they promised, "visit us from islands,   25
Are stalking, head-up, lovely, through our cities;
Now is the time to leave your wretched valleys
And sail with them across the lime-green water,
Sitting at their white sides, forget your sorrow,
The shadow cast across your lives by mountains"   30

———————

PAYSAGE MORALISÉ: *Title.* Landscape Moralized.

So many, doubtful, perished in the mountains,
Climbing up crags to get a view of islands,
So many, fearful, took with them their sorrow
Which stayed them when they reached unhappy cities,
So many, careless, dived and drowned in water,   35
So many, wretched, would not leave their valleys.

It is our sorrow. Shall it melt? Ah, water
Would gush, flush, green these mountains and these valleys,
And we rebuild our cities, not dream of islands.

NOW THE LEAVES ARE FALLING FAST
(1936)

Now the leaves are falling fast,
Nurse's flowers will not last;
Nurses to the graves are gone,
And the prams go rolling on.

Whispering neighbours, left and right,   5
Pluck us from the real delight;
And the active hands must freeze
Lonely on the separate knees.

Dead in hundreds at the back
Follow wooden in our track,   10
Arms raised stiffly to reprove
In false attitudes of love.

Starving through the leafless wood
Trolls run scolding for their food;
And the nightingale is dumb,   15
And the angel will not come.

Cold, impossible, ahead
Lifts the mountain's lovely head
Whose white waterfall could bless
Travellers in their last distress.   20

❧

WHO'S WHO

(1936)

A shilling life will give you all the facts:
How Father beat him, how he ran away,
What were the struggles of his youth, what acts
Made him the greatest figure of his day:
Of how he fought, fished, hunted, worked all night,   5
Though giddy, climbed new mountains; named a sea:
Some of the last researchers even write
Love made him weep his pints like you and me.

With all his honours on, he sighed for one
Who, say astonished critics, lived at home;   10
Did little jobs about the house with skill
And nothing else; could whistle; would sit still
Or potter round the garden; answered some
Of his long marvellous letters but kept none.

THE CLIMBERS

(1936)

Fleeing the short-haired mad executives,
The sad and useless faces round my home,
Upon the mountains of my fear I climb;
Above, the breakneck scorching rock, the caves,
No col, no water; with excuse concocted,   **5**
Soon on a lower alp I fall and pant,
Cooling my face there in the faults that flaunt
The life which they have stolen and perfected.

Climbing with you was easy as a vow:
We reached the top not hungry in the least,   **10**
But it was eyes we looked at, not the view,
Saw nothing but ourselves, left-handed, lost;
Returned to shore, the rich interior still
Unknown. Love gave the power, but took the will.

❧

THE CLIMBERS: 5. *col:* pass (in the mountains). 7. *faults:* (pun, on the geological and moral senses).

O WHO CAN EVER GAZE HIS FILL

(1937)

"Oh who can ever gaze his fill,"
  Farmer and fisherman say,
"On native shore and local hill,
Grudge aching limb or callus on the hand?
Fathers, grandfathers stood upon this land,   5
And here the pilgrims from our loins shall stand."
    So farmer and fisherman say
    In their fortunate heyday:
    But Death's soft answer drifts across
    Empty catch or harvest loss   10
      Or an unlucky May.
The earth is an oyster with nothing inside it,
  Not to be born is the best for man;
The end of toil is a bailiff's order,
  Throw down the mattock and dance while you can.   15

"O life's too short for friends who share,"
  Travellers think in their hearts,
"The city's common bed, the air,
The mountain bivouac and the bathing beach,
Where incidents draw every day from each   20
Memorable gesture and witty speech."
    So travellers think in their hearts,
    Till malice or circumstance parts
    Them from their constant humour:
    And slyly Death's coercive rumour   25
      In the silence starts.
A friend is the old old tale of Narcissus,
  Not to be born is the best for man;
An active partner in something disgraceful,
  Change your partner, dance while you can.   30

"O stretch your hands across the sea,"
  The impassioned lover cries,
"Stretch them towards your harm and me.
Our grass is green, and sensual our brief bed,

O WHO CAN EVER: 27. *Narcissus:* The Greek youth who fell in love with
his own image.

The stream sings at its foot, and at its head   35
The mild and vegetarian beasts are fed."
  So the impassioned lover cries
  Till his storm of pleasure dies:
  From the bedpost and the rocks
  Death's enticing echo mocks,   40
    And his voice replies.
The greater the love, the more false to its object,
  Not to be born is the best for man;
After the kiss comes the impulse to throttle,
  Break the embraces, dance while you can.   45

"I see the guilty world forgiven,"
  Dreamer and drunkard sing,
"The ladders let down out of heaven,
The laurel springing from the martyr's blood,
The children skipping where the weepers stood,   50
The lovers natural and the beasts all good."
  So dreamer and drunkard sing
  Till day their sobriety bring:
  Parrotwise with Death's reply
  From whelping fear and nesting lie,   55
    Woods and their echoes ring.
The desires of the heart are as crooked as corkscrews,
  Not to be born is the best for man;
The second-best is a formal order,
  The dance's pattern: Dance while you can.   60
Dance, dance, for the figure is easy,
  The tune is catching and will not stop;
Dance till the stars come down with the rafters;
  Dance, dance, dance till you drop.

IN TIME OF WAR

(1939)

I

So from the years the gifts were showered; each
Ran off with his at once into his life:
Bee took the politics that make a hive,
Fish swam as fish, peach settled into peach.

And were successful at the first endeavour;   5
The hour of birth their only time at college,
They were content with their precocious knowledge,
And knew their station and were good for ever.

Till finally there came a childish creature
On whom the years could model any feature,   10
And fake with ease a leopard or a dove;

Who by the lightest wind was changed and shaken,
And looked for truth and was continually mistaken,
And envied his few friends and chose his love.

II

They wondered why the fruit had been forbidden;   15
It taught them nothing new. They hid their pride,
But did not listen much when they were chidden;
They knew exactly what to do outside.

They left: immediately the memory faded
Of all they'd learnt; they could not understand   20
The dogs now who, before, had always aided;
The stream was dumb with whom they'd always planned.

They wept and quarrelled: freedom was so wild.
In front, maturity, as he ascended,
Retired like a horizon from the child;   25

The dangers and the punishments grew greater;
And the way back by angels was defended
Against the poet and the legislator.

XXI

The life of man is never quite completed;
The daring and the chatter will go on: 30
But, as an artist feels his power gone,
These walk the earth and know themselves defeated.

Some could not bear nor break the young and mourn for
The wounded myths that once made nations good,
Some lost a world they never understood,   35
Some saw too clearly all that man was born for.

Loss is their shadow-wife, Anxiety
Receives them like a grand hotel; but where
They may regret they must; their life, to hear

The call of the forbidden cities, see   40
The stranger watch them with a happy stare,
And Freedom hostile in each home and tree.

XXVII

Wandering lost upon the mountains of our choice,
Again and again we sigh for an ancient South,
For the warm nude ages of instinctive poise,   45
For the taste of joy in the innocent mouth.

Asleep in our huts, how we dream of a part
In the glorious balls of the future; each intricate maze
Has a plan, and the disciplined movements of the heart
Can follow for ever and ever its harmless ways.   50

We envy streams and houses that are sure:
But we are articled to error; we
Were never nude and calm like a great door,

And never will be perfect like the fountains;
We live in freedom by necessity,   55
A mountain people dwelling among mountains.

LAW LIKE LOVE
(1940)

Law, say the gardeners, is the sun,
Law is the one
All gardeners obey
Tomorrow, yesterday, today.

Law is the wisdom of the old   5
The impotent grandfathers shrilly scold;
The grandchildren put out a treble tongue,
Law is the senses of the young.

Law, says the priest with a priestly look,
Expounding to an unpriestly people,   10
Law is the words in my priestly book,
Law is my pulpit and my steeple.

Law, says the judge as he looks down his nose,
Speaking clearly and most severely,
Law is as I've told you before,   15
Law is as you know I suppose,
Law is but let me explain it once more,
Law is The Law.

Yet law-abiding scholars write;
Law is neither wrong nor right,   20
Law is only crimes
Punished by places and by times,
Law is the clothes men wear
Anytime, anywhere,
Law is Good-morning and Good-night.   25

Others say, Law is our Fate;
Others say, Law is our State;
Others say, others say
Law is no more
Law has gone away.   30

And always the loud angry crowd
Very angry and very loud

Law is We,
And always the soft idiot softly Me.

If we, dear, know we know no more   35
Than they about the law,
If I no more than you
Know what we should and should not do
Except that all agree
Gladly or miserably   40
That the law is
And that all know this,
If therefore thinking it absurd
To identify Law with some other word,
Unlike so many men   45
I cannot say Law is again,
No more than they can we suppress
The universal wish to guess
Or slip out of our own position
Into an unconcerned condition.   50
Although I can at least confine
Your vanity and mine
To stating timidly
A timid similarity,
We shall boast anyway: 55
Like love I say.

Like love we don't know where or why
Like love we can't compel or fly
Like love we often weep
Like love we seldom keep.

LAY YOUR SLEEPING HEAD, MY LOVE

(1940)

Lay your sleeping head, my love,
Human on my faithless arm;
Time and fevers burn away
Individual beauty from
Thoughtful children, and the grave   5
Proves the child ephemeral:
But in my arms till break of day
Let the living creature lie,
Mortal, guilty, but to me
The entirely beautiful.   10

Soul and body have no bounds:
To lovers as they lie upon
Her tolerant enchanted slope
In their ordinary swoon,
Grave the vision Venus sends   15
Of supernatural sympathy,
Universal love and hope;
While an abstract insight wakes
Among the glaciers and the rocks
The hermit's sensual ecstasy.   20

Certainty, fidelity
On the stroke of midnight pass
Like vibrations of a bell,
And fashionable madmen raise
Their pedantic boring cry: 25
Every farthing of the cost,
All the dreaded cards foretell,
Shall be paid, but from this night
Not a whisper, not a thought,
Not a kiss nor look be lost.   30

Beauty, midnight, vision dies:
Let the winds of dawn that blow
Softly round your dreaming head
Such a day of sweetness show

Eye and knocking heart may bless, 35
Find the mortal world enough;
Noons of dryness see you fed
By the involuntary powers,
Nights of insult let you pass
Watched by every human love. 40

MUSÉE DES BEAUX ARTS

(1940)

About suffering they were never wrong,
The Old Masters: how well they understood
Its human position; how it takes place
While someone else is eating or opening a window or just walk-
    ing dully along;
How, when the aged are reverently, passionately waiting   5
For the miraculous birth, there always must be
Children who did not specially want it to happen, skating
On a pond at the edge of the wood:
They never forgot
That even the dreadful martyrdom must run its course   10
Anyhow in a corner, some untidy spot
Where the dogs go on with their doggy life and the torturer's
    horse
Scratches its innocent behind on a tree.

In Brueghel's *Icarus,* for instance: how everything turns away
Quite leisurely from the disaster; the ploughman may   15
Have heard the splash, the forsaken cry,
But for him it was not an important failure; the sun shone
As it had to on the white legs disappearing into the green
Water; and the expensive delicate ship that must have seen
Something amazing, a boy falling out of the sky,   20
Had somewhere to get to and sailed calmly on.

❧

<hr>

MUSÉE DES BEAUX ARTS: 14. *Icarus:* "The Fall of Icarus," a painting by Pieter Brueghel (1525?-69).

CRISIS

(1940)

Where do They come from? Those whom we so much dread
As on our dearest location falls the chill
        Of their crooked wing and endangers
        The melting friend, the aqueduct, the flower.

Terrible Presences that the ponds reflect   5
Back at the famous, and when the blond boy
        Bites eagerly into the shining
        Apple, emerge in their shocking fury.

And we realise the woods are deaf and the sky
Nurses no one, and we are awake and these   10
        Like farmers have purpose and knowledge,
        And towards us their hate is directed.

We are the barren pastures to which they bring
The resentment of outcasts; on us they work
        Out their despair; they wear our weeping   15
        As the disgraceful badge of their exile.

O we conjured them here like a lying map;
Desiring the extravagant joy of life
        We lured with a mirage of orchards
        Fat in the lazy climate of refuge.   20

Our money sang like streams on the aloof peaks
Of our thinking that beckoned them on like girls;
        Our culture like a West of wonder
        Shone a solemn promise in their faces.

We expected the beautiful or the wise   25
Ready to see a charm in our childish fib,
        Pleased to find nothing but stones and
        Able at once to create a garden.

But those who come are not even children with
The big indiscriminate eyes we had lost,   30
        Occupying our narrow spaces
        With their anarchist vivid abandon.

They arrive, already adroit, having learned
Restraint at the table of a father's rage;
      In a mother's distorting mirror   35
      They discovered the Meaning of Knowledge.

These pioneers have long adapted themselves
To the night and the nightmare; they come equipped
      To reply to terror with terror,
      With lies to unmask the least deception.   40

For a future of marriage nevertheless
The bed is prepared; though all our whiteness shrinks
      From the hairy and clumsy bridegroom,
      We conceive in the shuddering instant.

For the barren must wish to bear though the Spring   45
Punish; and the crooked that dreads to be straight
      Cannot alter its prayer but summons
      Out of the dark a horrible rector.

O the striped and vigorous tiger can move
With style through the borough of murder; the ape   50
      Is really at home in the parish
      Of grimacing and licking: but we have

Failed as their pupils. Our tears well from a love
We have never outgrown; our cities predict
      More than we hope; even our armies   55
      Have to express our need of forgiveness.

AS I WALKED OUT ONE EVENING
(1940)

As I walked out one evening,
   Walking down Bristol Street,
The crowds upon the pavement
   Were fields of harvest wheat.

And down by the brimming river   5
   I heard a lover sing
Under an arch of the railway:
   "Love has no ending.

I'll love you, dear, I'll love you
   Till China and Africa meet,   10
And the river jumps over the mountain
   And the salmon sing in the street.

I'll love you till the ocean
   Is folded and hung up to dry,
And the seven stars go squawking   15
   Like geese about the sky.

The years shall run like rabbits,
   For in my arms I hold
The Flower of the Ages,
   And the first love of the world."   20

But all the clocks in the city
   Began to whirr and chime:
"O let not Time deceive you,
   You cannot conquer Time.

In the burrows of the Nightmare   25
   Where Justice naked is,
Time watches from the shadow
   And coughs when you would kiss.

In headaches and in worry
   Vaguely life leaks away,
And Time will have his fancy   30
   Tomorrow or today.

Into many a green valley
  Drifts the appalling snow;
Time breaks the threaded dances   35
  And the diver's brilliant bow.

O plunge your hands in water,
  Plunge them in up to the wrist;
Stare, stare in the basin
  And wonder what you've missed.   40

The glacier knocks in the cupboard,
  The desert sighs in the bed,
And the crack in the tea-cup opens
  A lane to the land of the dead.

Where the beggars raffle the banknotes   45
  And the Giant is enchanting to Jack,
And the Lilly-white Boy is a Roarer,
  And Jill goes down on her back.

O look, look in the mirror,
  O look in your distress;   50
Life remains a blessing
  Although you cannot bless.

O stand, stand at the window
  As the tears scald and start;
You shall love your crooked neighbor   55
  With your crooked heart."

It was late, late in the evening,
  The lovers they were gone;
The clocks had ceased their chiming,
  And the deep river ran on.   60

LET ME TELL YOU A LITTLE STORY

(*Tune: St. James' Infirmary*)

(1940)

Let me tell you a little story
   About Miss Edith Gee;
She lived in Clevedon Terrace
   At Number 83.

She'd a slight squint in her left eye,   5
   Her lips they were thin and small,
She had narrow sloping shoulders
   And she had no bust at all.

She'd a velvet hat with trimmings,
   And a dark-grey serge costume;   10
She lived in Clevedon Terrace
   In a small bed-sitting room.

She'd a purple mac for wet days,
   A green umbrella too to take,
She'd a bicycle with shopping basket   15
   And a harsh back-pedal brake.

The Church of Saint Aloysius
   Was not so very far;
She did a lot of knitting,
   Knitting for that Church Bazaar.   20

Miss Gee looked up at the starlight
   And said: "Does anyone care
That I live in Clevedon Terrace
   On one hundred pounds a year?"

She dreamed a dream one evening   25
   That she was the Queen of France
And the Vicar of Saint Aloysius
   Asked Her Majesty to dance.

LET ME TELL YOU. 13. *mac: i.e.,* mackintosh.

But a storm blew down the palace,
  She was biking through a field of corn,   30
And a bull with the face of the Vicar
  Was charging with lowered horn.

She could feel his hot breath behind her,
  He was going to overtake;
And the bicycle went slower and slower   35
  Because of that back-pedal brake.

Summer made the trees a picture,
  Winter made them a wreck;
She bicycled to the evening service
  With her clothes buttoned up to her neck.   40

She passed by the loving couples,
  She turned her head away;
She passed by the loving couples
  And they didn't ask her to stay.

Miss Gee sat down in the side-aisle,   45
  She heard the organ play;
And the choir it sang so sweetly
  At the ending of the day,

Miss Gee knelt down in the side-aisle,
  She knelt down on her knees;   50
"Lead me not into temptation
  But make me a good girl, please."

The days and nights went by her
  Like waves round a Cornish wreck;
She bicycled down to the doctor   55
  With her clothes buttoned up to her neck.

She bicycled down to the doctor,
  And rang the surgery bell;
"O, doctor, I've a pain inside me,
  And I don't feel very well."   60

Doctor Thomas looked her over,
  And then he looked some more;
Walked over to his wash-basin,
  Said, "Why didn't you come before?"

---

54. *Cornish wreck*: The coast of Cornwall is very dangerous to shipping.

Doctor Thomas sat over his dinner,   65
   Though his wife was waiting to ring;
Rolling his bread into pellets,
   Said, "Cancer's a funny thing.

"Nobody knows what the cause is,
   Though some pretend they do;   70
It's like some hidden assassin
   Waiting to strike at you.

"Childless women get it,
   And men when they retire;
It's as if there had to be some outlet   75
   For their foiled creative fire."

His wife she rang for the servant,
   Said, "Don't be so morbid, dear,"
He said; "I saw Miss Gee this evening
   And she's a goner, I fear."   80

They took Miss Gee to the hospital,
   She lay there a total wreck,
Lay in the ward for women
   With the bedclothes right up to her neck.

They laid her on the table,   85
   The students began to laugh;
And Mr. Rose the surgeon
   He cut Miss Gee in half.

Mr. Rose he turned to his students,
   Said; "Gentlemen, if you please,   90
We seldom see a sarcoma
   As far advanced as this."

They took her off the table,
   They wheeled away Miss Gee
Down to another department   95
   Where they study Anatomy.

They hung her from the ceiling,
   Yes, they hung up Miss Gee;
And a couple of Oxford Groupers
   Carefully dissected her knee.   100

---

91. *sarcoma:* cancerous growth. 99. *Oxford Groupers:* Name of the confessional religious cult established during the 1920's by Frank Buchman.

THE UNKNOWN CITIZEN

(To JS/07/M/378
This   Marble   Monument
Is Erected by the State)

(1940)

He was found by the Bureau of Statistics to be
One against whom there was no official complaint,
And all the reports on his conduct agree
That, in the modern sense of an old-fashioned word, he was a
  saint,
For in everything he did he served the Greater Community.   5
Except for the War till the day he retired
He worked in a factory and never got fired,
But satisfied his employers, Fudge Motors Inc.
Yet he wasn't a scab or odd in his views,
For his Union reports that he paid his dues,   10
(Our report on his Union shows it was sound)
And our Social Psychology workers found
That he was popular with his mates and liked a drink.
The Press are convinced that he bought a paper every day
And that his reactions to advertisements were normal in every
  way.   15
Policies taken out in his name prove that he was fully insured,
And his Health-card shows he was once in hospital but left it
  cured.
Both Producers Research and High-Grade Living declare
He was fully sensible to the advantages of the Instalment Plan
And had everything necessary to the Modern Man,   20
A phonograph, a radio, a car and a frigidaire.
Our researchers into Public Opinion are content
That he held the proper opinions for the time of year;
When there was peace, he was for peace; when there was war,
  he went.
He was married and added five children to the population,   25
Which our Eugenist says was the right number for a parent of
  his generation,
And our teachers report that he never interfered with their edu-
  cation.

Was he free? Was he happy? The question is absurd:
Had anything been wrong, we should certainly have heard.

IN MEMORY OF W. B. YEATS

(d. Jan. 1939)

(1940)

I

He disappeared in the dead of winter:
The brooks were frozen, the airports almost deserted,
And snow disfigured the public statues;
The mercury sank in the mouth of the dying day.
O all the instruments agree   5
The day of his death was a dark cold day.

Far from his illness
The wolves ran on through the evergreen forests,
The peasant river was untempted by the fashionable quays;
By mourning tongues   10
The death of the poet was kept from his poems.

But for him it was his last afternoon as himself,
An afternoon of nurses and rumours;
The provinces of his body revolted,
The squares of his mind were empty,   15
Silence invaded the suburbs,
The current of his feeling failed: he became his admirers.

Now he is scattered among a hundred cities
And wholly given over to unfamiliar affections;
To find his happiness in another kind of wood   20
And be punished under a foreign code of conscience.
The words of a dead man
Are modified in the guts of the living.

But in the importance and noise of tomorrow
When the brokers are roaring like beasts on the floor of the
        Bourse,   25
And the poor have the sufferings to which they are fairly accustomed,
And each in the cell of himself is almost convinced of his freedom;

IN MEMORY OF W. B. YEATS. 25. *Bourse:* the French stock-exchange.

A few thousand will think of this day
As one thinks of a day when one did something slightly unusual.
O all the instruments agree   30
The day of his death was a dark cold day.

2

You were silly like us: your gift survived it all;
The parish of rich women, physical decay,
Yourself; mad Ireland hurt you into poetry.
Now Ireland has her madness and her weather still,   35
For poetry makes nothing happen: it survives
In the valley of its saying where executives
Would never want to tamper; it flows south
From ranches of isolation and the busy griefs,
Raw towns that we believe and die in; it survives,   40
A way of happening, a mouth.

3

Earth, receive an honoured guest;
William Yeats is laid to rest:
Let the Irish vessel lie
Emptied of its poetry.   45

Time that is intolerant
Of the brave and innocent,
And indifferent in a week
To a beautiful physique,

Worships language and forgives   50
Everyone by whom it lives;
Pardons cowardice, conceit,
Lays its honours at their feet.

Time that with this strange excuse
Pardoned Kipling and his views,   55
And will pardon Paul Claudel,
Pardons him for writing well.

In the nightmare of the dark
All the dogs of Europe bark,
And the living nations wait,   60
Each sequestered in its hate;

---

55. *Kipling . . . views:* alluding to Kipling's imperialism. 56. *Claudel:* contemporary French poet and man of letters, very conservative politically.

Intellectual disgrace
Stares from every human face,
And the seas of pity lie
Locked and frozen in each eye.   65

Follow, poet, follow right
To the bottom of the night,
With your unconstraining voice
Still persuade us to rejoice;

With the farming of a verse   70
Make a vineyard of the curse,
Sing a human unsuccess
In a rapture of distress:

In the deserts of the heart
Let the healing fountain start,
In the prison of his days   75
Teach the free man how to praise.

FOR THE TIME BEING
A Christmas Oratorio
(1944)

*What shall we say then? Shall we continue
in sin, that grace may abound? God forbid.*
ROMANS VI.

ADVENT

I

Chorus

Darkness and snow descend;
The clock on the mantelpiece
Has nothing to recommend,
Nor does the face in the glass
Appear nobler than our own   5
As darkness and snow descend
On all personality.
Huge crowds mumble—"Alas,
Our angers do not increase,
Love is not what she used to be";   10
Portly Caesar yawns—"I know";
He falls asleep on his throne,
They shuffle off through the snow:
Darkness and snow descend.

Semi-Chorus

Can great Hercules keep his   15
Extraordinary promise
To reinvigorate the Empire?
Utterly lost, he cannot
Even locate his task but
Stands in some decaying orchard   20
Or the irregular shadow

Of a ruined temple, aware of
Being watched from the horrid mountains
By fanatical eyes yet
Seeing no one at all, only hearing   25
The silence softly broken
By the poisonous rustle
Of famishing Arachne.

Chorus

Winter completes an age
With its thorough levelling;   30
Heaven's tourbillons of rage
Abolish the watchman's tower
And delete the cedar grove.
As winter completes an age,
The eyes huddle like cattle, doubt   35
Seeps into the pores and power
Ebbs from the heavy signet ring;
The prophet's lantern is out
And gone the boundary stone,
Cold the heart and cold the stove,   40
Ice condenses on the bone:
Winter completes an age.

Semi-Chorus

Outside the civil garden
Of every day of love there
Crouches a wild passion   45
    To destroy and be destroyed.
O who to boast their power
Have challenged it to charge? Like
Wheat our souls are sifted
    And cast into the void.   50

Chorus

The evil and armed draw near;
The weather smells of their hate
And the houses smell of our fear;
Death has opened his white eye
And the black hole calls the thief   55
As the evil and armed draw near.

FOR THE TIME BEING: 28. *Arachne:* Greek word for spider.

Ravens alight on the wall,
Our plans have all gone awry,
The rains will arrive too late,
Our resourceful general   60
Fell down dead as he drank
And his horses died of grief,
Our navy sailed away and sank;
The evil and armed draw near.

II

Narrator

If, on account of the political situation,   65
There are quite a number of homes without roofs, and men
Lying about in the countryside neither drunk nor asleep,
If all sailings have been cancelled till further notice,
If it's unwise now to say much in letters, and if,
Under the subnormal temperatures prevailing,   70
The two sexes are at present the weak and the strong,
That is not at all unusual for this time of year.
If that were all we should know how to manage. Flood, fire,
The desiccation of grasslands, restraint of princes,
Piracy on the high seas, physical pain and fiscal grief,   75
These after all are our familiar tribulations,
And we have been through them all before, many, many times.
As events which belong to the natural world where
The occupation of space is the real and final fact
And time turns round itself in an obedient circle,   80
They occur again and again but only to pass
Again and again into their formal opposites,
From sword to ploughshare, coffin to cradle, war to work,
So that, taking the bad with the good, the pattern composed
By the ten thousand odd things that can possibly happen   85
Is permanent in a general average way.

   Till lately we knew of no other, and between us we seemed
To have what it took—the adrenal courage of the tiger,
The chameleon's discretion, the modesty of the doe,
Or the fern's devotion to spatial necessity: 90
To practise one's peculiar civic virtue was not
So impossible after all; to cut our losses
And bury our dead was really quite easy: That was why

We were always able to say: "We are children of God,
And our Father has never forsaken His people."   95

But then we were children: That was a moment ago,
Before an outrageous novelty had been introduced
Into our lives. Why were we never warned? Perhaps we were.
Perhaps that mysterious noise at the back of the brain
We noticed on certain occasions—sitting alone   100
In the waiting room of the country junction, looking
Up at the toilet window—was not indigestion
But this Horror starting already to scratch Its way in?
Just how, just when It succeeded we shall never know:
We can only say that now It is there and that nothing   105
We learnt before It was there is now of the slightest use,
For nothing like It has happened before. It's as if
We had left our house for five minutes to mail a letter,
And during that time the living room had changed places
With the room behind the mirror over the fireplace;   110
It's as if, waking up with a start, we discovered
Ourselves stretched out flat on the floor, watching our shadow
Sleepily stretching itself at the window. I mean
That the world of space where events re-occur is still there,
Only now it's no longer real; the real one is nowhere   115
Where time never moves and nothing can ever happen:
I mean that although there's a person we know all about
Still bearing our name and loving himself as before,
That person has become a fiction; our true existence
Is decided by no one and has no importance to love.   120
    That is why we despair; that is why we would welcome
The nursery bogey or the winecellar ghost, why even
The violent howling of winter and war has become
Like a juke-box tune that we dare not stop. We are afraid
Of pain but more afraid of silence; for no nightmare   125
Of hostile objects could be as terrible as this Void.
This is the Abomination. This is the wrath of God.

III

Chorus

Alone, alone, about a dreadful wood
Of conscious evil runs a lost mankind,
Dreading to find its Father lest it find   130

The Goodness it has dreaded is not good:
Alone, alone, about our dreadful wood.

Where is that Law for which we broke our own,
Where now that Justice for which Flesh resigned
Her hereditary right to passion, Mind   135
His will to absolute power? Gone. Gone.
Where is that Law for which we broke our own?

The Pilgrim Way has led to the Abyss.
Was it to meet such grinning evidence
We left our richly odoured ignorance?   140
Was the triumphant answer to be this?
The Pilgrim Way has led to the Abyss.

We who must die demand a miracle.
How could the Eternal do a temporal act,
The Infinite become a finite fact?
Nothing can save us that is possible:
We who must die demand a miracle.

IV

Recitative

If the muscle can feel repugnance, there is still a false move to be
    made;
If the mind can imagine tomorrow, there is still a defeat to remember;
As long as the self can say "I," it is impossible not to rebel;   150
As long as there is an accidental virtue, there is a necessary vice:
And the garden cannot exist, the miracle cannot occur.
For the garden is the only place there is, but you will not find it
Until you have looked for it everywhere and found nowhere that is
    not a desert;
The miracle is the only thing that happens, but to you it will not be
    apparent,   155
Until all events have been studied and nothing happens that you can-
    not explain;
And life is the destiny you are bound to refuse until you have con-
    sented to die.

Therefore, see without looking, hear without listening, breathe with-
    out asking:
The Inevitable is what will seem to happen to you purely by chance;
The Real is what will strike you as really absurd;   160

Unless you are certain you are dreaming, it is certainly a dream of
   your own;
Unless you exclaim—"There must be some mistake"—you must be
   mistaken.

v

Chorus

O where is that immortal and nameless Centre from which our
   points of
Definition and death are all equi-distant? Where
The well of our wish to wander, the everlasting fountain   165
   Of the waters of joy that our sorrow uses for tears?
O where is the garden of Being that is only known in Existence
   As the command to be never there, the sentence by which
Alephs of throbbing fact have been banished into position,
   The clock that dismisses the moment into the turbine of time?   170

O would I could mourn over Fate like the others, the resolute crea-
   tures,
   By seizing my chance to regret. The stone is content
With a formal anger and falls and falls; the plants are indignant
   With one dimension only and can only doubt   174
Whether light or darkness lies in the worse direction; and the subtler
   Exiles who try every path are satisfied
With proving that none have a goal: why must Man also acknowledge
   It is not enough to bear witness, for even protest is wrong?

Earth is cooled and fire is quenched by his unique excitement,
   All answers expire in the clench of his questioning hand,   180
His singular emphasis frustrates all possible order:
   Alas, his genius is wholly for envy; alas,
The vegetative sadness of lakes, the locomotive beauty
   Of choleric beasts of prey, are nearer than he

---

169. *Alephs:* A mathematical term designating relationships among trans-
finite cardinal numbers, and (in the singular) the name of the first letter
of the Hebrew alphabet. In Auden's context, it may be taken in the first
sense as roughly equivalent to "categories" (i.e., "throbbing fact" classified
into categories designated "aleph 1," "aleph 2," etc.): or, in the second sense,
as roughly equivalent to "discrete particles," "integers," "members," of
the alphabet. In either case the reference, as in the other clauses, is to
an ideal order or whole or source (a One), to which the heterogeneity of
experience (the Many) may be assimilated.

To the dreams that deprive him of sleep, the powers that compel him
    to idle,   185
  To his amorous nymphs and his sanguine athletic gods.

How can his knowledge protect his desire for truth from illusion?
  How can he wait without idols to worship, without
Their overwhelming persuasion that somewhere, over the high hill,
  Under the roots of the oak, in the depths of the sea,   190
Is a womb or a tomb wherein he may halt to express some attainment?
  How can he hope and not dream that his solitude
Shall disclose a vibrating flame at last and entrust him forever
  With its magic secret of how to extemporise life?

THE ANNUNCIATION

I

The Four Faculties

Over the life of Man   195
We watch and wait,
The Four who manage
His fallen estate:
We who are four were
Once but one,   200
Before his act of
Rebellion;
We were himself when
His will was free,
His error became our   205
Chance to be.
Powers of air and fire,
Water and earth,
Into our hands is given
Man from his birth: 210

Intuition

As a dwarf in the dark of
His belly I rest;

Feeling

A nymph, I inhabit
The heart in his breast;

Sensation

A giant, at the gates of   215
His body I stand;

Thought

His dreaming brain is
My fairyland.

Tutti

Invisible phantoms,
The forms we assume are   220
Adapted to each
Individual humour,
Beautiful facts or true
Generalisations,
Test cases in Law or   225
Market quotations:
As figures and formulae
Chemists have seen us,
Who to true lovers were
Putti of Venus.   230

Ambiguous causes
Of all temptation,
We lure men either
To death or salvation:
We alone may look over
The wall of that hidden
Garden whose entrance
To him is forbidden;
Must truthfully tell him
What happens inside,   240
But what it may mean he
Alone must decide.

---

230. *Putti:* little boys (with reference to the Cupid-like figures which throng
Renaissance Italian paintings).

II

Thought

The garden is unchanged, the silence is unbroken.
Truth has not yet intruded to possess
Its empty morning nor the promised hour   245
Shaken its lasting May.

Intuition

        The human night,
Whose messengers we are, cannot dispel
Its wanton dreams, and they are all we know.

Sensation

My senses are still coarse
From late engrossment in a fair. Old tunes   250
Reiterated, lights with repeated winks,
Were fascinating like a tic and brought
Whole populations running to a plain,
Making its lush alluvial meadows
One boisterous preposter. By the river   255
A whistling crowd had waited many hours
To see a naked woman swim upstream;
Honours and reckless medicines were served
In booths where interest was lost
As easily as money; at the back,   260
In a wet vacancy among the ash cans,
A waiter coupled sadly with a crow.

Feeling

I have but now escaped a raging landscape:
There woods were in a tremor from the shouts
Of hunchbacks hunting a hermaphrodite;   265
A burning village scampered down a lane;
Insects with ladders stormed a virgin's house:
On a green knoll littered with picnics
A mob of horses kicked a gull to death.

---

255. *preposter:* a coined word, suggesting something ridiculously different
from what should be—a preposterous spectacle.

Intuition

Remembrance of the moment before last   270
Is like a yawning drug. I have observed
The sombre valley of an industry
In dereliction. Conduits, ponds, canals,
Distressed with weeds; engines and furnaces
At rust in rotting sheds; and their strong users   275
Transformed to spongy heaps of drunken flesh.
Deep among dock and dusty nettle lay
Each ruin of a will; manors of mould
Grew into empires as a westering sun
Left the air chilly; not a sound disturbed   280
The autumn dusk except a stertorous snore
That over their drowned condition like a sea
Wept without grief.

Thought

My recent company
Was worse than your three visions. Where I was,
The haunting ghosts were figures with no ground,   285
Areas of wide omission and vast regions
Of passive colour; higher than any squeak,
One note went on for ever; an embarrassed sum
Stuck on the stutter of a decimal,
And points almost coincident already   290
Approached so slowly they could never meet.
There nothing could be stated or constructed:
To Be was an archaic nuisance.

Intuition

Look. There is someone in the garden.

Feeling

The garden is unchanged, the silence is unbroken   295
For she is still walking in her sleep of childhood:
Many before
Have wandered in, like her, then wandered out
Unconscious of their visit and unaltered,
The garden unchanged, the silence unbroken: 300
None may wake there but One who shall be woken.

The Angel Gabriel

Wake.

III

Gabriel

Mary, in a dream of love
Playing as all children play,
For unsuspecting children may   305
Express in comic make-believe
The wish that later they will know
Is tragic and impossible;
Hear, child, what I am sent to tell:
Love wills your dream to happen, so   310
Love's will on earth may be, through you,
No longer a pretend but true.

Mary

What dancing joy would whirl
My ignorance away?
Light blazes out of the stone,   315
The taciturn water
Burst into music,
And warm wings throb within
The motionless rose:
What sudden rush of Power   320
Commands me to command?

Gabriel

When Eve, in love with her own will,
Denied the will of Love and fell,
She turned the flesh Love knew so well
To knowledge of her love until   325

---

302. Luke, 1:26-31: "And in the sixth month the angel Gabriel was sent
from God unto a city of Galilee, named Nazareth, to a virgin espoused to
a man whose name was Joseph of the House of David; and the virgin's
name was Mary. And the angel came in unto her, and said, Hail, thou
that art highly favored, the Lord is with Thee: blessed art thou among
women. And when she saw him, she was troubled at his saying, and cast
in her mind what manner of salutation this should be. And the angel said
unto her, Fear not, Mary: for thou hast found favour with God. And,
behold, thou shalt conceive in thy womb, and bring forth a son, and shalt
call his name, JESUS."

Both love and knowledge were of sin:
What her negation wounded, may
Your affirmation heal today;
Love's will requires your own, that in
The flesh whose love you do not know,   330
Love's knowledge into flesh may grow.

Mary

My flesh in terror and fire
Rejoices that the Word
Who utters the world out of nothing,
As a pledge of His word to love her   335
Against her will, and to turn
Her desperate longing to love,
Should ask to wear me,
From now to their wedding day,
For an engagement ring.   340

Gabriel

Since Adam, being free to choose,
Chose to imagine he was free
To choose his own necessity,
Lost in his freedom, Man pursues
The shadow of his images: 345
Today the Unknown seeks the known;
What I am willed to ask, your own
Will has to answer; child, it lies
Within your power of choosing to
Conceive the Child who chooses you.   350

IV

Solo and Chorus

Let number and weight rejoice
In this hour of their translation
Into conscious happiness:
For the whole in every part,
The truth at the proper centre   355
(*There's a Way. There's a Voice.*)
Of language and distress
Is recognised in her heart
Singing and dancing.

Let even the great rejoice.   360
Though buffeted by admirers
And arrogant as noon,
The rich and the lovely have seen
For an infinitesimal moment
(*There's a Way. There's a Voice.*)   365
In another's eye till their own
Reflection came between,
Singing and dancing.

Let even the small rejoice
Though threatened from purple rostra   370
And dazed by the soldier's drum
Proclaiming total defeat,
The general loquacious Public
(*There's a Way. There's a Voice.*)
Have been puzzled and struck dumb,   375
Hearing in every street
Singing and dancing.

Let even the young rejoice
Lovers at their betrayal
Weeping alone in the night,   380
Have fallen asleep as they heard,
Though too far off to be certain
(*There's a Way. There's a Voice.*)
They had not imagined it,
Sounds that made grief absurd,   385
Singing and dancing.

Let even the old rejoice
The Bleak and the Dim, abandoned
By impulse and regret,
Are startled out of their lives;   390
For to footsteps long expected
(*There's a Way. There's a Voice.*)
Their ruins echo, yet
The Demolisher arrives
Singing and dancing.   395

---

370. *rostra:* platforms (for oratory)

THE TEMPTATION OF ST. JOSEPH

I

Joseph

My shoes were shined, my pants were cleaned and pressed,
And I was hurrying to meet
　My own true Love:
But a great crowd grew and grew
Till I could not push my way through,　　　　　　　400
　Because
A star had fallen down the street;
　When they saw who I was,
The police tried to do their best.

Chorus [*off*]

Joseph, you have heard　　　　　　　　　　　　405
What Mary says occurred;
Yes, it may be so.
Is it likely? No.

Joseph

The bar was gay, the lighting well-designed,
And I was sitting down to wait　　　　　　　　　410
　My own true Love:
A voice I'd heard before, I think,
Cried: "This is on the House. I drink
　To him
Who does not know it is too late";　　　　　　　415
　When I asked for the time,
Everyone was very kind.

Section title: *The Temptation:* Matthew 1: 18-20: "Now the birth of Jesus Christ was on this wise: When as his mother Mary was espoused to Joseph, before they came together, she was found with child of the Holy Ghost. Then Joseph her husband, being a just man, and not willing to make her a publick example was minded to put her away privily. But while he thought on these things, behold the angel of the Lord appeared unto him in a dream. . . ."

Chorus [*off*]

Mary may be pure,
But, Joseph, are you sure?
How is one to tell?   42c
Suppose, for instance . . . Well . . .

Joseph

Through cracks, up ladders, into waters deep,
I squeezed, I climbed, I swam to save
    My own true Love:
Under a dead apple tree   425
I saw an ass; when it saw me
    It brayed;
A hermit sat in the mouth of a cave;
    When I asked him the way,
He pretended to be asleep.   430

Chorus [*off*]

Maybe, maybe not.
But, Joseph, you know what
Your world, of course, will say
About you anyway.

Joseph

Where are you, Father, where?   435
Caught in the jealous trap
Of an empty house I hear
As I sit alone in the dark
Everything, everything,
The drip of the bathroom tap,   440
The creak of the sofa spring,
The wind in the air-shaft, all
Making the same remark
Stupidly, stupidly,
Over and over again.   445
Father, what have I done?
Answer me, Father, how
Can I answer the tactless wall
Or the pompous furniture now?
Answer them . . .   450

Gabriel

No, you must.

Joseph

How then am I to know,
Father, that you are just?
Give me one reason.

Gabriel

No.   455

Joseph

All I ask is one
Important and elegant proof
That what my Love had done
Was really at your will
And that your will is Love.   460

Gabriel

No, you must believe;
Be silent, and sit still.

II

Narrator

  For the perpetual excuse
Of Adam for his fall—"My little Eve,
God bless her, did beguile me and I ate,"   465
  For his insistence on a nurse,
All service, breast, and lap, for giving Fate
Feminine gender to make girls believe
That they can save him, you must now atone,
  Joseph, in silence and alone;   470
While she who loves you makes you shake with fright,
Your love for her must tuck you up and kiss good night.
  For likening Love to war, for all
The pay-off lines of limericks in which

---

462. *sit still:* Cf. Psalm 46: 10: "Be still and know that I am God"—and
also the prayer For Quiet Confidence in the Book of Common Prayer,
which echoes this.

The weak resentful bar-fly shows his sting,   475
   For talking of their spiritual
Beauty to chorus-girls, for flattering
The features of old gorgons who are rich,
For the impudent grin and Irish charm
   That hides a cold will to do harm,   480
Today the roles are altered; you must be
The Weaker Sex whose passion is passivity.

   For those delicious memories
Cigars and sips of brandy can restore
To old dried boys, for gallantry that scrawls   485
   In idolatrous detail and size
A symbol of aggression on toilet walls,
For having reasoned—"Woman is naturally pure
Since she has no moustache," for having said,
   "No woman has a business head,"   490
You must learn now that masculinity,
To Nature, is a non-essential luxury.

   Lest, finding it impossible
To judge its object now or throatily
Forgive it as eternal God forgives,   495
   Lust, tempted by this miracle
To more ingenious evil, should contrive
A heathen fetish from Virginity
To soothe the spiritual petulance
   Of worn-out rakes and maiden aunts,   500
Forgetting nothing and believing all,
You must behave as if this were not strange at all.

   Without a change in look or word,
You both must act exactly as before;
Joseph and Mary shall be man and wife   505
   Just as if nothing had occurred.
There is one World of Nature and one Life;
Sin fractures the Vision, not the Fact; for
The Exceptional is always usual
   And the Usual exceptional.   510
To choose what is difficult all one's days
As if it were easy, that is faith. Joseph, praise.

III

Semi-Chorus

Joseph, Mary, pray for those
Misled by moonlight and the rose,
For all in our perplexity.   515
Lovers who hear a distant bell
That tolls from somewhere in their head
Across the valley of their dream—
"All those who love excessively
Foot or thigh or arm or face   520
Pursue a louche and fatuous fire
And stumble into Hell"—
Yet what can such foreboding seem
But intellectual talk
So long as bodies walk   525
An earth where Time and Space
Turn Heaven to a finite bed
And Love into desire?
Pray for us, enchanted with
The green Bohemia of that myth   530
Where knowledge of the flesh can take
The guilt of being born away,
Simultaneous passions make
One eternal chastity:
Pray for us romantics, pray.   535

Boys' Semi-Chorus

Joseph, Mary, pray for us,
Independent embryos who,
Unconscious in another, do
Evil as each creature does
In every definite decision   540
To improve; for even in
The germ-cell's primary division
Innocence is lost and sin,
Already given as a fact,
Once more issues as an act.   545

---

521. *louche:* oblique, roving.

Semi-Chorus

Joseph, Mary, pray for all
The proper and conventional
Of whom this world approves.
Pray for us whose married loves
Acquire so readily   550
The indolent fidelity
Of unaired beds, for us to whom
Domestic hatred can become
A habit-forming drug, whose will
To civil anarchy,   555
Uses disease to disobey
And makes our private bodies ill.
O pray for our salvation
Who take the prudent way,
Believing we shall be exempted   560
From the general condemnation
Because our self-respect is tempted
To incest not adultery:
O pray for us, the bourgeoisie.

Boys' Semi-Chorus

Joseph, Mary, pray   565
For us children as in play
Upon the nursery floor
We gradually explore
Our members till our jealous lives
Have worked through to a clear   570
But trivial idea
Of that whence each derives
A vague but massive feel
Of being individual.
O pray for our redemption; for   575
The will that occupies
Our sensual infancy
Already is mature
And could immediately
Beget upon our flesh far more   580
Expressions of its disbelief
Than we shall manage to conceive
In a long life of lies.

Chorus

Blessed Woman,
Excellent Man,   585
Redeem for the dull the
Average Way,
That common ungifted
Natures may
Believe that their normal   590
Vision can
Walk to perfection.

THE SUMMONS

I

Star of the Nativity

I am that star most dreaded by the wise,
For they are drawn against their will to me,
Yet read in my procession through the skies   595
The doom of orthodox sophrosyne:
I shall discard their major preservation,
All that they know so long as no one asks;
I shall deprive them of their minor tasks
In free and legal households of sensation,   600
Of money, picnics, beer, and sanitation.

Beware. All those who follow me are led
Onto that Glassy Mountain where are no

Section title, *The Summons:* Matthew 2: 1-9: "Now when Jesus was born
in Bethlehem of Judaea in the days of Herod the king, behold, there came
wise men from the east to Jerusalem, saying, Where is he that is born
King of the Jews? for we have seen his star in the east and are come to
worship him. When Herod the king had heard these things, he was
troubled, and all Jerusalem with him. And when he had gathered all the
chief priests and scribes of the people together, he demanded of them
where Christ should be born. And they said unto him, In Bethlehem of
Judaea; for thus it is written by the prophet . . . Then Herod, when he
had privily called the wise men, inquired of them diligently what time the
star appeared. And he sent them to Bethlehem, and said, Go and search diligently for the young child: and when ye have found him, bring me word
again, that I may come and worship him also. When they had heard the
king, they departed: and, lo, the star, which they saw in the east, went
before them. . . ." 596. *sophrosyne:* the classical ethics of moderation.

Footholds for logic, to that Bridge of Dread
Where knowledge but increases vertigo: 605
Those who pursue me take a twisting lane
To find themselves immediately alone
With savage water or unfeeling stone,
In labyrinths where they must entertain
Confusion, cripples, tigers, thunder, pain.   610

The First Wise Man

To break down Her defences
    And profit from the vision
That plain men can predict through an
    Ascesis of their senses,
With rack and screw I put Nature through   615
    A thorough inquisition:
But She was so afraid that if I were disappointed
I should hurt Her more that Her answers were disjointed—
    I did. I didn't. I will. I won't.
She is just as big a liar, in fact, as we are.   620
    To discover how to be truthful now
    Is the reason I follow this star.

The Second Wise Man

My faith that in Time's constant
    Flow lay real assurance
Broke down on this analysis—   625
    At any given instant
All solids dissolve, no wheels revolve,
    And facts have no endurance—
And who knows if it is by design or pure inadvertence
That the Present destroys its inherited self-importance?   630
    With envy, terror, rage, regret,
We anticipate or remember but never are.
    To discover how to be living now
    Is the reason I follow this star.

The Third Wise Man

Observing how myopic   635
    Is the Venus of the Soma,
The concept Ought would make, I thought,

---

614. *Ascesis:* training. 636. *Soma:* the body.

Our passions philanthropic,
  And rectify in the sensual eye
    Both lens-flare and lens-coma: 640
But arriving at the Greatest Good by introspection
And counting the Greater Number, left no time for affection,
  Laughter, kisses, squeezing, smiles:
And I learned why the learnèd are as despised as they are.
  To discover how to be loving now   645
  Is the reason I follow this star.

The Three Wise Men

The weather has been awful,
  The countryside is dreary,
Marsh, jungle, rock; and echoes mock,
  Calling our hope unlawful;   650
But a silly song can help along
  Yours ever and sincerely:
At least we know for certain that we are three old sinners,
That this journey is much too long, that we want our dinners,
  And miss our wives, our books, our dogs,   655
But have only the vaguest idea why we are what we are.
  To discover how to be human now
  Is the reason we follow this star.

Star of the Nativity

Descend into the fosse of Tribulation,
Take the cold hand of Terror for a guide;   660
Below you in its swirling desolation
Hear tortured Horror roaring for a bride:
O do not falter at the last request
But, as the huge deformed head rears to kill,
Answer its craving with a clear I Will;   665
Then wake, a child in the rose-garden, pressed
Happy and sobbing to your lover's breast.

II

Narrator

Now let the wife look up from her stove, the husband
Interrupt his work, the child put down its toy,

---

640. *lens-flare* is a blur caused by interreflection between lens surfaces; *lens-coma* is a blur caused by spherical aberrations in the lens. 659. *fosse:* ditch.

That His voice may be heard in our Just Society 670
  Who under the sunlight
Of His calm, possessing the good earth, do well. Pray
Silence for Caesar: stand motionless and hear
In a concourse of body and concord of soul
  His proclamation. 675

Recitative

CITIZENS OF THE EMPIRE, GREETING. ALL MALE PERSONS WHO SHALL
HAVE ATTAINED THE AGE OF TWENTY-ONE YEARS OR OVER MUST PROCEED
IMMEDIATELY TO THE VILLAGE, TOWNSHIP, CITY, PRECINCT OR OTHER LOCAL
ADMINISTRATIVE AREA IN WHICH THEY WERE BORN AND THERE REGISTER
THEMSELVES AND THEIR DEPENDENTS IF ANY WITH THE POLICE. [680
WILFUL FAILURE TO COMPLY WITH THIS ORDER IS PUNISHABLE BY CON-
FISCATION OF GOODS AND LOSS OF CIVIL RIGHTS.

Narrator

You have been listening to the voice of Caesar
Who overcame implacable Necessity
By His endurance and by His skill has subdued the 685
  Welter of Fortune.
It is meet, therefore, that, before dispersing
In pious equanimity to obey His orders,
With well-tuned instruments and grateful voices
  We should praise Caesar. 690

III

Fugal-Chorus

Great is Caesar: He has conquered Seven Kingdoms.
The First was the Kingdom of Abstract Idea:
Last night it was Tom, Dick and Harry; tonight it is S's with P's:
Instead of inflexions and accents
There are prepositions and word-order; 695
Instead of aboriginal objects excluding each other
There are specimens reiterating a type;
Instead of wood-nymphs and river-demons,
There is one unconditioned ground of Being.
Great is Caesar: God must be with Him. 700

Fugal: having the character of a fugue.

Great is Caesar: He has conquered Seven Kingdoms.
The Second was the Kingdom of Natural Cause:
Last night it was Sixes and Sevens; tonight it is One and Two;
Instead of saying, "Strange are the whims of the Strong,"
We say, "Harsh is the Law but it is certain";   705
Instead of building temples, we build laboratories;
Instead of offering sacrifices, we perform experiments;
Instead of reciting prayers, we note pointer-readings;
Our lives are no longer erratic but efficient.
Great is Caesar: God must be with Him.   710

Great is Caesar; He has conquered Seven Kingdoms.
The Third was the Kingdom of Infinite Number:
Last night it was Rule-of-Thumb, tonight it is To-a-T;
Instead of Quite-a-lot, there is Exactly-so-many;
Instead of Only-a-few, there is Just-these;   715
Instead of saying, "You must wait until I have counted,"
We say, "Here you are. You will find this answer correct";
Instead of a nodding acquaintance with a few integers
The Transcendentals are our personal friends.
Great is Caesar: God must be with Him.   720

Great is Caesar: He has conquered Seven Kingdoms.
The Fourth was the Kingdom of Credit Exchange:
Last night it was Tit-for-Tat, tonight it is C.O.D.;
When we have a surplus, we need not meet someone with a deficit;
When we have a deficit, we need not meet someone with a surplus;
Instead of heavy treasures, there are paper symbols of value;   726
Instead of Pay at Once, there is Pay when you can;
Instead of My Neighbour, there is Our Customers;
Instead of Country Fair, there is World Market.
Great is Caesar: God must be with Him.   730

Great is Caesar; He has conquered Seven Kingdoms.
The Fifth was the Kingdom of Inorganic Giants:
Last night it was Heave-Ho, tonight it is Whee-Spree;
When we want anything, They make it;
When we dislike anything, They change it;   735
When we want to go anywhere, They carry us;
When the Barbarian invades us, They raise immovable shields;
When we invade the Barbarian, They brandish irresistible swords;
Fate is no longer a fiat of Matter, but a freedom of Mind.
Great is Caesar: God must be with Him.   740

Great is Caesar: He has conquered Seven Kingdoms.
The Sixth was the Kingdom of Organic Dwarfs:
Last night it was Ouch-Ouch, tonight it is Yum-Yum;
When diseases waylay us, They strike them dead;
When worries intrude on us, They throw them out;   745
When pain accosts us, They save us from embarrassment;
When we feel like sheep, They make us lions;
When we feel like geldings, They make us stallions;
Spirit is no longer under Flesh, but on top.
Great is Caesar: God must be with Him.   750

Great is Caesar: He has conquered Seven Kingdoms.
The Seventh was the Kingdom of Popular Soul:
Last night it was Order-Order, tonight it is Hear-Hear;
When he says, You are happy, we laugh;
When he says, You are wretched, we cry;   755
When he says, It is true, everyone believes it;
When he says, It is false, no one believes it;
When he says, This is good, this is loved;
When he says, That is bad, that is hated.
Great is Caesar: God must be with Him.   760

IV

Narrator

These are stirring times for the editors of newspapers:
History is in the making; Mankind is on the march.
The longest aqueduct in the world is already
Under construction; the Committees on Fen-Drainage
And Soil-Conservation will issue very shortly   765
Their Joint Report; even the problems of Trade Cycles
And Spiralling Prices are regarded by the experts
As practically solved; and the recent restrictions
Upon aliens and free-thinking Jews are beginning
To have a salutary effect upon public morale.   770
True, the Western seas are still infested with pirates,
And the rising power of the Barbarian in the North
Is giving some cause for uneasiness; but we are fully
Alive to these dangers; we are rapidly arming; and both
Will be taken care of in due course: then, united   775
In a sense of common advantage and common right,
Our great Empire shall be secure for a thousand years.

---

772. *North:* the traditional residence of Evil.

If we were never alone or always too busy,
Perhaps we might even believe what we know is not true:
But no one is taken in, at least not all of the time;   780
In our bath, or the subway, or the middle of the night,
We know very well we are not unlucky but evil,
That the dream of a Perfect State or No State at all,
To which we fly for refuge, is a part of our punishment.
    Let us therefore be contrite but without anxiety,   785
For Powers and Times are not gods but mortal gifts from God;
Let us acknowledge our defeats but without despair,
For all societies and epochs are transient details
Transmitting an everlasting opportunity
That the Kingdom of Heaven may come, not in our present   790
And not in our future, but in the Fullness of Time.
Let us pray.

v

Chorale *

Our Father, whose creative Will
    Asked Being for us all,
Confirm it that Thy Primal Love   795
May weave in us the freedom of
The actually deficient on
    The justly actual.

Though written by Thy children with
    A smudged and crooked line,
The Word is ever legible,   800
Thy Meaning unequivocal,
And for Thy Goodness even sin
    Is valid as a sign.

Inflict Thy promises with each   805
    Occasion of distress,
That from our incoherence we
May learn to put our trust in Thee,
And brutal fact persuade us to
    Adventure, Art, and Peace.   810

THE VISION OF THE SHEPHERDS

I

The First Shepherd

The winter night requires our constant attention,
  Watching that water and good-will,
Warmth and well-being, may still be there in the morning.

The Second Shepherd

  For behind the spontaneous joy of life
There is always a mechanism to keep going,   815

The Third Shepherd

  And someone like us is always there.

The First Shepherd

We observe that those who assure us their education
  And money would do us such harm,
How real we are just as we are, and how they envy us,
  For it is the centreless tree   820
And the uncivilised robin who are the truly happy,
  Have done pretty well for themselves:

The *Second Shepherd

Nor can we help noticing how those who insist that
  We ought to stand up for our rights,
And how important we are, keep insisting also   825
  That it doesn't matter a bit

Section title, *The Vision:* Luke 2: 8-14: "And there were in the same
country shepherds abiding in the field, keeping watch over their flock by
night. And, lo, the angel of the Lord came upon them, and the glory of the
Lord shone round about them: and they were sore afraid. And the angel
said unto them, Fear not: for, behold, I bring you good tidings of great
joy, which shall be to all people. For unto you is born this day in the city
of David a Saviour, which is Christ the Lord. And this shall be a sign
unto you: Ye shall find the babe wrapped in swaddling clothes, lying in
a manger. And suddenly there was with the angel, a multitude of the
heavenly host praising God and saying, Glory to God in the highest, and on
earth peace, good will toward men."

If one of us gets arrested or injured, for
It is only our numbers that count.

The Third Shepherd

In a way they are right,

The First Shepherd

But to behave like a cogwheel
When one knows one is no such thing,   830

The Second Shepherd

Merely to add to a crowd with one's passionate body,
Is not a virtue.

The Third Shepherd

What is real
About us all is that each of us is waiting.

The First Shepherd

That is why we are able to bear
Ready-made clothes, second-hand art and opinions   835
And being washed and ordered about;

The Second Shepherd

That is why you should not take our conversation
Too seriously, nor read too much
Into our songs;

The Third Shepherd

Their purpose is mainly to keep us
From watching the clock all the time.   840

The First Shepherd

For, though we cannot say why, we know that something
Will happen:

The Second Shepherd

What we cannot say,

The Third Shepherd

Except that it will not be a reporter's item
Of unusual human interest;

The First Shepherd

That always means something unpleasant.

The Second Shepherd

                     But one day or   845
The next we shall hear the Good News.

II

The Three Shepherds

Levers nudge the aching wrist;
   "You are free
   Not to be,
   Why exist?"   850
Wheels a thousand times a minute
   Mutter, stutter,
"End the self you cannot mend,
Did you, friend, begin it?"
   And the streets   855
   Sniff at our defeats.
Then who is the Unknown
Who answers for our fear
As if it were His own,
So that we reply   860
Till the day we die;
"No, I don't know why,
But I'm glad I'm here"?

III

Chorus of Angels

Unto you a Child,
A Son is given.   865
Praising, proclaiming
The ingression of Love,
Earth's darkness invents
The blaze of Heaven,
And frigid silence   870
Meditates a song;
For great joy has filled
The narrow and the sad,

While the emphasis
Of the rough and big,   875
The abiding crag
And wandering wave,
Is on forgiveness:
Sing Glory to God
And good-will to men,   880
All, all, all of them.
Run to Bethlehem.

Shepherds

Let us run to learn
How to love and run;
Let us run to Love.   885

Chorus

Now all things living,
Domestic or wild,
With whom you must share
Light, water, and air,
And suffer and shake   890
In physical need,
The sullen limpet,
The exuberant weed,
The mischievous cat,
And the timid bird,   895
Are glad for your sake
As the new-born Word
Declares that the old
Authoritarian
Constraint is replaced   900
By His Covenant,
And a city based
On love and consent
Suggested to men,
All, all, all of them.   905
Run to Bethlehem.

Shepherds

Let us run to learn
How to love and run;
Let us run to Love.

Chorus

The primitive dead   910
Progress in your blood,
And generations
Of the unborn, all
Are leaping for joy
In your reins today   915
When the Many shall,
Once in your common
Certainty of this
Child's lovableness,
Resemble the One,   920
That after today
The children of men
May be certain that
The Father Abyss
Is affectionate   925
To all Its creatures,
All, all, all of them.
Run to Bethlehem.

AT THE MANGER

I

Mary

O shut your bright eyes that mine must endanger
With their watchfulness; protected by its shade   930
Escape from my care: what can you discover
From my tender look but how to be afraid?
Love can but confirm the more it would deny.
    Close your bright eye.

Sleep. What have you learned from the womb that bore you   935
But an anxiety your Father cannot feel?
Sleep. What will the flesh that I gave do for you,
Or my mother love, but tempt you from His will?
Why was I chosen to teach His Son to weep?
    Little One, sleep.   940

_____
915. *reins:* loins.

Dream. In human dreams earth ascends to Heaven
Where no one need pray nor ever feel alone.
In your first few hours of life here, O have you
Chosen already what death must be your own?
How soon will you start on the Sorrowful Way?   945
  Dream while you may.

II

First Wise Man

Led by the light of an unusual star,
We hunted high and low.

Second Wise Man

                    Have travelled far,
For many days, a little group alone
With doubts, reproaches, boredom, the unknown.   950

Third Wise Man

Through stifling gorges.

First Wise Man

                    Over level lakes,

Second Wise Man

Tundras intense and irresponsive seas.

Third Wise Man

In vacant crowds and humming silences,

First Wise Man

By ruined arches and past modern shops,

Second Wise Man

Counting the miles,

Third Wise Man

                    And the absurd mistakes.   955

The Three Wise Men

O here and now our endless journey stops.

First Shepherd
We never left the place where we were born,

Second Shepherd
Have only lived one day, but every day,

Third Shepherd
Have walked a thousand miles yet only worn
The grass between our work and home away. 960

First Shepherd
Lonely we were though never left alone.

Second Shepherd
The solitude familiar to the poor
Is feeling that the family next door,
The way it talks, eats, dresses, loves, and hates,
Is indistinguishable from one's own. 965

Third Shepherd
Tonight for the first time the prison gates
Have opened.

First Shepherd
Music and sudden light

Second Shepherd
Have interrupted our routine tonight,

Third Shepherd
And swept the filth of habit from our hearts.

The Three Shepherds
O here and now our endless journey starts. 970

Wise Men
Our arrogant longing to attain the tomb,

Shepherds
Our sullen wish to go back to the womb,

Wise Men

To have no past,

Shepherds

No future,

Tutti

Is refused.
And yet, without our knowledge, Love has used
Our weakness as a guard and guide.

We bless   975

Wise Men

Our lives' impatience.

Shepherds

Our lives' laziness,

Tutti

And bless each other's sin, exchanging here

Wise Men

Exceptional conceit

Shepherds

With average fear.

Tutti

Released by Love from isolating wrong,
Let us for Love unite our various song,   980
Each with his gift according to his kind
Bringing this child his body and his mind.

III

Wise Men

Child, at whose birth we would do obsequy
For our tall errors of imagination,
Redeem our talents with your little cry.   985

Shepherds

Clinging like sheep to the earth for protection,
We have not ventured far in any direction:
   Wean, Child, our aging flesh away
   From its childish way.

Wise Men

Love is more serious than Philosophy   990
Who sees no humour in her observation
That Truth is knowing that we know we lie.

Shepherds

When, to escape what our memories are thinking,
We go out at nights and stay up drinking,
   Stay then with our sick pride and mind   995
   The forgetful mind.

Wise Men

Love does not will enraptured apathy;
Fate plays the passive role of dumb temptation
To wills where Love can doubt, affirm, deny.

Shepherds

When, chafing at the rule of old offences,   1000
We run away to the sea of the senses,
   On strange beds then O welcome home
   Our horror of home.

Wise Men

Love knows of no somatic tyranny;
For homes are built for Love's accommodation   1005
By bodies from the void they occupy.

Shepherds

When, exhausting our wills with our evil courses,
We demand the good-will of cards and horses,
   Be then our lucky certainty
   Of uncertainty.   1010

1004. *somatic:* bodily, physiological.

Wise Men

Love does not fear substantial anarchy,
But vividly expresses obligation
With movement and in spontaneity.

Shepherds

When, feeling the great boots of the rich on our faces,
We live in the hope of one day changing places,   1015
    Be then the truth of our abuse
    That we abuse.

Wise Men

The singular is not Love's enemy;
Love's possibilities of realisation
Require an Otherness that can say *I*   1020

Shepherds

When in dreams the beasts and cripples of resentment
Rampage and revel to our hearts' contentment,
    Be then the poetry of hate
    That replaces hate.

Wise Men

Not In but With our time Love's energy   1025
Exhibits Love's immediate operation;
The choice to love is open till we die.

Shepherds

O Living Love, by your birth we are able
Not only, like the ox and ass of the stable,
    To love with our live wills, but love,   1030
    Knowing we love.

Tutti

O Living Love replacing phantasy,
O Joy of life revealed in Love's creation;
Our mood of longing turns to indication:
Space is the Whom our loves are needed by,   1035
Time is our choice of How to love and Why.

THE MEDITATION OF SIMEON

Simeon

As long as the apple had not been entirely digested, as long as there remained the least understanding between Adam and the stars, rivers and horses with whom he had once known complete intimacy, as long as Eve could share in any way with the moods of the rose or   [1040 the ambitions of the swallow, there was still a hope that the effects of the poison would wear off, that the exile from Paradise was only a bad dream, that the Fall had not occurred in fact.

Chorus

When we woke, it was day; we went on weeping.

Simeon

As long as there were any roads to amnesia and anaesthesia   [1045 still to be explored, any rare wine or curiosity of cuisine as yet untested, any erotic variation as yet unimagined or unrealised, any method of torture as yet undevised, any style of conspicuous waste as yet unindulged, any eccentricity of mania or disease as yet unrepresented, there was still a hope that man had not been poisoned but trans-   [1050 formed, that Paradise was not an eternal state from which he had been forever expelled, but a childish state which he had permanently outgrown, that the Fall had occurred by necessity.

Chorus

We danced in the dark, but were not deceived.

Section title, *The Meditation*: Luke 2: 25-35: "And, behold there was a man in Jerusalem, whose name was Simeon: and the same man was just and devout, waiting for the consolation of Israel: and the Holy Ghost was upon him. And it was revealed unto him by the Holy Ghost that he should not see death, before he had seen the Lord's Christ. And he came by the spirit into the temple: and when the parents brought in the child Jesus, to do for him after the custom of the law, Then took he him up in his arms, and blessed God, and said Lord, now lettest thou thy servant depart in peace, according to thy word: For mine eyes have seen thy salvation . . . And Joseph and his mother marvelled at those things which were spoken of him. And Simeon blessed them and said unto Mary his mother, Behold, this child is set for the fall and the rising again of many in Israel; and for a sign which shall be spoken against; (Yea, a sword shall pierce through thy own soul also,) that the thoughts of many hearts may be revealed."

Simeon

As long as there were any experiments still to be under-   [1055
taken in restoring that order in which desire had once rejoiced to be
reflected, any code of equity and obligation upon which some society
had not yet been founded, any species of property of which the value
had not yet been appreciated, any talent that had not yet won private
devotion and public honour, any rational concept of the   [1060
Good or intuitive feeling for the Holy that had not yet found its
precise and beautiful expression, any technique of contemplation or
ritual of sacrifice and praise that had not yet been properly conducted,
any faculty of mind or body that had not yet been thoroughly disciplined, there was still a hope that some antidote might be   [1065
found, that the gates of Paradise had indeed slammed to, but with the
exercise of a little patience and ingenuity would be unlocked, that the
Fall had occurred by accident.

Chorus

Lions came loping into the lighted city.

Simeon

Before the Positive could manifest Itself specifically, it was   [1070
necessary that nothing should be left that negation could remove; the
emancipation of Time from Space had first to be complete, the Revolution of the Images, in which the memories rose up and cast into
subject on the senses by Whom hitherto they had been enslaved, successful beyond their wildest dreams, the mirror in which the   [1075
Soul expected to admire herself so perfectly polished that her natural
consolation of vagueness should be utterly withdrawn.

Chorus

We looked at our Shadow and, Lo, it was lame.

Simeon

Before the Infinite could manifest Itself in the finite, it was necessary that man should first have reached that point along his   [1080
road to Knowledge where, just as it rises from the swamps of Confusion onto the sunny slopes of Objectivity, it forks in opposite directions towards the One and the Many; where, therefore, in order to
proceed at all, he must decide which is Real and which only Appearance, yet at the same time cannot escape the knowledge that   [1085
his choice is arbitrary and subjective.

Chorus

Promising to meet, we parted forever.

Simeon

Before the Unconditional could manifest Itself under the conditions of existence, it was necessary that man should first have reached the ultimate frontier of consciousness, the secular limit of mem-   [1090 ory beyond which there remained but one thing for him to know, his Original Sin, but of this it is impossible for him to become conscious because it is itself what conditions his will to knowledge. For as long as he was in Paradise he could not sin by any conscious intention or act: his as yet unfallen will could only rebel against the   [1095 truth by taking flight into an unconscious lie; he could only eat of the Tree of the Knowledge of Good and Evil by forgetting that its exist-ence was a fiction of the Evil One, that there is only the Tree of Life.

Chorus

The bravest drew back on the brink of the Abyss.

Simeon

From the beginning until now God spoke through His   [1100 prophets. The Word aroused the uncomprehending depths of their flesh to a witnessing fury, and their witness was this: that the Word should be made Flesh. Yet their witness could only be received as long as it was vaguely misunderstood, as long as it seemed either to be neither impossible nor necessary, or necessary but not impos-   [1105 sible, or impossible but not necessary; and the prophecy could not there-fore be fulfilled. For it could only be fulfilled when it was no longer possible to receive, because it was clearly understood as absurd. The Word could not be made Flesh until men had reached a state of abso-lute contradiction between clarity and despair in which they   [1110 would have no choice but either to accept absolutely or to reject abso-lutely, yet in their choice there should be no element of luck, for they would be fully conscious of what they were accepting or rejecting.

Chorus

The eternal spaces were congested and depraved.

Simeon

But here and now the Word which is implicit in the Be-   [1115 ginning and in the End is become immediately explicit, and that which hitherto we could only passively fear as the incomprehensible I AM,

henceforth we may actively love with comprehension that THOU
ART. Wherefore, having seen Him, not in some prophetic vision of
what might be, but with the eyes of our own weakness as   [1120
to what actually is, we are bold to say that we have seen our salvation.

Chorus

Now and forever, we are not alone.

Simeon

By the event of this birth the true significance of all other events
is defined, for of every other occasion it can be said that it could have
been different, but of this birth it is the case that it could in   [1125
no way be other than it is. And by the existence of this Child, the
proper value of all other existences is given, for of every other creature
it can be said that it has extrinsic importance but of this Child it is
the case that He is in no sense a symbol.

Chorus

We have right to believe that we really exist.   1130

Simeon

By Him is dispelled the darkness wherein the fallen will cannot
distinguish between temptation and sin, for in Him we become fully
conscious of Necessity as our freedom to be tempted, and of Freedom
as our necessity to have faith. And by Him is illuminated the time
in which we execute those choices through which our free-   [1135
dom is realised or prevented, for the course of History is predictable
in the degree to which all men love themselves, and spontaneous
in the degree to which each man loves God and through Him his
neighbour.

Chorus

The distresses of choice are our chance to be blessed.   1140

Simeon

Because in Him the Flesh is united to the Word without magical
transformation, Imagination is redeemed from promiscuous fornication
with her own images. The tragic conflict of Virtue with Necessity
is no longer confined to the Exceptional Hero; for disaster is not the
impact of a curse upon a few great families, but issues con-   [1145
tinually from the hubris of every tainted will. Every invalid is Roland
defending the narrow pass against hopeless odds, every stenographer

Brunnhilde refusing to renounce her lover's ring which came into existence through the renunciation of love.

Nor is the Ridiculous a species any longer of the Ugly;   [1150 for since of themselves all men are without merit, all are ironically assisted to their comic bewilderment by the Grace of God. Every Cabinet Minister is the woodcutter's simple-minded son to whom the fishes and the crows are always whispering the whereabouts of the Dancing Water or the Singing Branch, every heiress the   [1155 washerwoman's butter-fingered daughter on whose pillow the fairy keeps laying the herb that could cure the Prince's mysterious illness.

Nor is there any situation which is essentially more or less interesting than another. Every tea-table is a battlefield littered with old catastrophes and haunted by the vague ghosts of vast issues,   [1160 every martyrdom an occasion for flip cracks and sententious oratory.

Because in Him all passions find a logical In-Order-That, by Him is the perpetual recurrence of Art assured.

Chorus

Safe in His silence, our songs are at play.

Simeon

Because in Him the Word is united to the Flesh without   [1165 loss of perfection, Reason is redeemed from incestuous fixation on her own Logic, for the One and the Many are simultaneously revealed as real. So that we may no longer, with the Barbarians, deny the Unity, asserting that there are as many gods as there are creatures, nor, with the philosophers, deny the Multiplicity, asserting that God is   [1170 One who has no need of friends and is indifferent to a World of Time and Quantity and Horror which He did not create, nor, with Israel, may we limit the co-inherence of the One and the Many to a special case, asserting that God is only concerned with and of concern to that People whom out of all that He created He has chosen for   [1175 His own.

For the Truth is indeed One, without which is no salvation, but the possibilities of real knowledge are as many as are the creatures in the very real and most exciting universe that God creates with and for His love, and it is not Nature which is one public illusion,   [1180 but we who have each our many private illusions about Nature.

Because in Him abstraction finds a passionate For-The-Sake-Of, by Him is the continuous development of Science assured.

Chorus

Our lost Appearances are saved by His love.

Simeon

And because of His visitation, we may no longer desire [1185
God as if He were lacking: our redemption is no longer a question of
pursuit but of surrender to Him who is always and everywhere present. Therefore at every moment we pray that, following Him, we may
depart from our anxiety into His peace.

Chorus

Its errors forgiven, may our Vision come home.   1190

THE MASSACRE OF THE INNOCENTS

I

Herod

Because I am bewildered, because I must decide, because my decision
must be in conformity with Nature and Necessity, let me honour those
through whom my nature is by necessity what it is.

To Fortune—that I have become Tetrarch, that I have escaped
assassination, that at sixty my head is clear and my digestion
sound.   1194
To my Father—for the means to gratify my love of travel and study.
To my Mother—for a straight nose.
To Eva, my coloured nurse—for regular habits.
To my brother, Sandy, who married a trapeze-artist and died of
drink—for so refuting the position of the Hedonists.
To Mr. Stewart, nicknamed The Carp, who instructed me in the
elements of geometry through which I came to perceive the
errors of the tragic poets.
To Professor Lighthouse—for his lectures on The Peloponnesian
War.   1200
To the stranger on the boat to Sicily—for recommending to me
Brown on Resolution.
To my secretary, Miss Button—for admitting that my speeches were
inaudible.

There is no visible disorder. No crime—what could be more innocent than the birth of an artisan's child? Today has been one of
those perfect winter days, cold, brilliant, and utterly still,   [1205
when the bark of a shepherd's dog carries for miles, and the great wild
mountains come up quite close to the city walls, and the mind feels
intensely awake, and this evening as I stand at this window high up
in the citadel there is nothing in the whole magnificent panorama of
plain and mountains to indicate that the Empire is threat-   [1210
ened by a danger more dreadful than any invasion of Tartars on
racing camels or conspiracy of the Praetorian Guard.

Barges are unloading soil fertilizer at the river wharves. Soft drinks
and sandwiches may be had in the inns at reasonable prices. Allot-
ment gardening has become popular. The highway to the   [1215
coast goes straight up over the mountains and the truck-drivers no
longer carry guns. Things are beginning to take shape. It is a long
time since anyone stole the park benches or murdered the swans. There
are children in this province who have never seen a louse, shopkeepers
who have never handled a counterfeit coin, women of   [1220
forty who have never hidden in a ditch except for fun. Yes, in twenty
years I have managed to do a little. Not enough, of course. There
are villages only a few miles from here where they still believe in
witches. There isn't a single town where a good bookshop would pay.
One could count on the fingers of one hand the people   [1225
capable of solving the problem of Achilles and the Tortoise. Still it is
a beginning. In twenty years the darkness has been pushed back a few
inches. And what, after all, is the whole Empire, with its few thousand
square miles on which it is possible to lead the Rational Life, but a tiny
patch of light compared with those immense areas of bar-   [1230
baric night that surround it on all sides, that incoherent wilderness of
rage and terror, where Mongolian idiots are regarded as sacred and
mothers who give birth to twins are instantly put to death, where
malaria is treated by yelling, where warriors of superb courage obey
the commands of hysterical female impersonators, where   [1235
the best cuts of meat are reserved for the dead, where, if a white
blackbird has been seen, no more work may be done that day, where

---

1226. *Achilles and the Tortoise:* an ancient logical paradox, founded on
the proposition that in a race between a runner and a tortoise—if the
tortoise is given a headstart—the runner can never overtake the tortoise.
(Suppose the headstart to be 100 feet: the runner will first cover half of
this (50 ft.), then half of the remainder (25 ft.), then half of that, and so
on indefinitely. Logically, there will always be half of some extremely
minute distance separating the runner from the tortoise).

it is firmly believed that the world was created by a giant with three heads or that the motions of the stars are controlled from the liver of a rogue elephant?   1240

Yet even inside this little civilised patch itself, where, at the cost of heaven knows how much grief and bloodshed, it has been made unnecessary for anyone over the age of twelve to believe in fairies or that First Causes reside in mortal and finite objects, so many are still homesick for that disorder wherein every passion formerly   [1245 enjoyed a frantic licence. Caesar flies to his hunting lodge pursued by ennui; in the faubourgs of the Capital, Society grows savage, corrupted by silks and scents, softened by sugar and hot water, made insolent by theatres and attractive slaves; and everywhere, including this province, new prophets spring up every day to sound the old barbaric   [1250 note.

I have tried everything. I have prohibited the sale of crystals and ouija-boards; I have slapped a heavy tax on playing cards; the courts are empowered to sentence alchemists to hard labour in the mines; it is a statutory offence to turn tables or feel bumps. But   [1255 nothing is really effective. How can I expect the masses to be sensible when, for instance, to my certain knowledge, the captain of my own guard wears an amulet against the Evil Eye, and the richest merchant in the city consults a medium over every important transaction?

Legislation is helpless against the wild prayer of longing   [1260 that rises, day in, day out, from all these households under my protection: "O God, put away justice and truth for we cannot understand them and do not want them. Eternity would bore us dreadfully. Leave Thy heavens and come down to our earth of waterclocks and hedges. Become our uncle. Look after Baby, amuse Grandfather,   [1265 escort Madam to the Opera, help Willy with his home-work, introduce Muriel to a handsome naval officer. Be interesting and weak like us, and we will love you as we love ourselves."

Reason is helpless, and now even the Poetic Compromise no longer works, all those lovely fairy tales in which Zeus, disguising   [1270 himself as a swan or a bull or a shower of rain or what-have-you, lay with some beautiful woman and begot a hero. For the Public has grown too sophisticated. Under all the charming metaphors and symbols, it detects the stern command, "Be and act heroically"; behind the myth of divine origin, it senses the real human excellence   [1275 that is a reproach to its own baseness. So, with a bellow of rage, it kicks Poetry downstairs and sends for Prophecy. "Your sister has just insulted me. I asked for a God who should be as like me as possible. What use to me is a God whose divinity consists in doing diffi-

cult things that I cannot do or saying clever things that I [1280
cannot understand? The God I want and intend to get must be someone I can recognise immediately without having to wait and see what
he says or does. There must be nothing in the least extraordinary about
him. Produce him at once, please. I'm sick of waiting."

Today, apparently, judging by the trio who came to see [1285
me this morning with an ecstatic grin on their scholarly faces, the job
has been done. "God has been born," they cried, "we have seen him
ourselves. The World is saved. Nothing else matters."

One needn't be much of a psychologist to realise that if this rumour
is not stamped out now, in a few years it is capable of diseas- [1290
ing the whole Empire, and one doesn't have to be a prophet to predict
the consequences if it should.

Reason will be replaced by Revelation. Instead of Rational Law, objective truths perceptible to any who will undergo the necessary intellectual discipline, and the same for all, Knowledge will de- [1295
generate into a riot of subjective visions—feelings in the solar plexus
induced by undernourishment, angelic images generated by fevers or
drugs, dream warnings inspired by the sound of falling water. Whole
cosmogonies will be created out of some forgotten personal resentment, complete epics written in private languages, the daubs [1300
of school children ranked above the greatest masterpieces.

Idealism will be replaced by Materialism. Priapus will only have to
move to a good address and call himself Eros to become the darling of
middle-aged women. Life after death will be an eternal dinner party
where all the guests are twenty years old. Diverted from [1305
its normal and wholesome outlet in patriotism and civic or family
pride, the need of the materialistic Masses for some visible Idol to
worship will be driven into totally unsocial channels where no education can reach it. Divine honours will be paid to silver teapots, shallow
depressions in the earth, names on maps, domestic pets, [1310
ruined windmills, even in extreme cases, which will become increas-
ingly common, to headaches, or malignant tumours, or four o'clock in
the afternoon.

Justice will be replaced by Pity as the cardinal human virtue, and
all fear of retribution will vanish. Every corner-boy will con- [1315
gratulate himself: "I'm such a sinner that God had to come down in
person to save me. I must be a devil of a fellow." Every crook will
argue: "I like committing crimes. God likes forgiving them. Really
the world is admirably arranged." And the ambition of every young

---

1302. *Priapus:* god of sexuality and fertility. 1303. *Eros:* god of love.

cop will be to secure a death-bed repentance. The New Aris-   [1320
tocracy will consist exclusively of hermits, bums, and permanent inva-
lids. The Rough Diamond, the Consumptive Whore, the bandit who
is good to his mother, the epileptic girl who has a way with animals
will be the heroes and heroines of the New Tragedy when the general,
the statesman, and the philosopher have become the butt of   [1325
every farce and satire.

Naturally this cannot be allowed to happen. Civilisation must be
saved even if this means sending for the military, as I suppose it does.
How dreary. Why is it that in the end civilisation always has to call
in these professional tidiers to whom it is all one whether   [1330
it be Pythagoras or a homicidal lunatic that they are instructed to
exterminate. O dear, Why couldn't this wretched infant be born
somewhere else? Why can't people be sensible? I don't want to be
horrid. Why can't they see that the notion of a finite God is absurd?
Because it is. And suppose, just for the sake of argument,   [1335
that it isn't, that this story is true, that this child is in some inexplicable manner both God and Man, that he grows up, lives, and dies,
without committing a single sin? Would that make life any better?
On the contrary it would make it far, far worse. For it could only
mean this; that once having shown them how, God would   [1340
expect every man, whatever his fortune, to lead a sinless life in the flesh
and on earth. Then indeed would the human race be plunged into
madness and despair. And for me personally at this moment it would
mean that God had given me the power to destroy Himself. I refuse
to be taken in. He could not play such a horrible practical   [1345
joke. Why should He dislike me so? I've worked like a slave. Ask
anyone you like. I read all official dispatches without skipping. I've
taken elocution lessons. I've hardly ever taken bribes. How dare He
allow me to decide? I've tried to be good. I brush my teeth every
night. I haven't had sex for a month. I object. I'm a liberal.   [1350
I want everyone to be happy. I wish I had never been born.

II

Soldiers

When the Sex War ended with the slaughter of the Grandmothers,
They found a bachelor's baby suffocating under them;

1331. *Pythagoras:* pre-Socratic philosopher.

Section title, *Soldiers:* Matthew 2: 16: Then Herod . . . was exceeding
wroth, and sent forth and slew all the children that were in Bethlehem,
and in all the coasts thereof, from two years old and under. . . .

Somebody called him George and that was the end of it:
  They hitched him up to the Army.   1355
  George, you old debutante,
  How did you get in the Army?

In the Retreat from Reason he deserted on his rocking-horse
And lived on a fairy's kindness till he tired of kicking her;   1359
He smashed her spectacles and stole her check-book and mackintosh
  Then cruised his way back to the Army.
  George, you old numero,
  How did you get in the Army?

Before the Diet of Sugar he was using razor-blades
And exited soon after with an allergy to maidenheads;   1365
He discovered a cure of his own, but no one would patent it,
  So he showed up again in the Army.
  George, you old flybynight,
  How did you get in the Army?   1369

When the Vice Crusades were over he was hired by some Muscovites
Prospecting for deodorants among the Eskimos;
He was caught by a common cold and condemned to the whiskey
    mines,
  But schemozzled back to the Army.
  George, you old Emperor,
  How did you get in the Army?   1375

Since Peace was signed with Honour he's been minding his business;
But, whoops, here comes His Idleness, buttoning his uniform;
Just in tidy time to massacre the Innocents;
  He's come home to roost in the Army.
  George, you old matador,   1380
  Welcome back to the Army.

III

Rachel

On the Left are grinning dogs, peering down into a solitude too deep
  to fill with roses.

Section title, *Rachel:* Matthew 2: 17-18: "Then was fulfilled that which
was spoken by Jeremy the prophet, saying, In Rama was there a voice
heard, lamentation and weeping, and great mourning, Rachel weeping for
her children and would not be comforted, because they are not."

On the Right are sensible sheep, gazing up at a pride where no dream
    can grow.
Somewhere in these unending wastes of delirium is a lost child, speak-
    ing of Long Ago in the language of wounds.
Tomorrow, perhaps, he will come to himself in Heaven.   1385
But here Grief turns her silence, neither in this direction, nor in that,
    nor for any reason.
And her coldness now is on the earth forever.

THE FLIGHT INTO EGYPT

I

Joseph

Mirror, let us through the glass
No authority can pass.

Mary

Echo, if the strong should come,   1390
Tell a white lie or be dumb.

Voices of the Desert

It was visitors' day at the vinegar works
In Tenderloin Town when I tore my time;
A sorrowful snapshot was my sinful wage:
Was that why you left me, elusive bones?   1395
   Come to our bracing desert
   Where eternity is eventful,
     For the weather-glass
     Is set at Alas,
   The thermometer at Resentful.   1400

Section title, *The Flight:* Matthew 2: 13-14: ". . . behold, the angel of
the lord appeareth to Joseph in a dream, saying, Arise, and take the young
child and his mother and flee into Egypt, and be thou there until I bring
thee word: for Herod will seek the young child to destroy him. When
he arose, he took the young child and his mother by night, and departed
into Egypt."

Mary

The Kingdom of the Robbers lies
Between Time and our memories;

Joseph

Fugitives from Space must cross
The waste of the Anonymous.

Voices of the Desert

How should he figure my fear of the dark?   1405
The moment he can he'll remember me,
The silly, he locked in the cellar for fun,
And his dear little doggie shall die in his arms.
  Come to our old-world desert
  Where everyone goes to pieces;   1410
    You can pick up tears
    For souvenirs
  Or genuine diseases.

Joseph

Geysers and volcanoes give
Sudden comical relief;   1415

Mary

And the vulture is a boon
On a dull hot afternoon.

Voices of the Desert

All Father's nightingales knew their place,
The gardens were loyal: look at them now.
The roads are so careless, the rivers so rude,   1420
My studs have been stolen; I must speak to the sea.
  Come to our well-run desert
  Where anguish arrives by cable,
    And the deadly sins
    May be bought in tins   1425
  With instructions on the label.

Mary

Skulls recurring every mile
Direct the thirsty to the Nile;

Joseph

And the jackal's eye at night
Forces Error to keep right.   1430

Voices of the Desert

In a land of lilies I lost my wits,
Nude as a number all night I ran
With a ghost for a guest along green canals;
By the waters of waking I wept for the weeds.
  Come to our jolly desert   1435
  Where even the dolls go whoring;
    Where cigarette-ends
    Become intimate friends,
  And it's always three in the morning.

Joseph and Mary

Safe in Egypt we shall sigh   1440
For lost insecurity;
Only when her terrors come
Does our flesh feel quite at home.

II

Recitative

Fly, Holy Family, from our immediate rage,
That our future may be freed from our past; retrace   1445
    The footsteps of law-giving
  Moses, back through the sterile waste,

Down to the rotten kingdom of Egypt, the damp
Tired delta where in her season of glory our
    Forefathers sighed in bondage;   1450
  Abscond with the Child to the place

That their children dare not revisit, to the time
They do not care to remember; hide from our pride
    In our humiliation;
  Fly from our death with our new life.   1455

III

Narrator

Well, so that is that. Now we must dismantle the tree,
Putting the decorations back into their cardboard boxes—
Some have got broken—and carrying them up to the attic.
The holly and the mistletoe must be taken down and burnt,
And the children got ready for school. There are enough   1460
Left-overs to do, warmed-up, for the rest of the week—
Not that we have much appetite, having drunk such a lot,
Stayed up so late, attempted—quite unsuccessfully—
To love all of our relatives, and in general
Grossly overestimated our powers. Once again   1465
As in previous years we have seen the actual Vision and failed
To do more than entertain it as an agreeable
Possibility, once again we have sent Him away,
Begging though to remain His disobedient servant,
The promising child who cannot keep His word for long.   1470
The Christmas Feast is already a fading memory,
And already the mind begins to be vaguely aware
Of an unpleasant whiff of apprehension at the thought
Of Lent and Good Friday which cannot, after all, now
Be very far off. But, for the time being, here we all are,   1475
Back in the moderate Aristotelian city
Of darning and the Eight-Fifteen, where Euclid's geometry
And Newton's mechanics would account for our experience,
And the kitchen table exists because I scrub it.
It seems to have shrunk during the holidays. The streets   1480
Are much narrower than we remembered; we had forgotten
The office was as depressing as this. To those who have seen
The Child, however dimly, however incredulously,
The Time Being is, in a sense, the most trying time of all.
For the innocent children who whispered so excitedly   1485
Outside the locked door where they knew the presents to be
Grew up when it opened. Now, recollecting that moment
We can repress the joy, but the guilt remains conscious;
Remembering the stable where for once in our lives
Everything became a You and nothing was an It.   1490
And craving the sensation but ignoring the cause,
We look round for something, no matter what, to inhibit
Our self-reflection, and the obvious thing for that purpose
Would be some great suffering. So, once we have met the Son,

We are tempted ever after to pray to the Father;   1495
"Lead us into temptation and evil for our sake."
They will come, all right, don't worry; probably in a form
That we do not expect, and certainly with a force
More dreadful than we can imagine. In the meantime
There are bills to be paid, machines to keep in repair,   1500
Irregular verbs to learn, the Time Being to redeem
From insignificance. The happy morning is over,
The night of agony still to come; the time is noon:
When the Spirit must practise his scales of rejoicing
Without even a hostile audience, and the Soul endure   1505
A silence that is neither for nor against her faith
That God's Will will be done, that, in spite of her prayers,
God will cheat no one, not even the world of its triumph.

IV

Chorus

He is the Way.
Follow Him through the Land of Unlikeness;   1510
You will see rare beasts, and have unique adventures.

He is the Truth.
Seek Him in the Kingdom of Anxiety;
You will come to a great city that has expected your return for years.

He is the Life.   1515
Love Him in the World of the Flesh;
And at your marriage all its occasions shall dance for joy.

Selected Modern Poems

Emily Dickinson

I LIKE TO SEE IT LAP THE MILES

(1890)

I like to hear it lap the miles,
And lick the valleys up,
And stop to feed itself at tanks;
And then, prodigious, step

Around a pile of mountains,   5
And, supercilious, peer
In shanties by the sides of roads;
And then a quarry pare

To fit its ribs, and crawl between,
Complaining all the while   10
In horrid, hooting stanza;
Then chase itself down hill

And neigh like Boanerges;
Then, punctual as a star,
Stop—docile and omnipotent—   15
At its own stable door.

❧

The selections from Emily Dickinson are used with the permission of Harvard University Press from THE POEMS OF EMILY DICKINSON, *Thomas H. Johnson, Editor, Cambridge, Mass.: Harvard University Press, copyright, 1951, 1955, by the President and Fellows of Harvard College.*

I LIKE TO SEE: 13. *Boanerges:* "sons of thunder": the name given by Christ to James and John (Mark iii: 17) because they offered to call down fire from heaven upon the inhospitable Samaritans (Luke 9: 54).

A NARROW FELLOW IN THE GRASS

(1890)

A narrow fellow in the grass
Occasionally rides;
You may have met him,—did you not?
His notice sudden is.

The grass divides as with a comb,   5
A spotted shaft is seen;
And then it closes at your feet
And opens further on.

He likes a boggy acre,
A floor too cool for corn.   10
But when a boy, and barefoot,
I more than once at noon

Have passed, I thought, a whip-lash
Unbraiding in the sun,—
When, stooping to secure it,   15
It wrinkled, and was gone.

Several of nature's people
I know, and they know me;
I feel for them a transport
Of cordiality;   20

But never met this fellow,
Attended or alone,
Without a tighter breathing,
And zero at the bone.

THERE'S A CERTAIN SLANT OF LIGHT
(1890)

There's a certain slant of light,
Winter afternoons,
That oppresses, like the heft
Of cathedral tunes.

Heavenly hurt it gives us;   5
We can find no scar,
But internal difference
Where the meanings are.

None may teach it—Any—
'Tis the seal, despair,—   10
An imperial affliction
Sent us of the air.

When it comes, the landscape listens,
Shadows hold their breath;
When it goes, 'tis like the distance   15
On the look of death.

I DIED FOR BEAUTY

(1890)

I died for beauty, but was scarce
Adjusted in the tomb,
When one who died for truth was lain
In an adjoining room.

He questioned softly why I failed?   5
"For beauty," I replied.
"And I for truth,—Themself are one;
We brethren are," he said.

And so, as kinsmen, met a night,
We talked between the rooms,   10
Until the moss had reached our lips,
And covered up our names.

BECAUSE I COULD NOT STOP FOR DEATH

(1890)

Because I could not stop for Death,
He kindly stopped for me;
The carriage held but just ourselves
And Immortality.

We slowly drove, he knew no haste,   5
And I had put away
My labor, and my leisure too,
For his civility.

We passed the school where children strove
At recess in the ring,   10
We passed the fields of gazing grain,
We passed the setting sun,

Or rather, he passed us—
The dews drew quivering and chill,
For only gossamer my gown,   15
My tippet only tulle.

We paused before a house that seemed
A swelling of the ground;
The roof was scarcely visible,
The cornice in the ground.   20

Since then—'tis centuries—and yet
Feels shorter than the day
I first surmised the horses' heads
Were toward eternity.

I HEARD A FLY BUZZ WHEN I DIED

(1890)

I heard a fly buzz when I died;
   The stillness in the room
Was like the stillness in the air
   Between the heaves of storm.

The eyes around had wrung them dry,   5
   And breaths were gathering firm
For that last onset, when the king
   Be witnessed in the room.

I willed my keepsakes, signed away
   What portion of me be   10
Assignable,—and then it was
   There interposed a fly,

With blue, uncertain, stumbling buzz,
   Between the light and me;
And then the windows failed, and then   15
   I could not see to see.

Thomas Hardy

THE RUINED MAID

(1866)

"O 'Melia, my dear, this does everything crown!
Who could have supposed I should meet you in Town?
And whence such fair garments, such prosperi—ty?"—
"O didn't you know I'd been ruined?" said she.

—"You left us in tatters, without shoes or socks,   5
Tired of digging potatoes, and spudding up docks;
And now you've gay bracelets and bright feathers three!"—
"Yes: that's how we dress when we're ruined," said she.

—"At home in the barton you said 'thee' and 'thou',
And 'thik oon', and 'theäs oon', and 't 'other'; but now   10
Your talking quite fits 'ee for high compa—ny!"—
"Some polish is gained with one's ruin," said she.

—"Your hands were like paws then, your face blue and bleak
But now I'm bewitched by your delicate cheek,
And your little gloves fit as on any la—dy!"—   15
"We never do work when we're ruined," says she.

—"You used to call home-life a hag-ridden dream,
And you'd sigh, and you'd sock; but at present you seem

THE RUINED MAID: 6. *spudding . . . docks:* digging out dockweed. 7.
feathers: i.e., a fancy headdress or hat. 9. *barton:* farm-yard. 18. *sock:*
sigh audibly. 19. *megrims:* low spirits, the dumps.

To know not of megrims or melancho—ly!"—
"True. One's pretty lively when ruined," said she.   20

—"I wish I had feathers, a fine sweeping gown,
And a delicate face, and could strut about Town!"—
"My dear—a raw country girl, such as you be,
Cannot quite expect that. You ain't ruined," said she.

THE DARKLING THRUSH

(1900)

I leaned upon a coppice gate
   When Frost was specter-gray,
And Winter's dregs made desolate
   The weakening eye of day.
The tangled bine-stems scored the sky   5
   Like strings from broken lyres,
And all mankind that haunted nigh
   Had sought their household fires.

The land's sharp features seemed to be
   The Century's corpse outleant;   10
His crypt the cloudy canopy,
   The wind his death-lament.
The ancient pulse of germ and birth
   Was shrunken hard and dry,
And every spirit upon earth   15
   Seemed fervorless as I.

At once a voice burst forth among
   The bleak twigs overhead
In a full-hearted evensong
   Of joy illimited;   20
An agèd thrush, frail, gaunt and small,
   In blast-beruffled plume,
Had chosen thus to fling his soul
   Upon the growing gloom.

So little cause for carolings   25
   Of such ecstatic sound
Was written on terrestrial things
   Afar or nigh around,
That I could think there trembled through
   His happy good-night air   30
Some blessed hope, whereof he knew
   And I was unaware.

THE DARKLING THRUSH: 10. *outleant:* leaned out, perhaps both in the sense of outstretched (into the twentieth century) and thinned down.

CHANNEL FIRING

(April 1914)

That night your great guns, unawares,
Shook all our coffins as we lay,
And broke the chancel window-squares,
We thought it was the Judgment-day

And sat upright. While drearisome   5
Arose the howl of wakened hounds:
The mouse let fall the altar-crumb,
The worms drew back into the mounds,

The glebe cow drooled. Till God called, "No;
It's gunnery practice out at sea   10
Just as before you went below;
The world is as it used to be:

"All nations striving strong to make
Red war yet redder. Mad as hatters
They do no more for Christés sake   15
Than you who are helpless in such matters.

"That this is not the judgment-hour
For some of them's a blessèd thing,
For if it were they'd have to scour
Hell's floor for so much threatening . . .   20

"Ha, ha. It will be warmer when
I blow the trumpet (if indeed
I ever do; for you are men,
And rest eternal sorely need)."

So down we lay again. "I wonder,   25
Will the world ever saner be,"
Said one, "than when He sent us under
In our indifferent century!"

And many a skeleton shook his head.
"Instead of preaching forty year,"   30

CHANNEL FIRING: 15. *Cristés:* medieval spelling, evoking, with more modern colloquialisms, the timeless world in which this colloquy takes place.

My neighbour Parson Thirdly said,
"I wish I had stuck to pipes and beer."

Again the guns disturbed the hour,
Roaring their readiness to avenge,
As far inland as Stourton Tower,   35
And Camelot, and starlit Stonehenge.

❧

35. *Stourton Tower:* tower near Stourton in Wiltshire commemorating
King Alfred's victories over the Danes. 36. *Camelot:* legendary city of
King Arthur and his Table Round. *Stonehenge:* well-known open-air
sanctuary of large standing stones on Salisbury Plain, formerly supposed
to be the work of the Druids.

A. E. Housman

ON WENLOCK EDGE

(1896)

On Wenlock Edge the wood's in trouble;
    His forest fleece the Wrekin heaves;
The gale, it plies the saplings double,
    And thick on Severn snow the leaves.

'Twould blow like this through holt and hanger   5
    When Uricon the city stood:
'Tis the old wind in the old anger,
    But then it threshed another wood.

Then, 'twas before my time, the Roman
    At yonder heaving hill would stare: 10
The blood that warms an English yeoman,
    The thoughts that hurt him, they were there.

ON WENLOCK EDGE: 1, 2, 6. *Wenlok Edge, Wrekin, Uricon:* Wenlock and Uricon are the English and old Roman names for a town in Shropshire, where there exists a rocky hill known as the Wrekin, and a ridge called Wenlock Edge. 5. *holt and hanger:* Both words mean a steep wooded hill.

There, like the wind through woods in riot,
  Through him the gale of life blew high;
The tree of man was never quiet: 15
  Then 'twas the Roman, now 'tis I.

The gale, it plies the saplings double,
  It blows so hard, 'twill soon be gone:
To-day the Roman and his trouble
  Are ashes under Uricon.   20

TO AN ATHLETE DYING YOUNG
(1896)

The time you won your town the race
We chaired you through the market-place;
Man and boy stood cheering by,
And home we brought you shoulder-high.

To-day, the road all runners come,   5
Shoulder-high we bring you home,
And set you at your threshold down,
Townsman of a stiller town.

Smart lad, to slip betimes away
From fields where glory does not stay   10
And early though the laurel grows
It withers quicker than the rose.

Eyes the shady night has shut
Cannot see the record cut,
And silence sounds no worse than cheers   15
After earth has stopped the ears:

Now you will not swell the rout
Of lads that wore their honours out,
Runners whom renown outran
And the name died before the man.   20

So set, before its echoes fade,
The fleet foot on the sill of shade,
And hold to the low lintel up
The still-defended challenge-cup.

And round that early-laurelled head   25
Will flock to gaze the strengthless dead,
And find unwithered on its curls
The garland briefer than a girl's.

THE NIGHT IS FREEZING FAST

(1922)

The night is freezing fast,
   To-morrow comes December;
      And winterfalls of old
Are with me from the past;
   And chiefly I remember   5
      How Dick would hate the cold.

Fall, winter, fall; for he,
   Prompt hand and headpiece clever,
      Has woven a winter robe,
And made of earth and sea   10
   His overcoat for ever,
      And wears the turning globe.

EPITAPH ON AN ARMY OF MERCENARIES

(1922)

These, in the day when heaven was falling,
    The hour when earth's foundations fled,
Followed their mercenary calling
    And took their wages and are dead.

Their shoulders held the sky suspended;   5
    They stood, and earth's foundations stay;
What God abandoned, these defended,
    And saved the sum of things for pay.

DIFFUGERE NIVES

HORACE: *Odes* iv, 7.

(1936)

The snows are fled away, leaves on the shaws
    And grasses in the mead renew their birth,
The river to the river-bed withdraws,
    And altered is the fashion of the earth.

The Nymphs and Graces three put off their fear   5
    And unapparelled in the woodland play.
The swift hour and the brief prime of the year
    Say to the soul, *Thou wast not born for aye.*

Thaw follows frost; hard on the heel of spring
    Treads summer sure to die, for hard on hers   10
Comes autumn, with his apples scattering;
    Then back to wintertide, when nothing stirs.

But oh, whate'er the sky-led seasons mar,
    Moon upon moon rebuilds it with her beams:
Come *we* where Tullus and where Ancus are,   15
    And good Aeneas, we are dust and dreams.

Torquatus, if the gods in heaven shall add
    The morrow to the day, what tongue has told?
Feast then thy heart, for what thy heart has had
    The fingers of no heir will ever hold.   20

When thou descendest once the shades among,
    The stern assize and equal judgment o'er,
Not thy long lineage nor thy golden tongue,
    No, nor thy righteousness, shall friend thee more.

Night holds Hippolytus the pure of stain,   25
    Diana steads him nothing, he must stay;

DIFFUGERE NIVES: *Title:* The first clause in Horace's ode, which Housman
follows closely. 15. Tullus (Hostilius) and Ancus (Martius) were the third
and fourth Roman emperors after Romulus. 17. Torquatus was a friend of
Horace's. 25-6. Hippolytus, son of Theseus and Hippolyta, queen of the
Amazons, repulsed the advances of his stepmother Phaedra. She accused

And Theseus leaves Pirithöus in the chain
The love of comrades cannot take away.

him of attempting to dishonor her, whereupon Theseus cursed his son, and as a result the sea god Poseidon sent a monster which frightened Hippolytus's horses, causing him to be dragged to death. Unable to restore him to life, Diana, goddess of chastity, placed his body in a grove where it was worshipped. 27-8. Theseus, king of Thebes and the conqueror of the Minotaur, the Centaurs, and the Amazons, descended into Hades with his heroic companion Pirithöus to free Persephone. They were held prisoner, and when Hercules attempted to rescue them, Pirithöus was wrenched from Theseus' grasp and left chained to a rock.

Edwin Arlington Robinson

MR FLOOD'S PARTY

(1921)

Old Eben Flood, climbing alone one night
Over the hill between the town below
And the forsaken upland hermitage
That held as much as he should ever know
On earth again of home, paused warily.   5
The road was his with not a native near;
And Eben, having leisure, said aloud,
For no man else in Tilbury Town to hear:

"Well, Mr Flood, we have the harvest moon
Again, and we may not have many more;   10
The bird is on the wing, the poet says,
And you and I have said it here before.
Drink to the bird." He raised up to the light
The jug that he had gone so far to fill,
And answered huskily: "Well, Mr Flood,   15
Since you propose it, I believe I will."

Alone, as if enduring to the end
A valiant armour of scarred hopes outworn,
He stood there in the middle of the road
Like Roland's ghost winding a silent horn.   20

The selections from Edwin Arlington Robinson are used with the permission of The Macmillan Company: "Mr. Flood's Party" is *from* COLLECTED POEMS of Edwin Arlington Robinson, *copyright 1921 by Edwin Arlington Robinson, copyright renewed 1949 by The Macmillan Company;* "New England" *is from* COLLECTED POEMS of Edward Arlington Robinson, *copyright 1925.*

MR. FLOOD'S PARTY: 8. *Tilbury Town:* fictional town inhabited by many of Robinson's characters. 11. *poet:* Edward Fitzgerald, in his Rubaiyat (1859), sta. 7. 20. *Roland:* hero of the *Chanson de Roland,* who, fighting a desperate and losing rearguard action (like Mr. Flood), blows his horn for help in vain.

Below him, in the town among the trees,
Where friends of other days had honored him,
A phantom salutation of the dead
Rang thinly till old Eben's eyes were dim.

Then, as a mother lays her sleeping child   25
Down tenderly, fearing it may awake,
He set the jug down slowly at his feet
With trembling care, knowing that most things break;
And only when assured that on firm earth
It stood, as the uncertain lives of men   30
Assuredly did not, he paced away,
And with his hand extended paused again:

"Well, Mr Flood, we have not met like this
In a long time; and many a change has come
To both of us, I fear, since last it was   35
We had a drop together. Welcome home!"
Convivially returning with himself,
Again he raised the jug up to the light;
And with an acquiescent quaver said:
"Well, Mr Flood, if you insist, I might.   40

"Only a very little, Mr Flood—
For auld lang syne. No more, sir; that will do."
So, for the time, apparently it did,
And Eben evidently thought so too;
For soon amid the silver loneliness   45
Of night he lifted up his voice and sang,
Secure, with only two moons listening,
Until the whole harmonious landscape rang—

'For auld lang syne.' The weary throat gave out,
The last word wavered, and the song was done.   50
He raised again the jug regretfully
And shook his head, and was again alone.
There was not much that was ahead of him,
And there was nothing in the town below—
Where strangers would have shut the many doors   55
That many friends had opened long ago.

NEW ENGLAND

(1925)

Here where the wind is always north-north-east
And children learn to walk on frozen toes,
Wonder begets an envy of all those
Who boil elsewhere with such a lyric yeast
Of love that you will hear them at a feast   5
Where demons would appeal for some repose,
Still clamouring where the chalice overflows
And crying wildest who have drunk the least.

Passion is here a soilure of the wits,
We're old, and Love a cross for them to bear;   10
Joy shivers in the corner where she knits
And Conscience always has the rocking-chair,
Cheerful as when she tortured into fits
The first cat that was ever killed by Care.

Wallace Stevens

PETER QUINCE AT THE CLAVIER

(1923)

I

Just as my fingers on these keys
Make music, so the selfsame sounds
On my spirit make a music, too.

Music is feeling, then, not sound;
And thus it is that what I feel,   5
Here in this room, desiring you,

Thinking of your blue-shadowed silk,
Is music. It is like the strain
Waked in the elders by Susanna.

Of a green evening, clear and warm,   10
She bathed in her still garden, while
The red-eyed elders watching, felt

The basses of their beings throb
In witching chords, and their thin blood
Pulse pizzicati of Hosanna.   15

The selections from Wallace Stevens are used by permission of Alfred A. Knopf, Inc.: "Peter Quince at the Clavier," "The Emperor of Ice-Cream," "The Snow Man," "The Idea of Order at Key West," "Connoisseur of Chaos," *and* "The Poems of Our Climate" *are from* THE COLLECTED POEMS OF WALLACE STEVENS, *copyright 1923, 1936, 1942 by Wallace Stevens. Renewed, 1951.*

PETER QUINCE: 9. *Susanna:* See Apocrypha. The innocent wife Susanna was spied on by the lascivious elders in her husband's absence; when she repulsed one of them, he accused her of adultery, but she was saved from death by Daniel, who exposed the elders.

II

In the green water, clear and warm,
Susanna lay.

She searched
The touch of springs,
And found   20
Concealed imaginings.
She sighed,
For so much melody.

Upon the bank, she stood
In the cool   25
Of spent emotions.
She felt, among the leaves,
The dew
Of old devotions.

She walked upon the grass,   30
Still quavering.
The winds were like her maids,
On timid feet,
Fetching her woven scarves,
Yet wavering.   35

A breath upon her hand
Muted the night.
She turned—
A cymbal crashed,
And roaring horns.   40

III

Soon, with a noise like tambourines,
Came her attendant Byzantines.

They wondered why Susanna cried
Against the elders by her side:

And as they whispered, the refrain   45
Was like a willow swept by rain.

Anon their lamps' uplifted flame
Revealed Susanna and her shame.

And then the simpering Byzantines,
Fled, with a noise like tambourines.   50

IV

Beauty is momentary in the mind—
The fitful tracing of a portal;
But in the flesh it is immortal.

The body dies; the body's beauty lives.
So evenings die, in their green going,　　　　　55
A wave, interminably flowing.

So gardens die, their meek breath scenting
The cowl of Winter, done repenting.
So maidens die to the auroral
Celebration of a maiden's choral.　　　　　60

Susanna's music touched the bawdy strings
Of those white elders; but, escaping,
Left only Death's ironic scraping.
Now in its immortality, it plays
On the clear viol of her memory,　　　　　65
And makes a constant sacrament of praise.

THE EMPEROR OF ICE-CREAM

(1923)

Call the roller of big cigars,
The muscular one, and bid him whip
In kitchen cups concupiscent curds.
Let the wenches dawdle in such dress
As they are used to wear, and let the boys   5
Bring flowers in last month's newspapers.
Let be be finale of seem.
The only emperor is the emperor of ice-cream.

Take from the dresser of deal,
Lacking the three glass knobs, that sheet   10
On which she embroidered fantails once
And spread it so as to cover her face.
If her horny feet protrude, they come
To show how cold she is, and dumb.
Let the lamp affix its beam.   15
The only emperor is the emperor of ice-cream.

THE SNOW MAN

(1923)

One must have a mind of winter
To regard the frost and the boughs
Of the pine-trees crusted with snow;

And have been cold a long time
To behold the junipers shagged with ice,   5
The spruces rough in the distant glitter

Of the January sun; and not to think
Of any misery in the sound of the wind,
In the sound of a few leaves,

Which is the sound of the land   10
Full of the same wind
That is blowing in the same bare place

For the listener, who listens in the snow,
And, nothing himself, beholds
Nothing that is not there and the nothing that is. 15

∾

THE IDEA OF ORDER AT KEY WEST

(1936)

She sang beyond the genius of the sea.
The water never formed to mind or voice,
Like a body wholly body, fluttering
Its empty sleeves; and yet its mimic motion
Made constant cry, caused constantly a cry,
That was not ours although we understood,
Inhuman, of the veritable ocean.

The sea was not a mask. No more was she.
The song and water were not medleyed sound
Even if what she sang was what she heard,
Since what she sang was uttered word by word.
It may be that in all her phrases stirred
The grinding water and the gasping wind;
But it was she and not the sea we heard.
For she was the maker of the song she sang,   **15**
The ever-hooded, tragic-gestured sea
Was merely a place by which she walked to sing.
Whose spirit is this? we said, because we knew
It was the spirit that we sought and knew
That we should ask this often as she sang.   **20**

If it was only the dark voice of the sea
That rose, or even colored by many waves;
If it was only the outer voice of sky
And cloud, of the sunken coral water-walled,
However clear, it would have been deep air,   **25**
The heaving speech of air, a summer sound
Repeated in a summer without end

And sound alone. But it was more than that,
More even than her voice, and ours, among
The meaningless plungings of water and the wind,   30
Theatrical distances, bronze shadows heaped
On high horizons, mountainous atmospheres
Of sky and sea.

           It was her voice that made
The sky acutest at its vanishing.   35
She measured to the hour its solitude.
She was the single artificer of the world
In which she sang. And when she sang, the sea,
Whatever self it had, became the self
That was her song, for she was the maker. Then we,   40
As we beheld her striding there alone,
Knew that there never was a world for her
Except the one she sang and, singing, made.

Ramon Fernandez, tell me, if you know,
Why, when the singing ended and we turned   45
Toward the town, tell why the glassy lights,
The lights in the fishing boats at anchor there,
As the night descended, tilting in the air,
Mastered the night and portioned out the sea,
Fixing emblazoned zones and fiery poles,   50
Arranging, deepening, enchanting night.
Oh! Blessed rage for order, pale Ramon,
The maker's rage to order words of the sea,
Words of the fragrant portals, dimly-starred,
And of ourselves and of our origins,   55
In ghostlier demarcations, keener sounds.

❧

——— ——— ———

THE IDEA OF ORDER: 44. Ramon Fernandez (1894-1944), French critic
whose influential *Messages* (1926) promulgates the doctrine that every
great writer manifests something very like what Stevens here calls a
rage for order, the necessity to achieve a personality and a world by
creative effort imposed on chaos.

CONNOISSEUR OF CHAOS

(1942)

I

A. A violent order is disorder; and
B. A great disorder is an order. These
Two things are one. (Pages of illustrations.)

II

If all the green of spring was blue, and it is;
If the flowers of South Africa were bright   5
On the tables of Connecticut, and they are;
If Englishmen lived without tea in Ceylon, and they do;
And if it all went on in an orderly way,
And it does; a law of inherent opposites,
Of essential unity, is as pleasant as port,   10
As pleasant as the brush-strokes of a bough,
An upper, particular bough in, say, Marchand.

III

After all the pretty contrast of life and death
Proves that these opposite things partake of one,
At least that was the theory, when bishops' books   15
Resolved the world. We cannot go back to that.
The squirming facts exceed the squamous mind,
If one may say so. And yet relation appears,
A small relation expanding like the shade
Of a cloud on sand, a shape on the side of a hill.   20

IV

A. Well, an old order is a violent one.
This proves nothing. Just one more truth, one more
Element in the immense disorder of truths.
B. It is April as I write. The wind
Is blowing after days of constant rain.   25
All this, of course, will come to summer soon.

CONNOISSEUR OF CHAOS: 12. *Marchand:* Jean Marchand (1883-1941),
French painter.

But suppose the disorder of truths should ever come
To an order, most Plantagenet, most fixed . . .
A great disorder is an order. Now, A
And B are not like statuary, posed   30
For a vista in the Louvre. They are things chalked
On the sidewalk so that the pensive man may see.

V

The pensive man . . . He sees that eagle float
For which the intricate Alps are a single nest.

---

28. *Plantagenet:* i.e., persisting, like the long line of Plantagenet kings on
the English throne.

THE POEMS OF OUR CLIMATE

(1942)

I

Clear water in a brilliant bowl,
Pink and white carnations. The light
In the room more like a snowy air,
Reflecting snow. A newly-fallen snow
At the end of winter when afternoons return.   5
Pink and white carnations—one desires
So much more than that. The day itself
Is simplified: a bowl of white,
Cold, a cold porcelain, low and round,
With nothing more than the carnations there.   10

II

Say even that this complete simplicity
Stripped one of all one's torments, concealed
The evilly compounded, vital I
And made it fresh in a world of white,
A world of clear water, brilliant-edged,   15
Still one would want more, one would need more,
More than a world of white and snowy scents.

III

There would still remain the never-resting mind,
So that one would want to escape, come back
To what had been so long composed.   20
The imperfect is our paradise.
Note that, in this bitterness, delight,
Since the imperfect is so hot in us,
Lies in flawed words and stubborn sounds.

William Carlos Williams

TRACT

(1917)

I WILL teach you my townspeople
how to perform a funeral—
for you have it over a troop
of artists—
unless one should scour the world—   5
you have the ground sense necessary.

See! the hearse leads.
I begin with a design for a hearse.
For Christ's sake not black—
nor white either—and not polished!   10
Let it be weathered—like a farm wagon—
with gilt wheels (this could be
applied fresh at small expense)
or no wheels at all:
a rough dray to drag over the ground.   15

Knock the glass out!
My God—glass, my townspeople!
For what purpose? Is it for the dead
to look out or for us to see
how well he is housed or to see
the flowers or the lack of them—   20
or what?
To keep the rain and snow from him?
He will have a heavier rain soon:

pebbles and dirt and what not.   25
Let there be no glass—
and no upholstery! phew!
and no little brass rollers
and small easy wheels on the bottom—
my townspeople what are you thinking of!   30
A rough plain hearse then
with gilt wheels and no top at all.
On this the coffin lies
by its own weight.

              No wreaths please—   35
especially no hot-house flowers.
Some common memento is better,
something he prized and is known by:
his old clothes—a few books perhaps—
God knows what! You realize   40
how we are about these things,
my townspeople—
something will be found—anything—
even flowers if he had come to that.
So much for the hearse.   45

For heaven's sake though see to the driver!
Take off the silk hat! In fact
that's no place at all for him
up there unceremoniously
dragging our friend out to his own dignity!   50
Bring him down—bring him down!
Low and inconspicuous! I'd not have him ride
on the wagon at all—damn him—
the undertaker's understrapper!
Let him hold the reins   55
and walk at the side
and inconspicuously too!

Then briefly as to yourselves:
Walk behind—as they do in France,
seventh class, or if you ride   60
Hell take curtains! Go with some show
of inconvenience; sit openly—
to the weather as to grief.
Or do you think you can shut grief in?
What—from us? We who have perhaps   65

nothing to lose? Share with us
share with us—it will be money
in your pockets.
                    Go now
I think you are ready.   70

David Herbert Lawrence

SNAKE

(1923)

A SNAKE came to my water-trough
On a hot, hot day, and I in pyjamas for the heat,
To drink there.

In the deep, strange-scented shade of the great dark carob-tree
I came down the steps with my pitcher   5
And must wait, must stand and wait, for there he was at the trough
    before me.
He reached down from a fissure in the earth-wall in the gloom
And trailed his yellow-brown slackness soft-bellied down, over the
    edge of the stone trough
And rested his throat upon the stone bottom,
And where the water had dripped from the tap, in a small clear-
    ness,   10
He sipped with his straight mouth,
Softly drank through his straight gums, into his slack long body,
Silently.

Someone was before me at my water-trough,
And I, like a second comer, waiting.   15

He lifted his head from his drinking, as cattle do,
And looked at me vaguely, as drinking cattle do,
And flickered his two-forked tongue from his lips, and mused a
    moment,
And stooped and drank a little more,

---

*The selection from D. H. Lawrence is used with the permission of The
Viking Press, Inc.: "Snake" is from* COLLECTED POEMS *by D. H. Lawrence,
copyright 1929 by Jonathan Cape and Harrison Smith, Inc.; copyright
1957 by Frieda Lawrence Ravagli.*

SNAKE: 66. *albatross:* in Coleridge's *Rime of the Ancient Mariner.*

Being earth brown, earth golden from the burning burning bowels
    of the earth   20
On the day of Sicilian July, with Etna smoking.

The voice of my education said to me
He must be killed,
For in Sicily the black, black snakes are innocent, the gold are
    venomous.

And voices in me said, If you were a man   25
You would take a stick and break him now, and finish him off.

But I must confess how I liked him,
How glad I was he had come like a guest in quiet, to drink at my
    water-trough
And depart peaceful, pacified, and thankless,
Into the burning bowels of this earth.   30

Was it cowardice, that I dared not kill him?
Was it perversity, that I longed to talk to him?
Was it humility, to feel so honoured?
I felt so honoured.

And yet those voices: 35
If you were not afraid, you would kill him!

And truly I was afraid, I was most afraid,
But even so, honoured still more
That he should seek my hospitality
From out the dark door of the secret earth.   40

He drank enough
And lifted his head, dreamily, as one who has drunken,
And flickered his tongue like a forked night on the air, so black,
Seeming to lick his lips,
And looked around like a god, unseeing, into the air,   45
And slowly turned his head,
And slowly, very slowly, as if thrice adream,
Proceeded to draw his slow length curving round
And climb again the broken bank of my wall-face.

And as he put his head into that dreadful hole,   50
And as he slowly drew up, snake-easing his shoulders, and entered
    farther,
A sort of horror, a sort of protest against his withdrawing into that
    horrid black hole,

Deliberately going into the blackness, and slowly drawing himself
    after,
Overcame me now his back was turned.
I looked round, I put down my pitcher   55
I picked up a clumsy log
And threw it at the water-trough with a clatter.

I think it did not hit him.
But suddenly that part of him that was left behind convulsed in
    undignified haste.
Writhed like lightning, and was gone   60
Into the black hole, the earth-lipped fissure in the wallfront,
At which, in the intense still noon, I stared with fascination.

And immediately I regretted it.
I thought how paltry, how vulgar, what a mean act!
I despised myself and the voices of my accursed human education. 65

And I thought of the albatross,
And I wished he would come back, my snake.

For he seemed to me again like a king,
Like a king in exile, uncrowned in the underworld,
Now due to be crowned again.   70

And so, I missed my chance with one of the lords
Of life.
And I have something to expiate;
A pettiness.

Ezra Pound

PORTRAIT D'UNE FEMME

(1912)

Your mind and you are our Sargasso Sea,
London has swept about you this score years
And bright ships left you this or that in fee:
Ideas, old gossip, oddments of all things,
Strange spars of knowledge and dimmed wares of price.   5
Great minds have sought you—lacking someone else.
You have been second always. Tragical?
No. You preferred it to the usual thing:
One dull man, dulling and uxorious,
One average mind—with one thought less, each year.   10
Oh, you are patient, I have seen you sit
Hours, where something might have floated up.
And now you pay one. Yes, you richly pay.
You are a person of some interest, one comes to you
And takes strange gain away: 15
Trophies fished up; some curious suggestion;
Fact that leads nowhere; and a tale or two,
Pregnant with mandrakes, or with something else
That might prove useful and yet never proves,
That never fits a corner or shows use,   20
Or finds its hour upon the loom of days:
The tarnished, gaudy, wonderful old work;
Idols and ambergris and rare inlays,
These are your riches, your great store; and yet
For all this sea-hoard of deciduous things,   25
Strange woods half sodden, and new brighter stuff:
In the slow float of differing light and deep,
No! there is nothing! In the whole and all,
Nothing that's quite your own.
                     Yet this is you.   30

THE LAKE ISLE

(1915)

O God, O Venus, O Mercury, patron of thieves,
Give me in due time, I beseech you, a little tobacco-shop,
With the little bright boxes
        piled up neatly upon the shelves
And the loose fragrant cavendish   5
        and the shag,
And the bright Virginia
        loose under the bright glass cases,
And a pair of scales not too greasy,
And the whores dropping in for a word or two in passing,   10
For a flip word, and to tidy their hair a bit.

O God, O Venus, O Mercury, patron of thieves,
Lend me a little tobacco-shop,
        or install me in any profession
Save this damned profession of writing,   15
        where one needs one's brains all the time.

❧

THE LAKE ISLE: an allusion to Yeats's *The Lake Isle of Innisfree.*

THE RIVER-MERCHANT'S WIFE:
A LETTER

(1915)

While my hair was still cut straight across my forehead
I played about the front gate, pulling flowers.
You came by on bamboo stilts, playing horse,
You walked about my seat, playing with blue plums.
And we went on living in the village of Chokan: 5
Two small people, without dislike or suspicion.

At fourteen I married My Lord you.
I never laughed, being bashful.
Lowering my head, I looked at the wall.
Called to, a thousand times, I never looked back.   10

At fifteen I stopped scowling,
I desired my dust to be mingled with yours
For ever and for ever and for ever.
Why should I climb the look out?

At sixteen you departed,   15
You went into far Ku-to-yen, by the river of swirling eddies,
And you have been gone five months.
The monkeys make sorrowful noise overhead.

You dragged your feet when you went out.
By the gate now, the moss is grown, the different mosses,   20
Too deep to clear them away!
The leaves fall early this autumn, in wind.
The paired butterflies are already yellow with August
Over the grass in the West garden;
They hurt me. I grow older.   25
If you are coming down through the narrows of the river Kiang,
Please let me know beforehand,
And I will come out to meet you
         As far as Cho-fu-Sa.

                                  By Rihaku

THE STUDY IN AESTHETICS

(1916)

The very small children in patched clothing,
Being smitten with an unusual wisdom,
Stopped in their play as she passed them
And cried up from their cobbles:
    Guarda! Ahi, guarda! ch' è be'a!   5

But three years after this
I heard the young Dante, whose last name I do not know—
For there are, in Sirmione, twenty-eight young Dantes and thirty-
    four Catulli;
And there had been a great catch of sardines,
And his elders   10
Were packing them in the great wooden boxes
For the market in Brescia, and he
Leapt about, snatching at the bright fish
And getting in both of their ways;
And in vain they commanded him to *sta fermo!*   15
And when they would not let him arrange
The fish in the boxes
He stroked those which were already arranged,
Murmuring for his own satisfaction
This identical phrase: 20
    Ch' è be'a.

And at this I was mildly abashed.

❧

THE STUDY: 5. *Guarda . . . be'a:* Look! Oh, look! That's beautiful! 15
sta fermo: be still!

E. P. ODE POUR L'ELECTION DE SON SÉPULCHRE

(1920)

I

For three years, out of key with his time,
He strove to resuscitate the dead art
Of poetry; to maintain "the sublime"
In the old sense. Wrong from the start—

No, hardly, but seeing he had been born   5
In a half-savage country, out of date;
Bent resolutely on wringing lilies from the acorn;
Capaneus; trout for factitious bait;

Ἴδμεν γάρ τοι πάνθ᾽, ὅσ᾽ ἐνὶ Τροίῃ
Caught in the unstopped ear;   10
Giving the rocks small lee-way
The chopped seas held him, therefore, that year.

His true Penelope was Flaubert,
He fished by obstinate isles;
Observed the elegance of Circe's hair   15
Rather than the mottoes on sundials.

Unaffected by "the march of events,"
He passed from men's memory in *l'an trentiesme,*
De son eage; the case presents
No adjunct to the Muses' diadem.   20

E. P. ODE: *Title:* The title—"E[zra] P[ound's] Ode for the Election of his Sepulchre"—is adapted from Pierre Ronsard's "Ode de l'élection de son sépulcre" (1550). 8. *Capaneus:* One of the seven heroes from Argos engaged in the assault against Thebes, on whose shield was written, "I shall burn the city" (Aeschylus, *Seven Against Thebes,* 434): a sentiment in which perhaps the poet sees a reflection of his own youthful ardor to set the world aflame. Capaneus was struck by a thunderbolt from Zeus when scaling the Theban walls. 9. "For we know all the things that in Troy [the Argives and Trojans suffered by the will of the gods]"—sung by the sirens to Odysseus (*Odyssey,* xii 189). The line may be read roughly as follows by those unfamiliar with the Greek alphabet: Ídmén gár tóy pánth hŏs (as in "dose") ăný Trói-áy. 18-19. *l'an . . . eage:* in the thirtieth year of his life—paraphrased from the French poet, Villon. "Trentiesme" is pronounced like modern French "trentième" and so does not affect the rhyme (with "diadem").

II

The age demanded an image
Of its accelerated grimace,
Something for the modern stage,
Not, at any rate, an Attic grace;

Not, not certainly, the obscure reveries   25
Of the inward gaze;
Better mendacities
Than the classics in paraphrase!

The "age demanded" chiefly a mould in plaster,
Made with no loss of time,   30
A prose kinema, not, not assuredly, alabaster
Or the "sculpture" of rhyme.

III

The tea-rose tea-gown, etc.
Supplants the mousseline of Cos,
The pianola "replaces"   35
Sappho's barbitos.

Christ follows Dionysus,
Phallic and ambrosial
Made way for macerations;
Caliban casts out Ariel.   40

All things are a flowing,
Sage Heracleitus says;
But a tawdry cheapness
Shall outlast our days.

Even the Christian beauty   45
Defects—after Samothrace;
We see τὸ καλὸν
Decreed in the market place.

---

31. *kinema:* movement (in contrast with the stillness and permanence suggested in "alabaster" and "sculpture." Cf. also, 41-2). 34. *mousseline of Cos:* an Aegean island, famous for its fine silk-like cloth. 36. *barbitos:* a kind of lyre or lute, symbol of lyric poetry. 41-2. See the notes to the epigraphs of Eliot's *Burnt Norton,* in this volume. 46. *Samothrace:* Aegean island, home of ancient religious mysteries and of the statue of the Winged Victory. 47. "The Beautiful."

Faun's flesh is not to us,
Nor the saint's vision.   50
We have the Press for wafer;
Franchise for circumcision.

All men, in law, are equals.
Free of Pisistratus,
We choose a knave or an eunuch   55
To rule over us.

O bright Apollo,
τίν' ἄνδρα, τίν' ἥρωα, τίνα θεὸν
What god, man, or hero
Shall I place a tin wreath upon!   60

IV

These fought in any case,
and some believing,
                    pro domo, in any case . . .

Some quick to arm,
some for adventure,   65
some for fear of weakness,
some from fear of censure,
some for love of slaughter, in imagination,
learning later . . .
some in fear, learning love of slaughter;   70

Died some, pro patria,
                    non "dulce" non "et decor" . . .
walked eye-deep in hell
believing in old men's lies, then unbelieving
came home, home to a lie,   75
home to many deceits,
home to old lies and new infamy;

---

54. *Pisistratus:* Athenian tyrant, B.C. 605-527. 58. "What man, what hero,
what god?" Pound invokes a more heroic age than our own by paraphras-
ing Pindar's Second Olympian Ode (on Theron of Agrigentum, l.2).
Transliteration of the Greek (tin andra, tin heroa, tina theon) reveals the
sardonic pun on "tin wreath" in l. 60.) 63. *pro domo:* "for home." 71-2.
pro . . . decor: "for their country, but not sweetly, nor in glory"—with
reference to Horace's famous line, *"Dulce et decorum est pro patria mori"*
(Sweet and fitting it is to die for one's country), *Odes* III ii 13.

usury age-old and age-thick
and liars in public places.

Daring as never before, wastage as never before.   80
Young blood and high blood,
fair cheeks, and fine bodies;

fortitude as never before,

frankness as never before,
disillusions as never told in the old days,   85
hysterias, trench confessions,
laughter out of dead bellies.

V

There died a myriad,
And of the best, among them,
For an old bitch gone in the teeth,   90
For a botched civilization,

Charm, smiling at the good mouth,
Quick eyes gone under earth's lid,

For two gross of broken statues,
For a few thousand battered books.   95

ENVOI (1919)
(1920)

Go, dumb-born book,
Tell her that sang me once that song of Lawes:
Hadst thou but song
As thou hast subjects known,
Then were there cause in thee that should condone   5
Even my faults that heavy upon me lie,
And build her glories their longevity.

Tell her that sheds
Such treasure in the air,
Recking naught else but that her graces give   10
Life to the moment,
I would bid them live
As roses might, in magic amber laid,
Red overwrought with orange and all made
One substance and one color   15
Braving time.

Tell her that goes
With song upon her lips
But sings not out the song, nor knows
The maker of it, some other mouth   20
May be as fair as hers,
Might, in new ages, gain her worshippers
When our two dusts with Waller's shall be laid,
Siftings on siftings in oblivion,
Till change hath broken down   25
All things save Beauty alone.

❧

ENVOI: 1. *Go . . . book:* Cf. Waller's "Go, lovely rose" (l. 23), set to music by Henry Lawes, the Elizabethan composer. See Vol. III.

HOMAGE TO SEXTUS PROPERTIUS
(1919)

VI

When, when, and whenever death closes our eyelids,
Moving naked over Acheron
Upon the one raft, victor and conquered together,
Marius and Jugurtha together,

                              one tangle of shadows.   5
Caesar plots against India,
Tigris and Euphrates shall, from now on, flow at his bidding,
Tibet shall be full of Roman policemen,
The Parthians shall get used to our statuary

                         and acquire a Roman religion; 10

One raft on the veiled flood of Acheron,
        Marius and Jugurtha together.
Nor at my funeral either will there be any long trail,
                bearing ancestral lares and images;
No trumpets filled with my emptiness,   15
Nor shall it be on an Atalic bed;
        The perfumed cloths shall be absent.
A small plebeian procession.
        Enough, enough and in plenty
There will be three books at my obsequies   20
Which I take, my not unworthy gift, to Persephone.

You will follow the bare scarified breast
Nor will you be weary of calling my name, nor too weary
        To place the last kiss on my lips
When the Syrian onyx is broken.   25

HOMAGE TO SEXTUS PROPERTIUS: This is the title of a collection of Pound's poems (1934) which are midway between translations of Propertius (a Roman poet writing from 30-15 B.C.) and original works placing modern (especially British) imperialism in a deflating context. 4. *Acheron:* river of the underworld. 4. *Marius and Jugurtha:* instances of death's catholicity (Marius of Rome being *victor* over Jugurtha of Numidia in 106 B.C.). 6. *Caesar:* Augustus, in whose reign the Roman Empire expanded rapidly eastward. 16. *Atalic:* i.e., rich (with reference to Attalus III, king of Pergamum, from whose splendor any great treasure was later called *Attalicus*). 21. *Persephone:* queen of the underworld. 25. *Syrian onyx:* ointment box made of Syrian onyx.

"He who is now vacant dust
                 Was once the slave of one passion:"
Give that much inscription
                 "Death why tardily come?"
You, sometimes, will lament a lost friend,   30
          For it is a custom:
This care for past men,

Since Adonis was gored in Idalia, and the Cytharean
Ran crying with out-spread hair,
          In vain, you call back the shade,   35
In vain, Cynthia. Vain call to unanswering shadow,
          Small talk comes from small bones.

---

33. *gored:* Adonis died from the thrust of a wild boar he was hunting,
after which not even his lover Aphrodite could restore him to life. 36.
Cynthia: any mourning lover (but specifically an aristocratic Roman
courtesan loved by Propertius, whose first book of poems is called by her
name).

From CANTO LXXXI

(1948)

libretto   Yet
Ere the season died a-cold
Borne upon a zephyr's shoulder
I rose through the aureate sky
        Lawes and Jenkyns guard thy rest   5
        Dolmetsch ever be thy guest,
Has he tempered the viol's wood
To enforce   both the grave   and the acute?
Has he curved us the bowl of the lute?
        Lawes and Jenkyns guard thy rest   10
        Dolmetsch ever be thy guest
Hast 'ou fashioned so airy a mood
   To draw up leaf from the root?
Hast 'ou found   a cloud   so light
   As seemed neither mist nor shade?   15

        Then resolve me, tell me aright
        If Waller sang or Dowland played,

   Your eyen two wol sleye me sodenly
   I may the beauté of hem nat susteyne

And for 180 years almost nothing.   20

Ed ascoltando al leggier mormorio
   there came new subtlety of eyes into my tent,

CANTO LXXXI: 5. *Lawes and Jenkyns:* Henry Lawes (1596-1662—but possibly also his brother William, b. 1645) and John Jenkins (1592-78), English composers. For Henry (?) Lawes and Waller (line 19), cf. Pound's *Envoi.* 6. *Dolmetsch:* Arnold Dolmetsch (1858-1940), French musician settled in London, maker of viols and other early instruments, a key figure in the revival of Renaissance and Baroque music. 9. *grave, acute:* musical terms meaning, respectively, lowered pitch and raised pitch. 17. *Waller, Dowland:* Edmund Waller (1608-87), Cavalier poet; John Dowland (1562?-1626?), greatest of English lutanists and composers for the lute. 18-19. Chaucer, *Merciles Beauté,* 6-7. 20. *180 years:* i.e., between Chaucer and the next great age of English poetry, the Elizabethan. 21. *Ed . . . mormorio:* "And listening to the light murmur." (Not a quotation but a phrase manufactured by Pound to suggest perhaps Dante, on whose account of the power of Beatrice's eyes he seems to draw in 22 ff.)

whether of spirit or hypostasis,
    but what the blindfold hides
or at carneval   25
                  nor any pair showed anger
    Saw but the eyes and stance between the eyes,
colour, diastasis,
      careless or unaware it had not the
    whole tent's room   30
nor was place for the full Εἰδώς
interpass, penetrate
      casting but shade beyond the other lights
        sky's clear
        night's sea   35
        green of the mountain pool
        shone from the unmasked eyes in half-mask's
          space.
What thou lovest well remains,
           the rest is dross
What thou lov'st well shall not be reft from thee   40
What thou lov'st well is thy true heritage
Whose world, or mine or theirs
        or is it of none?
First came the seen, then thus the palpable
    Elysium, though it were in the halls of hell,   45
What thou lovest well is thy true heritage

The ant's a centaur in his dragon world.
Pull down thy vanity, it is not man
Made courage, or made order, or made grace,
    Pull down thy vanity, I say pull down.   50
Learn of the green world what can be thy place
In scaled invention or true artistry,
Pull down thy vanity,
              Paquin pull down!
The green casque has outdone your elegance.   55

"Master thyself, then others shall thee beare"

---

28. *diastasis:* apartness, separation. 31. Εἰδώς: "knowing." 41. *heritage:*
what one inherits but also hands on. 54. *Paquin:* Parisian dress designer
of the 1920's. 55. *casque:* equally applicable to the perianth of orchids,
the so-called helmet of toucans (and certain other birds), and the fashions
of Paris. 56. Chaucer's *Balade de Bon Conseyl* (line 13), as paraphrased
in a pocket book of verse found by Pound in his prison camp at Pisa
when isolated from all other books.

      Pull down thy vanity
Thou art a beaten dog beneath the hail,
A swollen magpie in a fitful sun,
Half black half white
Nor knowst'ou wing from tail
Pull down thy vanity
            How mean thy hates
Fostered in falsity,
            Pull down thy vanity,   65
Rathe to destroy, niggard in charity,
Pull down thy vanity,
            I say pull down.

But to have done instead of not doing
            this is not vanity   70
To have, with decency, knocked
That a Blunt should open
      To have gathered from the air a live tradition
or from a fine old eye the unconquered flame
This is not vanity.   75
   Here error is all in the not done,
all in the diffidence that faltered,

❧

---

67. *rathe:* eager, quick (with possible pun on *wrath*). 72. *Blunt:* evidently
Wilfrid Scawen Blunt, poet and man of affairs, whom Pound saw much
of in his early days in London (possibly used with an allusion to "plain-
speaking"). 74. *eye:* probably the fine eye of William Butler Yeats. 77. The
Canto ends significantly with a comma.

Marianne Moore

POETRY

(1921)

I, too, dislike it: there are things that are important
        beyond all this fiddle.
Reading it, however, with a perfect contempt for it, one
        discovers in
it after all, a place for the genuine.
    Hands that can grasp, eyes
      that can dilate, hair that can rise   5
        if it must, these things are important not because a

high-sounding interpretation can be put upon them but because
        they are
useful. When they become so derivative as to become
        unintelligible,
the same thing may be said for all of us, that we
    do not admire what
    we cannot understand: the bat   10
        holding on upside down or in quest of something to

eat, elephants pushing, a wild horse taking a roll, a tireless
        wolf under
a tree, the immovable critic twitching his skin like a
        horse that feels a flea, the base-
ball fan, the statistician—   15
    nor is it valid
        to discriminate against "business documents and

school-books"; all these phenomena are important. One
        must make a distinction

*The selections from Marianne Moore are used with the permission of
The Macmillan Company:* "Poetry" *and* "The Grave" *are from* SELECTED
POEMS *by Marianne Moore, © 1935 by Marianne Moore.*

however: when dragged into prominence by half poets,
   the result is not poetry,
nor till the poets among us can be   20
  "literalists of
  the imagination"—above
   insolence and triviality and can present

for inspection, "imaginary gardens with real toads in them,"
   shall we have
it. In the meantime, if you demand on the one hand,   25
the raw material of poetry in
  all its rawness and
  that which is on the other hand
   genuine, you are interested in poetry.

A GRAVE

(1924)

Man looking into the sea,
taking the view from those who have as much right to it as you
      have to it yourself,
it is human nature to stand in the middle of a thing,
but you cannot stand in the middle of this;
the sea has nothing to give but a well excavated grave.   5
The firs stand in a procession, each with an emerald turkey-foot
      at the top,
reserved as their contours, saying nothing;
repression, however, is not the most obvious characteristic of
      the sea;
the sea is a collector, quick to return a rapacious look.
There are others besides you who have worn that look—   10
whose expression is no longer a protest; the fish no longer
      investigate them
for their bones have not lasted:
men lower nets, unconscious of the fact that they are desecrating
      a grave,
and row quickly away—the blades of the oars
moving together like the feet of water-spiders as if there were no 15
      such thing as death.
The wrinkles progress among themselves in a phalanx—beautiful
      under networks of foam,
and fade breathlessly while the sea rustles in and out of the
      seaweed;
the birds swim through the air at top speed, emitting catcalls as
      heretofore—
the tortoise-shell scourges about the feet of the cliffs, in motion
      beneath them;
and the ocean, under the pulsation of lighthouses and the noise 20
      of bell-buoys,
advances as usual, looking as if it were not that ocean in which
      dropped things are bound to sink—
in which if they turn and twist, it is neither with volition nor
      consciousness.

John Crowe Ransom

BELLS FOR JOHN WHITESIDES' DAUGHTER
(1924)

There was such speed in her little body,
And such lightness in her footfall,
It is no wonder that her brown study
Astonishes us all.

Her wars were bruited in our high window.   5
We looked among orchard trees and beyond,
Where she took arms against her shadow,
Or harried unto the pond

The lazy geese, like a snow cloud
Dripping their snow on the green grass,   10
Tricking and stopping, sleepy and proud,
Who cried in goose, Alas,

For the tireless heart within the little
Lady with rod that made them rise
From their noon apple-dreams, and scuttle   15
Goose-fashion under the skies!

But now go the bells, and we are ready;
In one house we are sternly stopped
To say we are vexed at her brown study,
Lying so primly propped.   20

THE EQUILIBRISTS

(1927)

Full of her long white arms and milky skin
He had a thousand times remembered sin.
Alone in the press of people travelled he,
Minding her jacinth and myrrh and ivory.

Mouth he remembered: the quaint orifice   5
From which came heat that flamed upon the kiss,
Till cold words came down spiral from the head,
Grey doves from the officious tower illsped.

Body: it was a white field ready for love.
On her body's field, with the gaunt tower above, 10
The lilies grew, beseeching him to take,
If he would pluck and wear them, bruise and break.

Eyes talking: Never mind the cruel words,
Embrace my flowers but not embrace the swords.
But what they said, the doves came straightway flying 15
And unsaid: Honor, Honor, they came crying.

Importunate her doves. Too pure, too wise,
Clambering on his shoulder, saying, Arise,
Leave me now, and never let us meet,
Eternal distance now command thy feet.   20

Predicament indeed, which thus discovers
Honor among thieves, Honor between lovers.
O such a little word is Honor, they feel!
But the grey word is between them cold as steel.

At length I saw these lovers fully were come   25
Into their torture of equilibrium:
Dreadfully had forsworn each other, and yet
They were bound each to each, and they did not forget.

And rigid as two painful stars, and twirled
About the clustered night their prison world,   30
They burned with fierce love always to come near,
But Honor beat them back and kept them clear.

Ah, the strict lovers, they are ruined now!
I cried in anger. But with puddled brow
Devising for those gibbeted and brave   35
Came I descanting: Man, what would you have?

For spin your period out, and draw your breath,
A kinder saeculum begins with Death.
Would you ascend to Heaven and bodiless dwell?
Or take your bodies honorless to Hell?   40

In Heaven you have heard no marriage is,
No white flesh tinder to your lecheries,
Your male and female tissue sweetly shaped
Sublimed away, and furious blood escaped.

Great lovers lie in Hell, the stubborn ones   45
Infatuate of the flesh upon the bones;
Stuprate, they rend each other when they kiss;
The pieces kiss again—no end to this.

But still I watched them spinning, orbited nice.
Their flames were not more radiant than their ice.   50
I dug in the quiet earth and wrought the tomb
And made these lines to memorize their doom:—

Equilibrists lie here; stranger, tread light;
Close, but untouching in each other's sight;
Mouldered the lips and ashy the tall skull,   55
Let them lie perilous and beautiful.

❧

Archibald MacLeish

THE END OF THE WORLD

(1926)

Quite unexpectedly, as Vasserot
The armless ambidextrian was lighting
A match between his great and second toe,
And Ralph the lion was engaged in biting
The neck of Madame Sossman while the drum   5
Pointed, and Teeny was about to cough
In waltz-time swinging Jocko by the thumb—
Quite unexpectedly the top blew off:

And there, there overhead, there, there hung over
Those thousands of white faces, those dazed eyes,   10
There in the starless dark the poise, the hover,
There with vast wings across the cancelled skies,
There in the sudden blackness the black pall
Of nothing, nothing, nothing—nothing at all.

The selections from Archibald MacLeish are used by permission of and arrangement with Houghton Mifflin Company, the authorized publishers: "End of the World," *from Archibald MacLeish,* STREETS IN THE MOON; "Eleven," *from Archibald MacLeish,* POEMS, 1924-33.

ELEVEN

(1933)

And summer mornings the mute child, rebellious,
Stupid, hating the words, the meanings, hating
The Think now, Think, the O but Think! would leave
On tiptoe the three chairs on the verandah
And crossing tree by tree the empty lawn   5
Push back the shed door and upon the sill
Stand pressing out the sunlight from his eyes
And enter and with outstretched fingers feel
The grindstone and behind it the bare wall
And turn and in the corner on the cool   10
Hard earth sit listening. And one by one,
Out of the dazzled shadow in the room
The shapes would gather, the brown plowshare, spades,
Mattocks, the polished helves of picks, a scythe
Hung from the rafters, shovels, slender tines   15
Glinting across the curve of sickles—shapes
Older than men were, the wise tools, the iron
Friendly with earth. And sit there quiet, breathing
The harsh dry smell of withered bulbs, the faint
Odor of dung, the silence. And outside   20
Beyond the half-shut door the blind leaves
And the corn moving. And at noon would come,
Up from the garden, his hard crooked hands
Gentle with earth, his knees still earth-stained, smelling
Of sun, of summer, the old gardener, like   25
A priest, like an interpreter, and bend
Over his baskets.
    And they would not speak:
They would say nothing. And the child would sit there
Happy as though he had no name, as though
He had been no one: like a leaf, a stem,   30
Like a root growing—

E. E. Cummings

CHANSON INNOCENTE

(1923)

in Just-
spring   when the world is mud-
luscious the little
lame balloonman

whistles   far   and wee   5

and eddieandbill come
running from marbles and
piracies and it's
spring

when the world is puddle-wonderful   10

the queer
old balloonman whistles
far   and   wee
and bettyandisbel come dancing
from hop-scotch and jump-rope and   15

it's
spring
and
        the

                goat-footed   20

balloonMan   whistles
far
and
wee

                        ⚬

A MAN WHO HAD FALLEN AMONG THIEVES

(1926)

a man who had fallen among thieves
lay by the roadside on his back
dressed in fifteenthrate ideas
wearing a round jeer for a hat

fate per a somewhat more than less   5
emancipated evening
had in return for consciousness
endowed him with a changeless grin

whereon a dozen staunch and leal
citizens did graze at pause   10
then fired by hypercivic zeal
sought newer pastures or because

swaddled with a frozen brook
of pinkest vomit out of eyes
which noticed nobody he looked   15
as if he did not care to rise

one hand did nothing on the vest
its wideflung friend clenched weakly dirt
while the mute trouserfly confessed
a button solemnly inert.   20

Brushing from whom the stiffened puke
i put him all into my arms
and staggered banged with terror through
a million billion trillion stars

❧

A MAN WHO HAD FALLEN: cf. Luke 10: 30 ff. 9. *leal:* loyal.

LOVE IS MORE THICKER
THAN FORGET

(1940)

love is more thicker than forget
more thinner than recall
more seldom than a wave is wet
more frequent than to fail

it is most mad and moonly   5
and less it shall unbe
than all the sea which only
is deeper than the sea

love is less always than to win
less never than alive   10
less bigger than the least begin
less littler than forgive

it is most sane and sunly
and more it cannot die
than all the sky which only   15
is higher than the sky

ANYONE LIVED IN A PRETTY HOW TOWN

(1940)

anyone lived in a pretty how town
(with up so floating many bells down)
spring summer autumn winter
he sang his didn't he danced his did.

Women and men(both little and small)   5
cared for anyone not at all
they sowed their isn't they reaped their same
sun moon stars rain

children guessed(but only a few
and down they forgot as up they grew   10
autumn winter spring summer)
that noone loved him more by more

when by now and tree by leaf
she laughed his joy she cried his grief
bird by snow and stir by still   15
anyone's any was all to her

someones married their everyones
laughed their cryings and did their dance
(sleep wake hope and then)they
said their nevers they slept their dream   20

stars rain sun moon
(and only the snow can begin to explain
how children are apt to forget to remember
with up so floating many bells down)

one day anyone died i guess   25
(and noone stooped to kiss his face)
busy folk buried them side by side
little by little and was by was

all by all and deep by deep
and more by more they dream their sleep   30
noone and anyone earth by april
wish by spirit and if by yes.

Women and men(both dong and ding)
summer autumn winter spring
reaped their sowing and went their came   35
sun moon stars rain

Allen Tate

ODE TO THE CONFEDERATE DEAD

(1937)

Row after row with strict impunity
The headstones yield their names to the element,
The wind whirrs without recollection;
In the riven troughs the splayed leaves
Pile up, of nature the casual sacrament   5
To the seasonal eternity of death;
Then driven by the fierce scrutiny
Of heaven to their election in the vast breath,
They sough the rumor of mortality.

ODE: *Title:* Tate discusses this poem in an essay entitled "Narcissus as Narcissus," reprinted in his *Reason in Madness* (1941) and *On the Limits of Poetry: Selected Essays, 1928-1948* (1948).

The speaker of the poem has stopped by the gate of a Confederate graveyard on a late autumn afternoon when the leaves are falling. Following a meditation on the destructiveness of time, he entertains in imagination the notion of an heroic age and an heroic society, sure enough of their convictions to permit the transcendence of self and death that heroic action requires. Of this notion, the leaves, when seen as soldiers, are symbolic. But the speaker is also aware that the necessary convictions are not his: as a child of the modern age he is a prisoner of the subjective, the self; he is a "locked-in ego"—of which the poem's symbols are the blind crab (energy without direction) and the jaguar (Narcissus) who leaps into the jungle pool, his own victim. For the man by the graveyard, therefore (*i.e.,* modern man in the world he has made for himself), the leaves can never be ultimately more than leaves, or death more than a chemical phenomenon stiffening "the saltier oblivion of the sea."

Autumn is desolation in the plot   10
Of a thousand acres where these memories grow
From the inexhaustible bodies that are not
Dead, but feed the grass row after rich row.
Think of the autumns that have come and gone!—
Ambitious November with the humors of the year,   15
With a particular zeal for every slab,
Staining the uncomfortable angels that rot
On the slabs, a wing chipped here, an arm there:
The brute curiosity of an angel's stare

Turns you, like them, to stone,
Transforms the heaving air
Till plunged to a heavier world below
You shift your sea-space blindly
Heaving, turning like the blind crab.

        Dazed by the wind, only the wind   25
        The leaves flying, plunge

You know who have waited by the wall
The twilight certainty of an animal,
Those midnight restitutions of the blood
You know—the immitigable pines, the smoky frieze   30
Of the sky, the sudden call: you know the rage,
The cold pool left by the mounting flood,
Of muted Zeno and Parmenides.
You who have waited for the angry resolution
Of those desires that should be yours tomorrow,   35
You know the unimportant shrift of death
And praise the vision
And praise the arrogant circumstance
Of those who fall
Rank upon rank, hurried beyond decision—   40
Here by the sagging gate, stopped by the wall.

---

33. *Zeno and Parmenides:* Parmenides and his disciple Zeno of Elea were
early Greek philosophers who opposed the Heracleitean doctrine of flux (see
the note to Eliot's *Burnt Norton*), and emphasized the stability, permanence,
and unity of things. Hence their names are invoked here in connection with
the heroic attitude, which only some such philosophy as theirs can nourish.
Muted refers perhaps to the way in which philosophies of this sort have
been silenced by the subjectiveness of our times; and also to the story that
Zeno, tortured by a tyrant for his attempt to restore the people's liberties, bit
off his own tongue in defiance and spat it at him.

Seeing, seeing only the leaves
Flying, plunge and expire

Turn your eyes to the immoderate past,
Turn to the inscrutable infantry rising   45
Demons out of the earth—they will not last.
Stonewall, Stonewall, and the sunken fields of hemp,
Shiloh, Antietam, Malvern Hill, Bull Run.
Lost in that orient of the thick and fast
You will curse the setting sun.   50

Cursing only the leaves crying
Like an old man in a storm

You hear the shout, the crazy hemlocks point
With troubled fingers to the silence which
Smothers you, a mummy, in time.   55

The hound bitch
Toothless and dying, in a musty cellar
Hears the wind only.

Now that the salt of their blood
Stiffens the saltier oblivion of the sea,   60
Seals the malignant purity of the flood,
What shall we who count our days and bow
Our heads with a commemorial woe
In the ribboned coats of grim felicity,
What shall we say of the bones, unclean,   65
Whose verdurous anonymity will grow?
The ragged arms, the ragged heads and eyes
Lost in these acres of the insane green?
The gray lean spiders come, they come and go;
In a tangle of willows without light   70
The singular screech-owl's tight
Invisible lyric seeds the mind
With the furious murmur of their chivalry.

We shall say only the leaves
Flying, plunge and expire   75

We shall say only the leaves whispering
In the improbable mist of nightfall
That flies on multiple wing:
Night is the beginning and the end
And in between the ends of distraction   80
Waits mute speculation, the patient curse

That stones the eyes, or like the jaguar leaps
For his own image in a jungle pool, his victim.

What shall we say who have knowledge
Carried to the heart? Shall we take the act 85
To the grave? Shall we, more hopeful, set up the grave
In the house? The ravenous grave?

Leave now
The shut gate and the decomposing wall:
The gentle serpent, green in the mulberry bush, 90
Riots with his tongue through the hush—
Sentinel of the grave who counts us all!

Richard Eberhart

THE FURY OF AERIAL BOMBARDMENT
(1944)

You would think the fury of aerial bombardment
Would rouse God to relent; the infinite spaces
Are still silent. He looks on shock-pried faces.
History, even, does not know what is meant.

You would feel that after so many centuries   5
God would give man to repent; yet he can kill
As Cain could, but with multitudinous will,
No farther advanced than in his ancient furies.

Was man made stupid to see his own stupidity?
Is God by definition indifferent, beyond us all?   10
Is the eternal truth man's fighting soul
Wherein the Beast ravens in its own avidity?

Of Van Wettering I speak, and Averill,
Names on a list, whose faces I do not recall
But they are gone to early death, who late in school   15
Distinguished the belt feed lever from the belt holding pawl.

❧

Robert Penn Warren

BEARDED OAKS

(1943)

The oaks, how subtle and marine,
Bearded, and all the layered light
Above them swims; and thus the scene,
Recessed, awaits the positive night.

So, waiting, we in the grass now lie   5
Beneath the languorous tread of light:
The grasses, kelp-like, satisfy
The nameless motions of the air.

Upon the floor of light, and time,
Unmurmuring, of polyp made,   10
We rest; we are, as light withdraws,
Twin atolls on a shelf of shade.

Ages to our construction went,
Dim architecture, hour by hour:
And violence, forgot now, lent   15
The present stillness all its power.

The storm of noon above us rolled,
Of light the fury, furious gold,
The long drag troubling us, the depth:
Dark is unrocking, unrippling, still.   20

Passion and slaughter, ruth, decay
Descend, minutely whispering down,
Silted down swaying streams, to lay
Foundation for our voicelessness.

All our debate is voiceless here,   25
As all our rage, the rage of stone;
If hope is hopeless, then fearless fear,
And history is thus undone.

Our feet once wrought the hollow street
With echo when the lamps were dead   30
At windows, once our headlight glare
Disturbed the doe that, leaping, fled.

I do not love you less that now
The caged heart makes iron stroke,
Or less that all that light once gave   35
The graduate dark should now revoke.

We live in time so little time
And we learn all so painfully,
That we may spare this hour's term
To practice for eternity.   40

Louis MacNeice

THE SUNLIGHT ON THE GARDEN
(1938)

The sunlight on the garden
Hardens and grows cold,
We cannot cage the minute
Within its nets of gold;
When all is told   5
We cannot beg for pardon.

Our freedom as free lances
Advances towards its end;
The earth compels, upon it
Sonnets and birds descend;   10
And soon, my friend,
We shall have no time for dances.

The sky was good for flying
Defying the church bells
And every evil iron   15
Siren and what it tells:
The earth compels,
We are dying, Egypt, dying

And not expecting pardon,
Hardened in heart anew,   20
But glad to have sat under
Thunder and rain with you,
And grateful too
For sunlight on the garden.

❧

The selections from Louis MacNeice are used with the permission of Random House, Inc., from POEMS, *1925-1940, by Louis MacNeice, copyright 1937, 1939, 1940, by Louis MacNeice.*

18. Cf. Antony's words to Cleopatra in *Antony and Cleopatra,* IV xiii.

LES SYLPHIDES

(1939-40)

Life in a day: he took his girl to the ballet;
Being shortsighted himself could hardly see it—
   The white skirts in the grey
   Glade and the swell of the music
   Lifting the white sails.   5

Calyx upon calyx, canterbury bells in the breeze
The flowers on the left mirror to the flowers on the right
   And the naked arms above
   The powdered faces moving
   Like seaweed in a pool.   10

Now, he thought, we are floating—ageless, oarless—
Now there is no separation, from now on
   You will be wearing white
   Satin and a red sash
   Under the waltzing trees.   15

But the music stopped, the dancers took their curtain,
The river had come to a lock—a shuffle of programmes—
   And we cannot continue down
   Stream unless we are ready
   To enter the lock and drop.   20

So they were married—to be the more together—
And found they were never again so much together,
   Divided by the morning tea,
   By the evening paper,
   By children and tradesmen's bills.   25

Waking at times in the night she found assurance
In his regular breathing but wondered whether
   It was really worth it and where
   The river had flowed away
   And where were the white flowers.   30

Theodore Roethke

THE WAKING

(1953)

I wake to sleep, and take my waking slow.
I feel my fate in what I cannot fear.
I learn by going where I have to go.

We think by feeling. What is there to know?
I hear my being dance from ear to ear. 5
I wake to sleep, and take my waking slow.

Of those so close beside me, which are you?
God bless the Ground! I shall walk softly there,
And learn by going where I have to go.

Light takes the Tree; but who can tell us how? 10
The lowly worm climbs up a winding stair;
I wake to sleep, and take my waking slow.

Great Nature has another thing to do
To you and me; so take the lively air,
And, lovely, learn by going where to go. 15

This shaking keeps me steady. I should know.
What falls away is always. And is near.
I wake to sleep, and take my waking slow.
I learn by going where I have to go.

I KNEW A WOMAN

(1954)

I knew a woman, lovely in her bon
When small birds sighed, she would sigh back at them;
Ah, when she moved, she moved more ways than one:
The shapes a bright container can contain!
Of her choice virtues only gods should speak,   5
Or English poets who grew up on Greek
(I'd have them sing in chorus, cheek to cheek).

How well her wishes went! She stroked my chin,
She taught me Turn, and Counter-turn, and Stand;
She taught me Touch, that undulant white skin;   10
I nibbled meekly from her proffered hand;
She was the sickle; I, poor I, the rake,
Coming behind her for her pretty sake
(But what prodigious mowing we did make).

Love likes a gander, and adores a goose: 15
Her full lips pursed, the errant note to seize;
She played it quick, she played it light and loose;
My eyes, they dazzled at her flowing knees;
Her several parts could keep a pure repose,
Or one hip quiver with a mobile nose   20
(She moved in circles, and those circles moved).

Let seed be grass, and grass turn into hay:
I'm martyr to a motion not my own;
What's freedom for? To know eternity.
I swear she cast a shadow white as stone.   25
But who would count eternity in days?
These old bones live to learn her wanton ways:
(I measure time by how a body sways).

The selections from Theodore Roethke are used with the permission of Doubleday & Company, Inc.: "The Waking" *is from* THE WAKING *by Theodore Roethke, copyright 1953 by Theodore Roethke;* "I Knew a Woman" *is from* WORDS FOR THE WIND *by Theodore Roethke, copyright 1954 by Theodore Roethke.*

Frank Templeton Prince

SOLDIERS BATHING

(1954)

The sea at evening moves across the sand,
And under a sunset sky I watch the freedom of a band
Of soldiers who belong to me. Stripped bare
For bathing in the sea, they shout and run in the warm air.
Their flesh, worn by the trade of war, revives   5
And my mind towards the meaning of it strives.

All's pathos now. The body that was gross,
Rank, ravening, disgusting in the act and in repose,
All fever, filth and sweat, all bestial strength
And bestial decay, by pain and labour grows at length   10
Fragile and luminous. "Poor bare forked animal,"
Conscious of his desires and needs and flesh that rise and fall,
Stands in the soft air, tasting after toil
The sweetness of his nakedness: letting the sea-waves coil
Their frothy tongues about his feet, forgets   15
His hatred of the war, its terrible pressure that begets
A machinery of death and slavery,
Each being a slave and making slaves of others: finds that he
Remembers his old freedom in a game
Mocking himself, and comically mimics fear and shame.   20

He plays with death and animality.
And reading in the shadows of his pallid flesh, I see
The idea of Michelangelo's cartoon

The selection, "Soldiers Bathing," published by Fortune Press, 1954, *is used with the permission of Frank Templeton Prince.*
SOLDIERS BATHING: 11. *"Poor . . . animal";* cf. *King Lear,* III iv 113. 23. *Cartoon:* Michelangelo's lost cartoon of "The Battle of Cascina," of which a copy is reproduced in L. Goldscheider's *Michel Angelo* (1953), Plate xxiv.

Of soldiers bathing, breaking off before they were half done
At some sortie of the enemy, an episode   25
Of the Pisan wars with Florence. I remember how he showed
Their muscular limbs that clamber from the water,
And heads that turn across the shoulder, eager for the slaughter,
Forgetful of their bodies that are bare,
And hot to buckle on and use the weapons lying there.   30
And I think too of the theme another found
When, shadowing lean bodies on a sinister red ground—
Another Florentine, Pollaiuolo,
Painted a naked battle: warriors straddled, hacked the foe,
Dug their bare toes into the soil and slew   35
The brother-naked man who lay between their feet and drew
His lips back from his teeth in a grimace.

They were Italians who knew war's sorrow and disgrace
And showed the thing suspended, stripped, a theme
Born out of the experience of war's horrible extreme   40
Beneath a sky where even the air flows
With *lachrimae Christi;* and that rage, that bitterness, those blows,
That hatred of the slain, what could they be
But indirectly or directly a commentary
On the crucifixion? And the picture burns   45
With indignation and pity and despair by turns
Because it is the obverse of the scene
Where Christ hangs murdered, stripped, upon the Cross: I mean,
That is the explanation of its rage.

And we too have our bitterness and pity that engage   50
Blood, spirit in this war. But night begins,
Night of the mind: who nowadays is conscious of our sins?
Though every human deed concerns our blood,
And even we must know what no one yet has understood,
That some great love is over what we do,   55
And that is what has driven us to this fury, for so few
Can suffer all the terror of that love:
The terror of that love has set us spinning in this groove
Greased with our blood.

              These dry themselves and dress,
Combing their hair, forget the fear and shame of nakedness.   60
Because to love is frightening we prefer

---

39. *naked battle:* Pollaiuolo's "Battle of the Nudes" in the Uffizi, Florence,
reproduced in Berenson's *Italian Painters of the Renaissance* (1952).

The freedom of our crimes. Yet as I drink the dusky air,
I feel a strange delight that fills me full,
A gratitude, as if evil itself were beautiful;
And kiss the wound in thought, while in the west   65
I watch a streak of red that might have issued from Christ's breast.

George Barker

TO MY MOTHER

(1941)

Most near, most dear, most loved and most far,
Under the window where I often found her
Sitting as huge as Asia, seismic with laughter,
Gin and chicken helpless in her Irish hand,
Irresistible as Rabelais, but most tender for   5
The lame dogs and hurt birds that surround her,—
She is a procession no one can follow after
But be like a little dog following a brass band.

She will not glance up at the bomber, or condescend
To drop her gin and scuttle to a cellar,   10
But lean on the mahogany table like a mountain
Whom only faith can move, and so I send
O all my faith and all my love to tell her
That she will move from mourning into morning.

&

The selection from George Barker is used with the permission of Faber
& Faber Ltd.: "To My Mother" is from EROS IN DOGMA (1944).
TO MY MOTHER: 5. *Rabelais:* French Renaissance writer of an inex-
haustible comic imagination.

John Frederick Nims

PENNY ARCADE

(1947)

This pale and dusty palace under the El
The ragged bankers of one coin frequent,
Beggars of joy, and in a box of glass
Control the destiny of some bright event.
Men black and bitter shuffle, grin like boys,   5
Recovering Christmas and elaborate toys.

The clerk controls the air gun's poodle puff
Or briefly the blue excalibur of a Colt,
Sweeps alien raiders from a painted sky,
And sees supreme the tin flotilla bolt.   10
Hard lightning in his eye, the hero smiles,
Steady MacArthur of the doodad is'es.

The trucker arrogant for his Sunday gal
Clouts the machine, is clocked as 'Superman!'
The stunted negro makes the mauler whirl   15
Toy iron limbs; his wizen features plan
The lunge of Louis, or, no longer black,
Send to the Pampas battering Firpo back.

Some for a penny in the slot of love
Fondle the bosom of aluminum whores,   20
Through hollow eye of lenses dryly suck
Beatitude of blondes and fallen drawers.

The selection from John Frederick Nims is used with the permission of William Sloane Associates: "Penny Arcade" *is from* THE IRON PASTORAL *by John Frederick Nims, copyright 1947 by John Frederick Nims.*

PENNY ARCADE: 1. *El:* elevated railway. 12. *MacArthur:* U. S. commander in Pacific during World War II. 17. *Louis:* Joe Louis, heavyweight boxing champion, 1937-1949. 18. *Firpo:* South American heavyweight contender, 1923-4.

For this Cithaeron wailed and Tempe sighed,
David was doomed, and young Actaeon died.

Who gather here will never move the stars,   25
Give law to nations, track the atom down.
For lack of love or vitamins or cash
All the red robins of their year have gone.
Here heaven ticks: the weariest tramp can buy
Glass mansions in the juke-seraphic sky.   30

~❧

23. *Cithaeron:* mountain where Actaeon died (24); *Tempe:* celebrated
Thessalian valley (but the instance of "spying" has not been identified).
24. *David:* King David, who watched Bathsheba bathing, disposed of
her husband, took her to wife, and "displeased the Lord" (2 Samuel 11).
Actaeon: who came upon Diana bathing and in punishment was turned
to a stag, whom his own dogs devoured.

Henry Reed

LESSONS OF THE WAR
To Alan Michell
(1947)

Vixi duellis nuper idoneus
Et militavi non sine gloria

I. Naming of Parts

To-day we have naming of parts. Yesterday,
We had daily cleaning. And to-morrow morning,
We shall have what to do after firing. But to-day,
To-day we have naming of parts. Japonica   5
Glistens like coral in all of the neighbouring gardens,
    And to-day we have naming of parts.

This is the lower sling swivel. And this
Is the upper sling swivel, whose use you will see,
When you are given your slings. And this is the piling swivel,   10
Which in your case you have not got. The branches
Hold in the gardens their silent, eloquent gestures,
    Which in our case we have not got.

This is the safety-catch, which is always released

The selection from Henry Reed is used with the permission of Harcourt, Brace, and Company, Inc. and Jonathan Cape Limited: "Lessons of The War" (I. Naming of Parts) *is from* A MAP OF VERONA *And Other Poems, copyright 1947 by Henry Reed.*

LESSONS OF THE WAR: Epigraph: "I have lived lately fit for the wars and have plied the soldier's trade not without glory" (Horace, *Odes,* III 26). Some MSS. of Horace have *puellis* (the girls) for *duellis* (the wars), and, in view of Reed's allusions in the poem, this fact may add an extra relevance to his use of this passage.

With an easy flick of the thumb. And please do not let me   15
See anyone using his finger. You can do it quite easy
If you have any strength in your thumb. The blossoms
Are fragile and motionless, never letting anyone see
    Any of them using their finger.

And this you can see is the bolt. The purpose of this   20
Is to open the breech, as you see. We can slide it
Rapidly backwards and forwards: we call this
Easing the spring. And rapidly backwards and forwards
The early bees are assaulting and fumbling the flowers:
    They call it easing the Spring.   25

They call it easing the Spring: it is perfectly easy
If you have any strength in your thumb: like the bolt,
And the breech, and the cocking-piece, and the point of balance,
Which in our case we have not; and the almond-blossom
Silent in all of the gardens and the bees going backwards and   30
    forwards,
    For to-day we have naming of parts.

Dylan Thomas

THE FORCE THAT THROUGH THE GREEN FUSE
DRIVES THE FLOWER

(1939)

The force that through the green fuse drives the flower
Drives my green age; that blasts the roots of trees
Is my destroyer.
And I am dumb to tell the crooked rose
My youth is bent by the same wintry fever.   5

The force that drives the water through the rocks
Drives my red blood; that dries the mouthing streams
Turns mine to wax.
And I am dumb to mouth unto my veins
How at the mountain spring the same mouth sucks.   10

The hand that whirls the water in the pool
Stirs the quicksand; that ropes the blowing wind
Hauls my shroud sail.
And I am dumb to tell the hanging man
How of my clay is made the hangman's lime.   15

The lips of time leech to the fountain head;
Love drips and gathers, but the fallen blood
Shall calm her sores.

The selections from Dylan Thomas are used with the permission of New Directions and J. M. Dent & Sons Ltd.: "The Force That Through the Green Fuse Drive the Flower" *and* "And Death Shall Have No Dominion" *are from* THE WORLD I BREATHE *by Dylan Thomas;* "Fern Hill" *and* "Do Not Go Gentle into That Good Night" *are from* THE COLLECTED POEMS OF DYLAN THOMAS, *copyright 1952, 1953 by Dylan Thomas.*

And I am dumb to tell a weather's wind
How time has ticked a heaven round the stars.   20

And I am dumb to tell the lover's tomb
How at my sheet goes the same crooked worm.

AND DEATH SHALL HAVE NO DOMINION
(1942)

And death shall have no dominion.
Dead men naked they shall be one
With the man in the wind and the west moon;
When their bones are picked clean and the clean bones gone,
They shall have stars at elbow and foot;   5
Though they go mad they shall be sane,
Though they sink through the sea they shall rise again;
Though lovers be lost love shall not;
And death shall have no dominion.

And death shall have no dominion.   10
Under the windings of the sea
They lying long shall not die windily;
Twisting on racks when sinews give way,
Strapped to a wheel, yet they shall not break;
Faith in their hands shall snap in two,   15
And the unicorn evils run them through;
Split all ends up they shan't crack;
And death shall have no dominion.

And death shall have no dominion.
No more may gulls cry at their ears   20
Or waves break loud on the seashores;
Where blew a flower may a flower no more
Lift its head to the blows of the rain;
Though they be mad and dead as nails,
Heads of the characters hammer through daisies;   25
Break in the sun till the sun breaks down,
And death shall have no dominion.

FERN HILL

(1946)

Now as I was young and easy under the apple boughs
About the lilting house and happy as the grass was green,
   The night above the dingle starry,
     Time let me hail and climb
   Golden in the heydays of his eyes,   5
And honoured among wagons I was prince of the apple towns
And once below a time I lordly had the trees and leaves
     Trail with daisies and barley
   Down the rivers of the windfall light.

And as I was green and carefree, famous among the barns   10
About the happy yard and singing as the farm was home,
   In the sun that is young once only,
     Time let me play and be
   Golden in the mercy of his means,   14
And green and golden I was huntsman and herdsman, the calves
Sang to my horn, the foxes on the hills barked clear and cold,
    And the sabbeth rang slowly
   In the pebbles of the holy streams.

All the sun long it was running, it was lovely, the hay-
Fields high as the house, the tunes from the chimneys, it was air
   And playing, lovely and watery   21
     And fire green as grass.
   And nightly under the simple stars
As I rode to sleep the owls were bearing the farm away,
All the moon long I heard, blessèd among stables, the night-jars
   Flying with the ricks, and the horses   26
     Flashing into the dark.

And then to awake, and the farm, like a wanderer white
With the dew, come back, the cock on his shoulder: it was all
   Shining, it was Adam and maiden,   30
     The sky gathered again
   And the sun grew round that very day.
So it must have been after the birth of the simple light
In the first, spinning place, the spellbound horses walking warm
   Out of the whinnying green stable   35
   On to the fields of praise.

And honoured among foxes and pheasants by the gay house
Under the new made clouds and happy as the heart was lon
  In the sun born over and over,
    I ran my heedless ways,   40
  My wishes raced through the house-high hay
And nothing I cared, at my sky blue trades, that time allows
In all his tuneful turning so few and such morning songs
  Before the children green and golden
    Follow him out of grace,   45

Nothing I cared, in the lamb white days, that time would take me
Up to the swallow thronged loft by the shadow of my hand,
  In the moon that is always rising,
    Nor that riding to sleep
  I should hear him fly with the high fields   50
And wake to the farm forever fled from the childless land.
Oh as I was young and easy in the mercy of his means,
    Time held me green and dying
  Though I sang in my chains like the sea.

DO NOT GO GENTLE INTO
THAT GOOD NIGHT

(1946)

Do not go gentle into that good night,
Old age should burn and rave at close of day;
Rage, rage against the dying of the light.

Though wise men at their end know dark is right,
Because their words have forked no lightning they   5
Do not go gentle into that good night.

Good men, the last wave by, crying how bright
Their frail deeds might have danced in a green bay,
Rage, rage against the dying of the light.

Wild men who caught and sang the sun in flight,   10
And learn, too late, they grieved it on its way,
Do not go gentle into that good night.

Grave men, near death, who see with blinding sight
Blind eyes could blaze like meteors and be gay,
Rage, rage against the dying of the light.   15

And you, my father, there on the sad height,
Curse, bless, me now with your fierce tears, I pray.
Do not go gentle into that good night.
Rage, rage against the dying of the light.

Robert Lowell

THE DRUNKEN FISHERMAN
(1946)

Wallowing in this bloody sty,
I cast for fish that pleased my eye
(Truly Jehovah's bow suspends
No pots of gold to weight its ends);
Only the blood-mouthed rainbow trout   5
Rose to my bait. They flopped about
My canvas creel until the moth
Corrupted its unstable cloth.

A calendar to tell the day;
A handkerchief to wave away   10
The gnats; a couch unstuffed with storm
Pouching a bottle in one arm;
A whiskey bottle full of worms;
And bedroom slacks: are these fit terms
To mete the worm whose molten rage   15
Boils in the belly of old age?

Once fishing was a rabbit's foot—
O wind blow cold, O wind blow hot,
Let suns stay in or suns step out:
Life danced a jig on the sperm-whale's spout— 20
The fisher's fluent and obscene
Catches kept his conscience clean.
Children, the raging memory drools
Over the glory of past pools.

Now the hot river, ebbing, hauls   25

Its bloody waters into holes;
A grain of sand inside my shoe
Mimics the moon that might undo
Man and Creation too; remorse,
Stinking, has puddled up its source;   30
Here tantrums thrash to a whale's rage.
This is the pot-hole of old age.

Is there no way to cast my hook
Out of this dynamited brook?
The Fisher's sons must cast about   35
When shallow waters peter out.
I will catch Christ with a greased worm,
And when the Prince of Darkness stalks
My bloodstream to its Stygian term . . .
On water the Man-Fisher walks.   40

❧

Richard Wilbur

BEASTS

(1955)

Beasts in their major freedom
Slumber in peace tonight. The gull on his ledge
Dreams in the guts of himself the moon-plucked waves below,
And the sunfish leans on a stone, slept
By the lyric water; 5

In which the spotless feet
Of deer make dulcet splashes, and to which
The ripped mouse, safe in the owl's talon, cries
Concordance. Here there is no such harm
And no such darkness 10

As the self-same moon observes
Where, warped in window-glass, it sponsors now
The werewolf's painful change. Turning his head away
On the sweaty bolster, he tries to remember
The mood of manhood, 15

But lies at last, as always,
Letting it happen, the fierce fur soft to his face,
Hearing with sharper ears the wind's exciting minors,
The leaves' panic, and the degradation
Of the heavy streams. 20

Meantime, at high windows
Far from thicket and pad-fall, suitors of excellence
Sigh and turn from their work to construe again the painful
Beauty of heaven, the lucid moon
And the risen hunter, 25

Making such dreams for men
As told will break their hearts as always, bringing
Monsters into the city, crows on the public statues,
Navies fed to the fish in the dark
Unbridled waters.   30

Kingsley Amis

A DREAM OF FAIR WOMEN

(1953)

The door still swinging to, and girls revive,
Aeronauts in the utmost altitudes
    Of boredom fainting, dive
Into the bright oxygen of my nod;
Angels as well, a squadron of draped nudes,   5
    They roar towards their god.

Militant all, they fight to take my hat,
No more as yet; the other men retire
    Insulted, gestured at;
Each girl presses on me her share of what   10
Makes up the barn-door target of desire:
    And I am a crack shot.

Speech fails them, amorous, but each one's look,
Endorsed in other ways, begs me to sign
    Her body's autograph-book;   15
"Me first, Kingsley; I'm cleverest" each declares,
But no gourmet races downstairs to dine,
    Nor will I race upstairs.

Feigning aplomb, perhaps for half an hour,
I hover, and am shown by each princess   20
    The entrance to her tower;
Open, in that its tenant throws the key
At once to anyone, but not unless
    The anyone is me.

The selection from Kingsley Amis is used with the permission of Harcourt, Brace, and Company, Inc. and Victor Gollancz, Ltd.: "A Dream of Fair Women" *is from* A CASE OF SAMPLES: Poems 1946-1956, © *1956 by Kingsley Amis.*

Now from the corridor their fathers cheer,   25
Their brothers, their young men; the cheers increase
    As soon as I appear;
From each I win a handshake and sincere
Congratulations; from the chief of police
    A nod, a wink, a leer.   30

This over, all delay is over too;
The first eight girls (the roster now agreed)
    Leap on me, and undo . . .
But honesty impels me to confess
That this is 'all a dream', which was, indeed,   35
    Not difficult to guess.

But wait; not 'just a dream', because, though good
And beautiful, it is also true, and hence
    Is rarely understood;
Who would choose any feasible ideal   40
In here and now's giant circumference,
    If that small room were real?

Only the best; the others find, have found
Love's ordinary distances too great,
    And, eager, stand their ground;   45
Map-drunk explorers, dry-land sailors, they
See no arrival that can compensate
    For boredom on the way;

And, seeming doctrinaire, but really weak,
Limelighted dolls guttering in their brain,   50
    They come with me, to seek
The halls of theoretical delight,
The women of that ever-fresh terrain,
    The night after to-night.

Philip Larkin

CHURCH GOING

(1955)

Once I am sure there's nothing going on
I step inside, letting the door thud shut.
Another church: matting, seats, and stone,
And little books; sprawlings of flowers, cut
For Sunday, brownish now; some brass and stuff   5
Up at the holy end; the small neat organ;
And a tense, musty, unignorable silence,
Brewed God knows how long. Hatless, I take off
My cycle-clips in awkward reverence,

Move forward, run my hand around the font.   10
From where I stand, the roof looks almost new—
Cleaned or restored? Someone would know: I don't.
Mounting the lectern, I peruse a few
Hectoring large-scale verses, and pronounce
'Here endeth' much more loudly than I meant.   15
The echoes snigger briefly. Back at the door
I sign the book, donate an Irish sixpence,
Reflect the place was not worth stopping for.

Yet stop I did: in fact I often do,
And always end much at a loss like this,   20
Wondering what to look for; wondering, too,
When churches fall completely out of use
What we shall turn them into, if we shall keep
A few cathedrals chronically on show,
Their parchment, plate and pyx in locked cases,   25
And let the rest rent-free to rain and sheep.
Shall we avoid them as unlucky places?

The selection from Philip Larkin is used with the permission of The Marvell Press, Hessle, Yorkshire, England: "Church Going" *is from* THE LESS DECEIVED *by Philip Larkin.*

Or, after dark, will dubious women come
To make their children touch a particular stone;
Pick simples for a cancer; or in some   30
Advised night see walking a dead one?
Power of some sort or other will go on
In games, in riddles, seemingly at random;
But superstition, like belief, must die,
And what remains when disbelief has gone?   35
Grass, weedy pavement, brambles, buttress, sky,

A shape less recognisable each week,
A purpose more obscure, I wonder who
Will be the last, the very last, to seek
This place for what it was: one of the crew   40
That tap and jot and know what rood-lofts were?
Some ruin-bibber, randy for antique,
Or Christmas-addict, counting on a whiff
Of gown-and-bands and organ-pipes and myrrh?
Or will he be my representative,   45

Bored, uninformed, knowing the ghostly silt
Dispersed, yet tending to this cross of ground
Through suburb scrub because it held unspilt
So long and equably what since is found
Only in separation—marriage, and birth,   50
And deaths, and thoughts of these—for whom was built
This special shell? For, though I've no idea
What this accoutred frowsty barn is worth,
It pleases me to stand in silence here;

A serious house on serious earth it is,   55
In whose blent air all our compulsions meet,
Are recognized, and robed as destinies.
And that much never can be obsolete,
Since someone will forever be surprising
A hunger in himself to be more serious,   60
And gravitating with it to this ground,
Which, he once heard, was proper to grow wise in,
If only that so many dead lie round.

Biographical and Bibliographical References

KINGSLEY WILLIAM AMIS

LIFE: Born 16 April 1922 in Clapham district of London, the son of an office clerk of Baptist stock. Educated at City of London School to 1941. Army service 1942-45. Received degree, First Class, in English language and literature from St. John's College, Oxford, in 1947. Postgraduate thesis on English poetry and the Victorian reading public. Married in 1948; has three children. Has taught English at the University College of Swansea in Wales since 1949. Won Somerset Maugham Award with first novel in 1955; was widely praised and denounced in England.

CHIEF WRITINGS: VERSE: *A Frame of Mind* (1953); *A Case of Samples: Poems, 1946-56* NOVELS: *Lucky Jim* (1954); *That Uncertain Feeling* (1955); *I Like It Here* (1958).

BIOGRAPHY AND CRITICISM: BIOGRAPHY: None. CRITICISM: John Wain, "English Poetry: The Immediate Situation," *Sewanee Review,* 65 (1957).

WYSTAN HUGH AUDEN

LIFE: Born in York, England, 21 February 1907, the son of a doctor. Educated at Gresham's School, Holt, 1920-25, and Christ Church, Oxford, 1925-28. Visited Berlin, taught school in England and Scotland, visited Iceland with Louis MacNeice, drove ambulance for Loyalists in Spain in 1937, was in China with Christopher Isherwood in 1938. Has made the United States his home since 1939 and is an American citizen. Has taught at various colleges, won the Pulitzer Prize in 1948, and was made Professor of Poetry at Oxford in 1955.

CHIEF WRITINGS: VERSE: *Poems* (1930); *Look, Stranger* or *On This Island* (1936); *The Double Man* or *New Year Letter* (1941); *For The Time Being* (1944); *Collected Poetry* (1945); *The Age of Anxiety* (1947); *Nones* (1951); *The Shield of Achilles* (1955); *The Old Man's Road* (1957), *Homage to Clio* (1960). VERSE PLAYS (with C. Isherwood): *The Dog Beneath the Skin* (1935); *The Ascent of F6* (1936); *On the Frontier* (1938). OPERA: *The Rake's Progress* (with Igor Stravinsky) (1957). CRITI-CISM: *The Enchàfed Flood* (1950); *Making, Knowing, and Judging* (1957).

BIOGRAPHY AND CRITICISM: BIOGRAPHIES: None. CRITICISM: F. R. Leavis, *New Bearings in English Poetry* (1950); Cleanth Brooks, *Modern*

Poetry and the Tradition (1939); F. Scarfe, *Auden and After: The Libera-tion of Poetry, 1930-1941* (1942); D. S. Savage, *The Personal Principle* (1944); D. Schwartz, "The Two Audens," *Kenyon Review* i (1939); R. Jarrell, "Stages of Auden's Ideology," *Partisan Review* xii (1945); D. Stauf-fer, "The Search for Beliefs in Auden's Poetry," *Virginia Quarterly Review*, xxii (1946); A. Mizener, "Ideas on Auden," in *Accent Anthology* (1947); G. R. Hamilton, *The Tell-Tale Article* (1950); Richard Hoggart, *Auden* (1951); John Bayley, *The Romantic Survival* (1957); J. W. Beach, *The Making of the Auden Canon* (1957). BIBLIOGRAHY: Edward Callan, *An-notated Checklist of the Works of Auden* (1958); J. P. Clancy, "A W. H. Auden Bibliography," *Thought,* xxx (1955).

GEORGE BARKER

LIFE: Born 26 February 1913, and educated at the London County Coun-cil School, Chelsea, and Regent Street Polytechnic, which he left when he was fourteen. In 1939 he was professor of English at the Imperial Tohoku University, Japan, and visited the United States, 1940-43. He was married in 1933, has six children, and lives in the country in England writing novels and plays as well as poetry.

CHIEF WRITINGS: *Collected Poems, 1930-55* (1957).

EDWARD ESTLIN CUMMINGS

LIFE: Born 14 October 1894 in Cambridge, Mass. His father taught at Harvard and became minister of the Old South Church in Boston. He took his A.B. at Harvard in 1915 and his M.A. in 1916. An ambulance driver in France during the First World War, he was held in a French detention camp for three months through a censor's error, and this gave him material for *The Enormous Room*. He studied art in Paris, and has lived as a poet and painter mainly in New York since 1924. He delivered the Charles Eliot Norton lectures in poetry at Harvard in 1952-3, and won the Bollingen prize in poetry in 1957. He is married to Marion Morehouse.

CHIEF WRITINGS: VERSE: *Poems 1923-54* (1954); *95 Poems* (1958). PROSE: *The Enormous Room* (1922); *Eimi* (1933); *i: six nonlectures* (1953); *A Miscellany* (1958). PLAYS: *Him* (1927); *Santa Claus* (1946).

BIOGRAPHY AND CRITICISM: Charles Norman, *The Magic-Maker: E. E. Cummings* (1958); *The Harvard Wake,* "Cummings Number," No. 5 (1946); Rudolph Von Abele, " 'Only to Grow': Change in the Poetry of E. E. Cummings," *PMLA,* lxx (1955); Norman Friedman, *E. E. Cum-mings: The Art of His Poetry* (1960). BIBLIOGRAPHY: Paul Lauter, *E. E. Cummings: Index to First Lines and Bibliography of Works by and about the Poet* (1955); George J. Frimage, *E. E. Cummings: A Bibliography* (1960).

EMILY DICKINSON

LIFE: Born 10 December 1830, in Amherst, Massachusetts, daughter of Edward Dickinson, a prominent lawyer influential in state politics and a Congressmen for two terms. At seventeen entered Mount Holyoke Female Seminary; when she was twenty-three, she visited her father in Washington. On her return through Philadelphia she met the Reverend Charles Wadsworth, who at this time, May 1854, was forty years old, happily married, and a devout and dynamic preacher. Emily was intensely attracted to him, and although they met only three times, it is clear from her correspondence that he was the central figure in her thoughts for many years. After 1856 she led a secluded and eccentric life in the family home in Amherst, where, until her death 15 May 1886, she carried on a voluminous correspondence and wrote the poems that ensure her fame. Only four of her poems appeared during her lifetime. The first volume was published in 1890.

CHIEF WRITINGS: Since Emily Dickinson's manuscript texts were often radically altered by her earlier editors, the only fully reliable edition is T. H. Johnson's *The Complete Poems of Emily Dickinson* (1955).

BIOGRAPHY AND CRITICISM: G. F. Wicher, *This Was a Poet: A Critical Biography of Emily Dickinson* (1938); H. W. Wells, *Introduction to Emily Dickinson* (1947); Richard Chase, *Emily Dickinson* (1951); R. P. Blackmur, *Language as Gesture* (1952); T. H. Johnson, *Emily Dickinson, An Interpretive Biography* (1955); J. C. Ransom, "Emily Dickinson, A Poet Restored," *Perspectives USA*, No. 15 (1956); T. C. Hoepfner, "Because I Could Not Stop for Death," *American Literature*, 29 (1957).

RICHARD G. EBERHART

LIFE: Born 5 April 1904 in Austin, Minnesota. He graduated from Dartmouth in 1926, took an A.B. and M.A. at St. John's College, Cambridge University, in 1929 and 1933, and studied at Harvard in 1933. From 1933-41 he taught English at St. Mark's School. He was an instructor in naval aircraft gunnery during world War II, and was discharged as a Lt. Commander in 1946. For the next six years he was an assistant manager of the Butcher Polish Co. of Boston. He held visiting professorships at the Universities of Washington and Connecticut, Wheaton College, and Princeton University, and in 1956 was appointed professor of English and Poet in Residence at Dartmouth. He is now on leave in his second year as Consultant in Poetry at the Library of Congress. He was married in 1941 to Elizabeth Butcher, and has two children.

CHIEF WRITINGS: *A Bravery of Earth* (1930); *Reading the Spirit* (1936): *Song and Idea* (1940); *Poems New and Selected* (1944); *Burr*

Oaks (1947); *Undercliff: Poems 1946-53* (1953); *Great Praises* (1957); *Collected Poems, 1930-60* (1960).

BIOGRAPHY AND CRITICISM: Selden Rodman, "The Poetry of Richard Eberhart," *Perspectives USA*, No. 10 (1955); Arthur Mizener, "The Earnest Victorian," *Poetry*, 73 (1949); James Hall, "Richard Eberhart: The Sociable Naturalist," *Western Review*, 18 (1954).

THOMAS STEARNS ELIOT

LIFE: Born 26 September 1888, to Henry Ware Eliot and Charlotte Chauncy Eliot, in St. Louis, Missouri. Educated in St. Louis schools, at Milton Academy, and at Harvard: B.A. 1909; M.A. 1910; further graduate study at the Sorbonne (1911), Harvard (1911-14), Merton College, Oxford (1914-15). Married first (1915) Vivienne Haigh (died 1947), second (1957) Esmé Valerie Fletcher. Taught at Highgate School in London, worked in Lloyd's Bank, founded *The Criterion* (1922), entered the publishing house of Faber and Faber, of which he is now a director. Became a British subject, 1927. Received the Nobel prize for literature, 1948.

CHIEF WRITINGS: VERSE: *Prufrock and Other Observations* (1917); *Ara Vos Prec* (1920); *The Waste Land* (1922); *Collected Poems, 1909-35* (1936); *Four Quartets* (1944); *Complete Poems and Plays, 1909-1950* (1952). VERSE PLAYS: *The Rock* (1934); *Murder in the Cathedral* (1935); *The Family Reunion* (1939); *The Cocktail Party* (1950); *The Confidential Clerk* (1954); *The Elder Statesman* (1959). CRITICISM: *The Sacred Wood* (1920); *Selected Essays* (1932); *The Use of Poetry and the Use of Criticism* (1933); *Elizabethan Essays* (1934); *Essays Ancient and Modern* (1936); *Poetry and Drama* (1951); *The Three Voices of Poetry* (1954); *On Poetry and Poets* (1957). GENERAL: *The Idea of a Christian Society* (1939); *Notes Towards the Definition of Culture* (1949).

BIOGRAPHY AND CRITICISM: BIOGRAPHY: There is a short account of Eliot's life in F. O. Matthiessen's *The Achievement of T. S. Eliot* (1935; revised edition 1947), and some miscellaneous biographical material in *T. S. Eliot, A Symposium,* ed. R. March, 1948. CRITICISM: T. McGreevy, *Thomas Stearns Eliot, a Study* (1931); F. R. Leavis, *New Bearings in English Poetry* (1932); H. R. Williamson, *The Poetry of T. S. Eliot* (1932); R. Preston, *Four Quartets Rehearsed* (1946); *T. S. Eliot, a Study of His Writings by Several Hands,* ed. B. Rajan (1947); *T. S. Eliot: A Selected Critique,* ed. L. Unger (1948); E. A. Drew, *T. S. Eliot, the Design of His Poetry* (1949); H. L. Gardner, *The Art of T. S. Eliot* (1949); R. H. Robbins, *The T. S. Eliot Myth* (1951); D. E. S. Maxwell, *The Poetry of T. S. Eliot* (1952); George Williamson, *Reader's Guide to T. S. Eliot* (1953); G. C. Smith, *T. S. Eliot's Poetry and Plays* (1956); Neville Braybrooke, *T. S. Eliot: A Symposium for His Seventieth Birthday* (1958); W. H. Kenner, *The Invisible Poet: T. S. Eliot* (1959); D. C. Gallup, *T. S. Eliot: A Bibliography* (1952).

ROBERT FROST

LIFE: Born 25 March 1874, in San Francisco, son of a Harvard graduate and a champion of States Rights and the South who had moved west during the Civil War; he named his son after General Lee. When the father died of tuberculosis in 1885, the mother, who had come from Scotland at fifteen, took her son Robert and returned to New England, where the first Frost had settled in 1634. Robert lived with his mother and Grandfather Frost in Lawrence, Massachusetts, and graduated in 1893 from the local high school as valedictorian. After a few months at Dartmouth, he left to work in Lawrence as a bobbin boy and a reporter. In 1895 he married his high school sweetheart, Elinor Miriam White, who had just graduated from St. Lawrence University, and in 1897 they moved to Cambridge, where Frost studied at Harvard for two years. After another try at mill and newspaper work, he settled on a farm near Derry, New Hampshire, but left there in 1905 to teach in Pinkerton Academy and then for a year, 1911-12, in the New Hampshire State Normal School at Plymouth. In September, 1912, the Frosts and their four children sailed for England, where they moved in literary circles and where Frost's poetry, which had been ignored in America, was first acclaimed and published in book form. With his reputation established by *A Boy's Will* (1913) and *North of Boston* (1914), the Frosts returned to America at the start of the First World War. Since then Frost has lived in New England, teaching informally at Amherst and other schools, and writing the poems that have made him the most widely honored of modern American poets.

CHIEF WRITINGS: *A Boy's Will* (1913); *North of Boston* (1914); *Mountain Interval* (1916); New Hampshire: A Poem (1923); *West-Running Brook* (1928); *A Further Range* (1936); *A Witness Tree* (1942); *A Masque of Reason* (1945); *Steeple Bush* (1947); *A Masque of Mercy* (1947); *Collected Poems* (1949).

BIOGRAPHY AND CRITICISM: W. B. S. Clymer and C. R. Green, *Robert Frost: A Bibliography* (1937); L. & E. Mertins, *The Intervals of R. F.: A Critical Bibliography* (1947); G. B. Munson, *Robert Frost, A Study in Sensibility and Good Sense* (1939); L. Thompson, *Fire and Ice: The Art and Thought of Robert Frost* (1942); R. Thornton, ed., *Recognition of Robert Frost* (1937); R. P. Warren, "The Themes of Robert Frost," *The Writer and His Craft* (1954); Sidney Cox, *A Swinger of Birches* (1957); Yvor Winters, "Robert Frost or, The Spiritual Drifter as Poet," *Function of Criticism* (1957); R. L. Cook, *The Dimensions of Robert Frost* (1958); L. R. Thompson, *Robert Frost* (1959); J. F. Lynen, *The Pastoral Art of Robert Frost* (1960); G. W. Nitchie, *Human Values in the Poetry of Robert Frost* (1960); E. S. Sergeant, *Robert Frost: The Trial by Existence* (1960).

THOMAS HARDY

LIFE: Born 2 June 1840 in Dorset, England. Educated at local school, 1848-54; apprenticed to local ecclesiastical architect, 1856-61; worked for London architect, 1862-67. Published first short story in 1865. First novel (1869) was rejected, but led to interview with George Meredith, who advised a second with more plot. Hardy began bringing out novels in 1871 and had produced fourteen by 1895, when the controversy aroused by his treatment of sex and marriage in the last two, *Tess* and *Jude,* caused him to abandon fiction for poetry. He was married twice and lived in Dorchester from 1885 on, becoming world-famous in later life. Died 11 January 1928. Somerset Maugham's *Cakes and Ale* (1930) is thought to include a fictionalized portrait of Hardy.

CHIEF WRITINGS: NOVELS: *Far From the Madding Crowd* (1874); *The Return of the Native* (1878); *The Mayor of Casterbridge* (1886); *The Woodlanders* (1887); *Tess of the D'Urbervilles* (1891); *Jude the Obscure* (1895). VERSE: *Wessex Poems* (1898); *Poems of the Past and the Present* (1902); *Satires of Circumstance* (1914); *Winter Words* (1928); *Collected Poems* (1953); *The Dynasts* (1903-08).

BIOGRAPHY AND CRITICISM: BIOGRAPHY: F. E. Hardy, *Early Life* (1928), *Later Years* (1930); C. J. Weber, *Hardy of Wessex* (1940); E. Hardy, *Thomas Hardy, A Critical Biography* (1954). CRITICISM: L. P. Johnson, *The Art of Thomas Hardy* (1894); L. Abercrombie, *Thomas Hardy: A Critical Study* (1912); H. C. Webster, *On a Darkling Plain* (1947); J. G. Southworth, *The Poetry of Thomas Hardy* (1947); John Holloway, "Hardy," in *The Victorian Sage* (1953); D. Brown, *Thomas Hardy* (1954); R. P. Blackmur, "The Shorter Poems of Thomas Hardy," *Form and Value in Modern Poetry* (1957); Mark Van Doren, "The Poems of Thomas Hardy," *Four Poets on Poetry* (1959). BIBLIOGRAPHY: R. L. Purdy, *Thomas Hardy: A Bibliographical Study* (1954).

GERARD MANLEY HOPKINS

LIFE: Born 11 June 1844, to Manley Hopkins and Catherine Smith Hopkins, in Stratford (Essex), England. Educated at home, at Highgate Grammar School, and at Baliol College, Oxford (B.A. 1867). Received into the Roman Catholic Church, 21 October 1866; entered Jesuit Novitiate, 1868; ordained priest, 1877. Preacher to various parishes, 1877-82. Teacher of classics at Stonyhurst College (Jesuit), 1882-4. Chair of Greek at the Royal University, Dublin, 1884-9. Died 8 June, 1889.

CHIEF WRITINGS: On entering the Jesuit Novitiate, 1868, Hopkins destroyed all the poetry he had previously written. What survives now is the poetry he wrote after 1876 when he again returned to writing. This was published in 1918 by Robert Bridges, Poet Laureate and friend of Hopkins, into whose hands it had come at Hopkins's death. A second and somewhat enlarged edition was published in 1930, and a third in 1948. Though a Victorian chronologically, Hopkins belongs with the modern poets, partly because of the tardy publication of his work, but chiefly because this work has exerted a very considerable influence on present-day poets.

BIOGRAPHY AND CRITICISM: BIOGRAPHIES: G. F. Lahey, *Gerard Manley Hopkins* (1930); E. Ruggles, *Gerard Manley Hopkins, A Life* (1944). BIBLIOGRAPHIES: Norman Weyand, "A Chronological Hopkins Bibliography," in *Immortal Diamond* (1949); Maurice Charney, "A Bibliographical Study of Hopkins Criticism," *Thought*, xxv (1950). CRITICISM: John Pick, *Gerard Manley Hopkins, Priest and Poet* (1942); The Kenyon Critics. *Gerard Manley Hopkins* (1945); W. H. Gardner, *Gerard Manley Hopkins, 1844-1889*, 2 vols. (1944-9); W. A. M. Peters, *Gerard Manley Hopkins, a Critical Essay Towards the Understanding of His Poetry* (1948); N. Weyand, ed., *Immortal Diamond: Studies in Gerard Manley Hopkins* (1949); G. H. Hartman, *The Unmediated Vision . . . Hopkins, Rilke, and Valery* (1954); Yvor Winters, "The Poetry of Gerard Manley Hopkins," *The Function of Criticism* (1957).

A. E. HOUSMAN

LIFE: Born 26 March 1859 in Worcestershire, England, the son of a lawyer. Entered St. John's College, Oxford, on a scholarship in 1877 and took his degree in classical studies. From 1882 to 1892, studied privately and worked in the Government Patent Office until his appointment as professor of Latin in University College, London. In 1911 he became Kennedy Professor of Latin in Trinity College, Cambridge, a position which he held with great distinction until his death 30 April 1936. He led a single and austere life, devoting himself to study, scholarly controversy, travel, and poetry, most of which was composed after he was thirty-five.

CHIEF WRITINGS: *A Shropshire Lad* (1896); *Last Poems* (1922); *More Poems* (1936); *Collected Poems* (1939); *The Name and Nature of Poetry* (1933).

BIOGRAPHY AND CRITICISM: BIOGRAPHIES: A. S. F. Gow, *A. E. Housman: A Sketch* (1937); L. Housman, *My Brother, A. E. Housman* (1938); G. Richard, *Housman, 1897-1936* (1941); P. Withers, *A Buried Life: Personal Recollections of A. E. Housman* (1940); G. Watson, *A. E. Housman: A Divided Life* (1957). BIBLIOGRAPHIES: R. W. Stallman, "Annotated Bibliography of A. E. Housman: A Critical Study," *PMLA*, lv (1945); J. Carter and J. Sparrow, *A. E. Housman: An Annotated Handlist* (1952). CRITICISM: R. Jarrell, "Texts from Housman," *Kenyon Review*, i (1939); Ian Scott-Kilvert, *A. E. Housman* (1955); M. M. Hawkins, *A. E. Housman* (1958); N. Marlow, *A. E. Housman: Scholar and Poet* (1958); Edmund Wilson, "A. E. Housman" in *The Triple Thinkers* (1938, 1952).

PHILIP LARKIN

LIFE: Born 9 August 1922 in England. He was educated at St. John's College, Oxford. He has been in library work since 1943, and is now Librarian of the University of Hull.

CHIEF WRITINGS: VERSE: *The North Ship* (1943); *The Less Deceived* (1955). NOVELS: *Jill* (1946); *A Girl in Winter* (1947).

CRITICISM: See Wain's article listed under Amis.

D. H. LAWRENCE

LIFE: Born 11 September 1885 in Eastwood, a mining town in Nottinghamshire, England; mother a schoolmistress, father a coal miner. Educated at Nottingham High School, 1896-99, and University College, 1906-08. Taught school; suffered attacks of pneumonia. Ran away with (1912) and married (1914) Frieda von Richthofen Weekly, wife of a university professor and mother of three small children. In 1915 was attacked for alleged obscenity in *The Rainbow* and alleged pro-German sympathies. Travel and residence in Italy, Sardinia, Australia, Mexico, and New Mexico (Taos), 1919-1928. Returned to England; controversy over *Lady Chatterley's Lover* (1928). Died 2 March 1930 in Vence, southern France. Mark Rampion in Aldous Huxley's *Point Counterpoint* (1928) is a fictional portrait of Lawrence.

CHIEF WRITINGS: VERSE: *Love Poems and Others* (1913); *Amores* (1916); *Look! We Have Come Through!* (1917); *New Poems* (1918); *Bay* (1919); *Tortoises* (1921); *Birds, Beasts, and Flowers* (1923); *Collected Poems* (1928); *Pansies* (1929); *Nettles* (1930); *The Triumph of the Machine* (1930); *Last Poems* (1932); *Fire and Other Poems* (1940); FICTION: *Sons and Lovers* (1913); *The Prussian Officer and Other Stories* (1914); *The Rainbow* (1915); *Women in Love* (1920). CRITICISM: *Studies in Classic American Literature* (1923).

BIOGRAPHY AND CRITICISM: BIOGRAPHIES: H. T. Moore, *The Intelligent Heart* (1954); Edward Nehls, *D. H. Lawrence: A Composite Biography* (1957-59). CRITICISM: Martin Jarrett-Kerr, *D. H. Lawrence and Human Existence* (1951); Horace Gregory, "The Poetry of D. H. Lawrence," and Richard Ellman, "Barbed Wire and Coming Through," both in Hoffman and Moore's *Achievement of D. H. Lawrence* (1953); F. R. Leavis, *D. H. Lawrence, Novelist* (1955); H. T. Moore, *A D. H. Lawrence Miscellany* (1959). BIBLIOGRAPHY: Earl Tannenbaum, *D. H. Lawrence: An Exhibition of First Editions . . .* (1958); W. White, *D. H. Lawrence: A Checklist, 1931-50* (1950).

ROBERT LOWELL

LIFE: Born 1 March 1917 in Boston, the great-grandnephew of James Russell Lowell. Educated at St. Mark's School, Harvard (two years), Kenyon College (A.B. 1940 in classics), and Louisiana State University. He has taught English at Iowa, the Kenyon School of English, and Boston University. In 1947 he won the Pulitzer prize for poetry and was Consultant in Poetry at the Library of Congress. He is married to the writer, Elizabeth Hardwick.

CHIEF WRITINGS: *Land of Unlikeness* (1944); *Lord Weary's Castle* (1946, 1947); *The Mills of the Kavanaughs* (1951); *Poems, 1938-49* (1950); *Life Studies* (1959).

BIOGRAPHY AND CRITICISM: John McCornick, "Falling Asleep Over Grillparzer: An Interview with Robert Lowell," *Poetry*, lxxxi (1953); W. C. Jumper, "Whom Seek Ye? A Note on Robert Lowell's Poetry," *Hudson Review*, ix (1956); John Hollander, "Robert Lowell's New Book," *Poetry*, xcv (1959); H. B. Staples, "Robert Lowell: Bibliography 1939-59, with an Illustrative Critique," *Harvard Library Bulletin*, xiii (1959).

ARCHIBALD MACLEISH

LIFE: Born 7 May 1892, to Andrew MacLeish and Martha Hilliard MacLeish, in Glencoe, Illinois. Educated Hotchkiss School, Yale University (B.A. 1915), and Harvard Law School. Married Ada Hitchcock, 1916. Served in First World War, 1917-18. Taught government at Harvard, 1919-21. Law practice, 1920-23. Residence in France, 1927-28. Editor of *Fortune*, 1929-38. Librarian of Congress, 1939-44. Assistant Secretary of State, 1944-45. Boylston Professor of Rhetoric, Harvard University, 1949.

CHIEF WRITINGS: VERSE: *The Pot of Earth* (1925); *The Hamlet of A. MacLeish* (1928); *Conquistador* (1930) [Pulitzer prize]; *Frescoes for Mr. Rockefeller's City* (1933); *Poems, 1924-1933* (1933); *Public Speech* (1936); *America Was Promises* (1939); *Actfive and Other Poems* (1948); *Collected Poems, 1917-1952* (1952); *Songs for Eve* (1954). VERSE PLAYS: *Panic* (1935); *The Fall of the City* (1937); *Air Raid* (1938); *JB* (1958).

LOUIS MACNEICE

LIFE: Born 12 September 1907, in Belfast, Ireland, the son of an Anglican clergyman who later became Bishop of Belfast. Educated in England, graduating in 1930 with highest honors in classical studies from Merton College, Oxford. Taught at the University of Birmingham (1930-36), Bedford College for Women (1936-40), and Cornell University (1941-42). Has been married twice and has two children. In addition to poetry, MacNeice has translated Aeschylus's *Agamemnon*, and has written books on modern poetry (1938) and Yeats (1941).

CHIEF WRITINGS: *Poems, 1925-1940* (1940); *Springboard* (1945); *Holes in the Sky* (1948); *Collected Poems, 1925-48* (1949); *Ten Burnt Offerings* (1952); *Autumn Sequel* (1954); *Visitations* (1957); *Eighty-five Poems* (1959).

CRITICISM: Delmore Schwartz, "Adroitly Naïve," *Poetry*, 48 (May 1936); see Drew and Scarfe under General Criticism.

MARIANNE MOORE

LIFE: Born 15 November 1887 in St. Louis, and brought up in Carlisle, Pa., where she taught in the government Indian school (1911-15) after graduating from Bryn Mawr College in 1909. After working in the New York Public Library, she was acting editor of the *Dial* from 1925 to 1929. She lives in Brooklyn, N. Y.

CHIEF WRITINGS: VERSE: *Poems* (1921); *Observations* (1924); *The Pangolin* (1936); *What Are Years* (1941); *Nevertheless* (1944); *Collected Poems* (1951); *Like a Bulwark* (1956); *Fables of La Fontaine* (translation) (1954). PROSE: *Predilections* (1955).

CRITICISM: H. Monroe, "Symposium on Marianne Moore," *Poetry*, xix (1922); W. C. Williams, "Marianne Moore," *Dial*, lxxviii (1925), reprinted in his Selected Essays, 1954; K. Burke, "Motives and Motifs in the Poetry of Marianne Moore," *Accent*, ii (1942); *Quarterly Review of Literature*, "Marianne Moore Issue," iv (1948); W. Fowlie, "Marianne Moore," *Sewanee Review*, lx (1952); F. J. Hoffman, "Marianne Moore: Imaginary Gardens and Real Toads," *Poetry*, lxxxiii (1953); R. P. Blackmur, "Marianne Moore," *Form and Value in Modern Poetry* (1957). BIBLIOGRAPHY: E. P. Sheehy & K. A. Lohf, *The Achievement of Marianne Moore: A Bibliography, 1907-57* (1958).

JOHN FREDERICK NIMS

LIFE: Born 20 November 1913 in Muskegon, Michigan. He was educated at Leo High School in Chicago, DePaul University (two years), Notre Dame (A.B. 1937, M.A. 1939), and the University of Chicago (Ph.D. 1945). He has taught English at Notre Dame since 1939. He was married in 1947 and has three sons.

CHIEF WRITINGS: *The Iron Pastoral* (1947); *A Fountain in Kentucky* (1950).

EZRA POUND

LIFE: Born 30 October 1885, to Homer Loomis Pound and Isabel Weston Pound, in Hailey, Idaho. Educated at University of Pennsylvania, 1901-03; Hamilton College, 1903-05 (B.A. 1905); University of Pennsylvania (M.A. 1906). Travel and residence abroad (except for visits to America), 1907-45. Married Dorothy Shakespear, 1914. Editor of *The Little Review* in London, 1917-19. Paris correspondent of *The Dial*, 1920-24. Residence at Rapallo, Italy, since 1924. Brought from Italy to America to stand trial for treason, 1945; declared mentally unsound by U. S. district court, February 1946. Bollingen award for poetry, 1949. Treason charge dismissed 18 April 1958, and Pound released from St. Elizabeth's Hospital to live with his family in Italy.

CHIEF WRITINGS: VERSE: *Personae* (1909); *Cathay* (1915); *Lustra and Other Poems* (1917); *Quia Pauper Amavi* (1919); *Umbra* [collected early poems] (1920); *Hugh Selwyn Mauberley* (1920); *Cantos* (published in groups from 1919 to 1948; collected edition, 1948); *Personae* [collected poems] (1926, 1949); *A Selection of Poems* (1940); *Section: Rock-Drill: Cantos 85-95* (1956); *Thrones: Cantos 96-109* (1959). CRITICISM: *Pavannes and Divisions* (1918); *Polite Essays* (1937); *Literary Essays,* ed. by T. S. Eliot (1954); *Letters of Ezra Pound: 1907-41* (1950); *The Translations of Ezra Pound* (1954).

BIOGRAPHY AND CRITICISM: BIOGRAPHIES: None. CRITICISM: T. S. Eliot, *Ezra Pound, His Metric and Poetry* (1917), introduction to Pound's *Selected Poems* (1928), and "Ezra Pound," *Poetry,* lxviii (1946); F. R. Leavis, *New Bearings in English Poetry* (1932); R. P. Blackmur, *The Double Agent* (1935); W. B. Yeats, "A Packet for Ezra Pound: Rapallo," in *A Vision* (1938); J. Berryman, "The Poetry of Ezra Pound," *Partisan Review,* xvi (1949); *An Examination of Ezra Pound: A Collection of Essays,* ed. by P. Russell (1950); H. Kenner, *The Poetry of Ezra Pound* (1951); H. H. Watts, *Ezra Pound and the Cantos* (1951); J. J. Espey, *Ezra Pound's "Mauberley": A Study in Composition* (1955); *A Casebook on Ezra Pound* (with checklist), ed. by W. V. O'Connor and E. Stone (1959); John Edwards, *A Preliminary Checklist of the Writings of Ezra Pound* (1953); J. H. Edwards and W. W. Vasse, *Annotated Index to the Cantos of Ezra Pound* (1957).

FRANK T. PRINCE

LIFE: Born in South Africa 13 September 1912. He was educated at Baliol College, Oxford, and was a graduate fellow at Princeton 1935-6. Since serving with the British Army Intelligence Corps (1940-46), he has taught English at Southampton University. He was married in 1943, and has two daughters.

CHIEF WRITINGS: VERSE: *Poems* (1938); *Soldiers Bathing* (1954).

JOHN CROWE RANSOM

LIFE: Born 30 April 1888, in Pulaski, Tennessee, the son of a Methodist preacher. After taking his A.B. at Vanderbilt University in 1909, was a Rhodes Scholar at Oxford from 1910 to 1913. Returned to teach English at Vanderbilt, where he founded and edited *The Fugitive* (1922-1925) and helped to develop a group of important Southern writers, including Allen Tate and Robert Penn Warren. In 1937 left Vanderbilt for Kenyon College, where he founded the *Kenyon Review* in 1939, and where he has devoted himself in late years to teaching and literary criticism.

CHIEF WRITINGS: *Poems about God* (1919); *Chills and Fever* (1924); *Two Gentlemen in Bonds* (1927); *Selected Poems* (1945); *Poems and Essays* (1955).

BIOGRAPHY AND CRITICISM: BIOGRAPHIES: None. CRITICISM: R. W. Stallman, "John Crowe Ransom: A Checklist," *Sewanee Review*, 56 (Summer 1948); R. P. Warren, "John Crowe Ransom," *Virginia Quarterly Review*, 11 (January 1935); "Homage to John Crowe Ransom," *Sewanee Review*, lvi (1948); Vivienne Koch, "The Achievement of John Crowe Ransom," *Sewanee Review*, lviii (1950); I. Gamble, "Ceremonies of Bravery: John Crowe Ransom," *Hopkins Review*, vi (1953).

HENRY REED

LIFE: Born in Birmingham, England, 22 February 1914, and educated at the University of Birmingham. Except for war service with the British Army and Foreign Office (1941-45), he has been a journalist, broadcaster, and writer of radio scripts.

CHIEF WRITINGS: VERSE: *A Map of Verona* (1946).

EDWIN ARLINGTON ROBINSON

LIFE: Born 22 December 1869 in Head Tide, Maine. Educated in Gardiner, Maine, through high school; college career at Harvard interrupted in 1893 by father's death. After mother's death in 1896 lived chiefly in New York, a bachelor scraping a livelihood from jobs such as train checking for the subway, but also writing and publishing verse. Through President Theodore Roosevelt's interest in him, worked in the customs house from 1905 to 1909. After 1911, with increasing recognition and financial aid from friends, he lived partly at the MacDowell Colony in New Hampshire. Pulitzer prizes 1921, 1924, and 1927. Died 6 April 1935 in New York City.

CHIEF WRITINGS: *Tristram* (1927); *Cavender's House* (1929); *Modred* (1929); *Glory of the Nightingales* (1930); *Nicodemus* (1932); *Talifer* (1933); *Collected Poems* (1937).

BIOGRAPHY AND CRITICISM: BIOGRAPHIES: Hermann Hagedorn, *E. A. Robinson: A Biography* (1938); Emery Neff, *Edwin Arlington Robinson* (1948). CRITICISM: Mark Van Doren, *Edwin Arlington Robinson* (1927); R. P. T. Coffin, *New Poetry of New England: Frost and Robinson* (1938); Yvor Winters, *Edwin Arlington Robinson* (1946); Ellsworth Barnard, *Edwin Arlington Robinson, A Critical Study* (1952); E. S. Fussell, *Edwin Arlington Robinson: The Literary Background of a Traditional Poet* (1954); W. D. Jacobs, "E. A. Robinson's 'Mr. Flood's Party,'" *College English*, 12 (1950); W. T. Scott, "To See Robinson," *New Mexico Quarterly*, xxvi (1956).

THEODORE ROETHKE

LIFE: Born 25 May 1908 in Saginaw, Michigan. He was educated at the University of Michigan (A.B. 1929, M.A. 1936) and at Harvard (1930-31). He has taught English at Lafayette College, Penn State University, Bennington, and, since 1943, the University of Washington. He won the Pulitzer prize for poetry in 1953 and the Bollingen prize in 1958. He was married in 1953.

CHIEF WRITINGS: *Open House* (1941); *The Lost Son* (1948); *Praise to the End!* (1951); *The Waking* (1953).

CRITICISM: S. Kunitz, "News of the Root," *Poetry*, lxxiii (1949); K. Burke, "The Vegetal Radicalism of Theodore Roethke," *Sewanee Review*, lviii (1950); H. Kramer, "The Poetry of Theodore Roethke," *Western Review*, xviii (1954); D. Schwartz, "The Cunning and the Craft of the Unconscious and the Preconscious," *Poetry*, xciv (1959).

WALLACE STEVENS

LIFE: Born 2 October 1879, to Garrett Barckalow Stevens and Mary Catherine Zeller Stevens, in Reading, Pennsylvania. Educated at Harvard, 1897-1900; New York Law School, 1900-1904. Admitted to the bar, 1904. 1916-1934, employed in the legal department of the Hartford Accident and Indemnity Insurance Co. 1934-1955, vice-president of the firm. Married. He won the Bollingen prize in 1950 and the Pulitzer prize in 1955. Died 2 August 1955 in Hartford.

CHIEF WRITINGS: VERSE: *Harmonium* (1923); *Ideas of Order* (1936); *Man with the Blue Guitar* (1937); *Parts of a World* (1942); *Transport to Summer* (1947); *The Auroras of Autumn* (1950); *Opus Posthumous*, ed. by S. F. Morse (1957). PROSE: *The Necessary Angel: Essays on Reality and Imagination* (1951).

BIOGRAPHY AND CRITICISM: BIOGRAPHIES: None. CRITICISM: *The Harvard Advocate*, Wallace Stevens issue (December 1940); R. P. Blackmur, *The Double Agent* (1935); Hi Simons, "The Genre of Wallace Stevens," *Sewanee Review*, liii (1945); L. L. Martz, "Wallace Stevens: The Romance of the Precise," *Yale Poetry Review*, 5 (1946); M. Bewley, "The Poetry of Wallace Stevens," *Partisan Review*, xvi (1949); W. V. O'Connor, *The Shaping Spirit: A Study of Wallace Stevens* (1950); S. F. Morse, "Motive for Metaphor," *Origin*, ii (1952); "Wallace Stevens Issue," *Perspective*, vii (1954); N. Frye, "The Realistic Oriole: A Study of Wallace Stevens," *Hudson Review*, x (1957); Frank Doggett, *"Wallace Stevens's Later Poetry," ELH*, xxv (1958); L. L. Martz, "Wallace Stevens: The World as Meditation," *Yale Rev.*, xlvii (1958); R. Pack, *Wallace Stevens: An Approach to His Poetry and Thought* (1958).

ALLEN TATE

LIFE: Born 19 November 1899, to John Orley Tate and Nellie Varnell Tate, in Winchester, Kentucky. Educated at home and in private schools in Louisville. B.A. Vanderbilt, 1922. Married the novelist Caroline Gordon, 1924. 1925-1951, lecturer and teacher at many colleges and universities; since 1951 professor of English, University of Minnesota.

CHIEF WRITINGS: VERSE: *Mr. Pope and Other Poems* (1928); *The Mediterranean and Other Poems* (1935); *The Winter Seas* (1944); *Poems, 1922-1947* (1948). CRITICISM: *Reactionary Essays on Poetry and Ideas* (1936); *Reason in Madness* (1941); *On the Limits of Poetry* (1948); *The Hovering Fly and Other Essays* (1949); *The Forlorn Demon* (1953); *The Man of Letters in the Modern World* (1955). BIOGRAPHY: *Stonewall Jackson, the Good Soldier* (1928); *Jefferson Davis, His Rise and Fall* (1929). FICTION: *The Fathers* (1938).

BIOGRAPHY AND CRITICISM: BIOGRAPHIES: None. CRITICISM: C. Brooks, *Modern Poetry and the Tradition* (1939); F. C. Flint, "Five Poets," *Southern Review*, i (1936); D. Schwartz, "The Poetry of Allen Tate," *Southern Review*, v (1940); "Homage to Allen Tate," *Sewanee Review*, lxvii (1959).

DYLAN THOMAS

LIFE: Born 22 October 1914 in Wales, the son of an English teacher. He was educated at the Swansea Grammar School, did some reporting and broadcasting, wrote radio and movie scripts, and gave many poetry readings. He died 9 November 1953 in New York on his third reading tour of the United States. He was survived by his wife, Caitlin Macnamara Thomas, and three children.

CHIEF WRITINGS: VERSE: *18 Poems* (1934); *Twenty-five Poems* (1936); *The Map of Love* (1939); *New Poems* (1943); *Deaths and Entrances*

(1940); *In Country Sleep* (1951); *Collected Poems 1934-52* (1953). DRAMA: *Under Milkwood* (1954, 1960). PROSE: *Portrait of The Artist As a Young Dog* (1940); *Quite Early One Morning* (1954); *Adventures In the Skin Trade* (1955); *Letters to Vernon Watkins* (1957).

BIOGRAPHY AND CRITICISM: J. M. Brinnin, *Dylan Thomas In America* (1955); Caitlin Thomas, *Leftover Life to Kill* (1957); *A Casebook on Dylan Thomas* (with checklist), ed. by J. M. Brinnin (1960); E. Olson, *The Poetry of Dylan Thomas* (with Bibliography by W. H. Huff) (1954); J. Rolph, *Dylan Thomas: A Bibliography* (1956).

ROBERT PENN WARREN

LIFE: Born 24 April 1905 in Guthrie, Kentucky. A. B. Vanderbilt 1925, M. A. California 1927, Yale Graduate School 1927-8, Rhodes scholar at Oxford (B. Litt., 1930). Taught at Vanderbilt, 1931-34; Louisiana State University, 1934-42, where he founded and edited (with Cleanth Brooks) *The Southern Review;* University of Minnesota, 1942-50; Yale, 1950-56. From 1947, when he won the Pulitzer prize for fiction, increasing recognition as a novelist. Married first (1930) Emma Brescia; second, Eleanor Clark (1952); two children.

CHIEF WRITINGS: VERSE: *Selected Poems 1923-44* (1944); *Brother to Dragons* (1953); *Promises, Poems 1954-56* (1957). NOVELS: *Night Rider* (1939); *At Heaven's Gate* (1943); *All the King's Men* (1946); *The Circus in the Attic and Other Stories* (1948); *World Enough and Time* (1950); *Band of Angels* (1955); *The Cave* (1959). ESSAYS: *Segregation* (1956); *Selected Essays* (1958).

BIOGRAPHY AND CRITICISM: Morgan Blum, "Promises as Fulfillment," *Kenyon Review, xxi* (1959); Leonard Casper, *The Dark and Bloody Ground* (with checklist of writings and criticism) (1960).

RICHARD WILBUR

LIFE: Born 1 March 1921 in New York City. He was educated at Amherst (A.B. 1942) and, after military service, at Harvard (M.A. 1947, Junior Fellow 1947-50). He taught English at Harvard (1950-54) and Wellesley College (1955-57), and is now a professor at Wesleyan University. He was married in 1942 and has four children. He won the Pulitzer prize for poetry in 1957.

CHIEF WRITINGS: *The Beautiful Changes* (1947); *Ceremony* (1950); *A Bestiary* (1955); translation of Molière's *Le Misanthrope* (1955); *Things of This World* (1956); *Poems 1943-56* (1957); *Candide* (a comic opera with Lillian Hellman) (1957).

CRITICISM: R. Jarrell, *Poetry and the Age* (1955); F. W. Warlow, "Richard Wilbur," *Bucknell Review,* vii (1958).

WILLIAM CARLOS WILLIAMS

LIFE: Born 17 September 1883 in Rutherford, New Jersey, the son of William George Williams, a bilingual (English and Spanish) Englishman brought up in the West Indies, and Raquel Helène (Hobeb) Williams, a Puerto Rican of French and Basque parentage. Educated at Horace Mann High School in New York City; in Paris; at the University of Pennsylvania (M.D., 1906), where his friendship with Ezra Pound began; and at Leipzig, where he did postgraduate work in pediatrics, 1907. Married Florence Herman 12 December 1912; two sons. Has pursued a double career as doctor and writer since 1910 in Rutherford, a few miles from industrial Paterson, the subject of his most substantial poem.

CHIEF WRITINGS: VERSE: *Collected Earlier Poems* (1951); *Collected Later Poems* (1950); *The Desert Music* (1954); *Journey to Love* (1955); *Paterson* (1948-58). PROSE: *In the American Grain* (1925); *Autobiography* (1951); *Make Light of It: Collected Stories* (1950); *Selected Essays* (1954); *Yes, Mrs. Williams* (1959).

BIOGRAPHY AND CRITICISM: "Williams Number," *Briarcliff Quarterly,* iii (1946); Vivienne Koch, *William Carlos Williams* (1950); Sister M. Bernetta Quinn, "William Carlos Williams: A Testament of Perpetual Change," *PMLA,* lxx (1955); Hugh Kenner, *Gnomon* (1958); Denis Donoghue, "For a Redeeming Language," *Twentieth Century,* 163 (1958).

WILLIAM BUTLER YEATS

LIFE: Born 13 June 1865, the son of the artist John B. Yeats, in Sandymount, Ireland, near Dublin. His childhood summers were spent in the wilds of County Sligo, his parents' birthplace. Attended a London day school, which he remembered as rough but challenging; when he was fifteen, returned with his family to Dublin, where he continued his education at the Erasmus Smith School. Began writing poetry by the time he was eighteen; his first book, *Mosada: A Poem,* appeared in 1886. After that he lived much in London, where he founded the Rhymers' Club, and associated with the writers of the nineties who were championing art for art's sake against the didacticism of Victorian poetry. Among his friends were William Morris, W. E. Henley, Lionel Johnson, Ernest Dowson, Oscar Wilde, and Arthur Symons, who introduced him 'to the writings of Mallarmé and the French Symbolists. At the same time his interest in Celtic materials was growing. Influenced by the Fenian leader John O'Leary, and associated with Synge and Lady Gregory, he founded the Abbey Theater in Dublin (1900), for which he wrote many plays, and worked in the national cultural movement known as the Irish Renaissance. He was by now writing voluminously in many forms, chiefly on Irish subjects; and he had become devoted to the lovely revolutionist,

Maude Gonne. After the turn of the century, however, Yeats began to drift away from the Celtic mistiness of his early poetry toward the dramatic lyric, toward a more colloquial language, a more realistic psychology, and a new set of symbols. With the change in style went an attempt to work out a private mythology as an extension of his poetic symbols. This attempt, which led to the publication of *A Vision* (1925), was supported by his wife and former secretary, Miss Hyde-Lees, whom he married 21 October 1917. Ezra Pound was best man. After the summer of 1922, during which the Republican and National armies visited Yeats' summer place in Ballylee (the occasion of the poem "Meditations in Time of Civil War"), he was appointed to the Senate of the Irish Free State and served for six years. In December 1923, awarded the Nobel Prize in Literature. The first congratulatory telegram was from James Joyce. Yeats continued to write and revise with great vigor until his death, 28 January 1939.

CHIEF WRITINGS: *The Wanderings of Oisin* (1889); *The Countess Kathleen* (1892); *The Wind Among the Reeds* (1899); *In the Seven Woods* (1903); *The Green Helmet* (1910); *Responsibilities: Poems and a Play* (1914); *The Wild Swans at Coole* (1919); *Michael Robartes and the Dancer* (1921); *The Tower* (1928); *Words for Music Perhaps and Other Poems* (1932); *The Winding Stair* (1933); *New Poems* (1938); *Last Poems and Plays* (1940); *The Collected Poems of W. B. Yeats* (1956); Variorum edition of *Poems,* ed. by P. Allt and R. K. Alspach (1957); *Collected Plays* (rev. 1952); *A Vision* (rev. 1937); *Autobiography* (1938); *Letters,* ed. by Allan Wade (1954).

BIOGRAPHY AND CRITICISM: Richard Ellmann, *Yeats, the Man and the Masks* (1948); Joseph Hone, *W. B. Yeats* (1943); A. N. Jeffares, *W. B. Yeats, Man and Poet* (1949); Louis MacNeice, *The Poetry of W. B. Yeats* (1941); *The Permanence of Yeats,* ed. by J. Hall and M. Steinman (1950); Donald Stauffer, *The Golden Nightingale* (1949); Vivienne Koch, *William Butler Yeats, The Tragic Phase: A Study of the Last Poems* (1951); T. F. Parkinson, *William Butler Yeats as Self-Critic* (1951); T. R. Henn, *The Lonely Tower* (1952); Arland Ussher, *Three Great Irishmen: Shaw, Yeats, Joyce* (1953); Una Ellis-Fermor, *The Irish Dramatic Movement* (1954); Richard Ellman, *The Identity of Yeats* (1954); John Bayley, *The Romantic Survival* (1957); Frank Kermode, *The Romantic Image* (1957); G. B. Saul, *Prolegomena to the Study of Yeats's Poems* (1957), *Plays* (1958); F. A. C. Wilson, *William Butler Yeats and Tradition* (1958); Allan Wade, *Bibliography of the Writings of William Butler Yeats* (rev. 1958).

A SELECTIVE BIBLIOGRAPHY OF BOOKS
ON MODERN POETRY

Conrad Aiken, *Scepticism, Notes on Contemporary Poetry*, New York and London, 1919.

A. Alvarez, *The Shaping Spirit: Studies in Modern English and American Poets*, London, 1958; N. Y. (*Stewards of Excellence*), 1958.

George Arms & J. M. Kuntz, *Poetry Explication*, N. Y., 1950.

D. V. Baker, ed., *Writers of Today*, London, 1946.

Ruth Bailey, *A Dialogue on Modern Poetry*, Oxford, 1939.

Owen Barfield, *Poetic Diction: A Study in Meaning*, London, 1928.

Roy P. Basler, *Sex, Symbolism, and Psychology in Literature*, New Brunswick, N. J., 1948.

John Bayley, *The Romantic Survival*, London, 1957.

Eric Bentley, ed., *The Importance of Scrutiny*, New York, 1948.

R. P. Blackmur, *The Double Agent: Essays in Craft and Elucidation*, New York, 1935.

————, *The Expense of Greatness*, New York, 1940.

————, *Language as Gesture*, London, 1954 (17 essays reprinted in *Form and Value in Modern Poetry*, New York, 1957).

Maud Bodkin, *Archetypal Patterns in Poetry*, Oxford, 1934.

C. M. Bowra, *The Heritage of Symbolism*, Toronto, 1943; London, 1947.

————, *The Creative Experiment*, New York, 1949.

Cleanth Brooks, *Modern Poetry and the Tradition*, Chapel Hill, N. C., 1939.

————, *The Well Wrought Urn*, New York, 1947.

Geoffrey Bullough, *The Trend of Modern Poetry*, London, 1934; rev. ed., 1941.

Kenneth Burke, *Counter-Statement*, New York, 1931.

————, *The Philosophy of Literary Form*, Baton Rouge, La., 1941.

————, *A Grammar of Motives*, New York, 1945.

David Daiches, *Poetry and the Modern World*, Chicago, 1940.

C. Day Lewis, *A Hope for Poetry*, Oxford, 1934.

————, "A Hope for Poetry," in *Collected Poems: 1929-1933*, New York, 1935; 2d ed., London, 1945.

————, *The Poetic Image*, London, 1947.

Babette Deutsch, *This Modern Poetry*, New York, 1935; London, 1936.

Elizabeth Drew, *Discovering Poetry*, New York, 1933.

———— and J. L. Sweeney, *Directions in Modern Poetry*, New York, 1940.

Max Eastman, *Enjoyment of Poetry*, New York, 1939.

T. S. Eliot, *Selected Essays: 1917-1932*, London and New York, 1932.

————, *Essays Ancient and Modern*, London and New York, 1936.

G. R. Elliott, *The Cycle of Modern Poetry*, Princeton, N. J., 1929.

William Empson, *Seven Types of Ambiguity*, London, 1930; Norfolk, Conn., 1947.

Lloyd Frankenburg, *Pleasure Dome*, Boston, 1949.

G. S. Fraser, *Vision and Rhetoric: Studies in Modern Poetry*, London, 1959.

Robert Graves, *On English Poetry*, London and New York, 1922.

———— and Laura Riding, *A Survey of Modernist Poetry*, London, 1927; New York, 1928.

Horace Gregory, *The Shield of Achilles: Essays on Belief in Poetry*, New York, 1944.

———— and Marya Zaturenska, *A History of American Poetry: 1900-1940*, New York, 1946.

Philip Henderson, *The Poet and Society*, London, 1939.

Frederick Hoffman, *Freudianism and the Literary Mind*, Baton Rouge, La., 1945.

A. E. Housman, *The Name and Nature of Poetry*, Cambridge, 1933, 1948.

Glenn Hughes, *Imagism and the Imagists*, Stanford University, Calif., 1941.

T. E. Hulme, *Speculations*, ed. Herbert Read, London and New York, 1924, 1936.

D. G. James, *Scepticism and Poetry. An Essay on the Poetic Imagination,* London, 1937.

Randall Jarrell, *Poetry and the Age,* N. Y., 1955.

Hugh Kenner, *Gnomon: Essays on Contemporary Literature,* N. Y., 1958.

Frank Kermode, *The Romantic Image,* London, 1957.

L. C. Knights, *Explorations,* New York, 1947.

Robert Langbaum, *The Poetry of Experience: the Dramatic Monologue in Modern Literary Tradition,* London, 1957.

F. R. Levis, *New Bearings in English Poetry,* London, 1932, 1950.

Louis MacNeice, *Modern Poetry: A Personal Essay,* Oxford, 1938.

R. L. Megroz, *Modern English Poetry: 1882-1932,* London, 1933.

William Van O'Connor, *Sense and Sensibility in Modern Poetry,* Chicago, 1948.

Poets at Work: Essays by W. H. Auden, Karl Shapiro, Rudolph Arnheim, Donald A. Stauffer; introduction Charles D. Abbott, New York, 1948.

Frederick A. Pottle, *The Idiom of Poetry,* Ithaca, N. Y., 1942; rev. ed., 1946.

Sister M. B. Quinn, *The Metamorphic Tradition in Modern Poetry,* Rutgers U. P., 1955.

John Crowe Ransom, *The World's Body,* New York, 1938.

Herbert Read, *Form in Modern Poetry,* London, 1932.

I. A. Richards, *Principles of Literary Criticism,* London, 1924; New York, 1925, 1929; 5th ed., 1934; re-issued 1938, 1948.

———, *Practical Criticism,* London and New York, 1929, 1930, 1935.

Michael Roberts, *Critique of Poetry,* London, 1934.

D. S. Savage, *The Personal Principle; Studies in Modern Poetry,* London, 1944.

Francis Scarfe, *Auden and After: The Liberation of Poetry: 1930-1941,* London, 1942.

Edith Sitwell, *Aspects of Poetry,* London, 1934.

James G. Southworth, *Sowing the Spring,* Oxford, 1940.

John Sparrow, *Sense and Poetry,* London and New Haven, Conn., 1934.

Stephen Spender, *The Destructive Element*, London, 1935; Boston, 1936.

——, *Life and the Poet*, London, 1942.

——, *Poetry Since 1939*, London, 1949.

Donald A. Stauffer, *The Nature of Poetry*, New York, 1946.

Allen Tate, *On the Limits of Poetry: Selected Essays*, New York, 1948.

——, *The Hovering Fly*, Cummington, Mass., 1948.

E. M. W. Tillyard, *Poetry Direct and Oblique*, London, 1934, 1945.

William Tindall, *Forces in Modern British Literature: 1885-1946*, New York, 1947.

Mark Van Doren, *The Private Reader*, New York, 1942.

H. H. Waggoner, *The Heel of Elohim: Science and Values in Modern American Poetry*, U. of Oklahoma P., 1950.

Austin Warren, *Rage for Order: Essays in Criticism*, Chicago, 1948.

Henry W. Wells, *New Poets From Old: A Study in Literary Genetics*, New York, 1940.

——, *The American Way of Poetry*, New York, 1943.

Charles Williams, *Poetry at Present*, Oxford, 1930.

Edmund Wilson, *Axel's Castle: A Study in the Imaginative Literature of 1870-1930*, New York, 1931, 1947.

——, *The Wound and the Bow: Seven Studies*, Boston, 1941; London, 1942; New York, 1947.

Yvor Winters, *The Function of Criticism*, Denver, 1957.

——, *In Defense of Reason*, New York, 1947. Reprints *Primitivism and Decadence*, *Maule's Curse*, and *The Anatomy of Nonsense*. New essay is "The Significance of [Hart Crane's] *The Bridge*."

Morton Dauwen Zabel, *Literary Opinion in America*, New York, 1937.